The Sermon on the Mount

The Sermon on the Mount

An Exegetical Commentary

GEORG STRECKER

TRANSLATED BY

O. C. Dean, Jr.

T & T Clark
EDINBURGH

Translation from the German language of Georg Strecker, DIE BERGPRE-
DIGT (zweite auflage, 1985) with the approval of the Publishing House
Vandenhoeck and Ruprecht, Göttingen, West Germany, © Vandenhoeck &
Ruprecht, Göttingen.
English translation copyright © 1988 Abingdon Press, Nashville, U.S.A.

Manufactured by the Parthenon Press at Nashville, Tennessee, U.S.A. for
T & T Clark Ltd, 59 George Street, Edinburgh EH2 2LQ, Scotland.

British Library Cataloguing in Publication Data
Strecker, Georg
 The Sermon on the Mount.
 1. Sermon on the Mount - Expositions
 I. Title II. Die Bergpredigt. *English* 226'.906

ISBN 0 567 29152 9

Contents

Preface

To every new generation is given the task of asking what the Sermon on the Mount means. In an age which more than any other claims to champion the cause of peace, yet in which the reality is one of confrontation between highly militarized superpowers and of numerous regional military conflicts, it is necessary to consider not only the religious, but also the political dimension of the Sermon on the Mount and, not least of all, the demand of its Preacher to become peacemakers. Nevertheless, the intention of the present volume is not to set forth another topical interpretation of the Sermon on the Mount. Its goal is rather—in the words of the subtitle of Hans Windisch's investigation—to make a contribution to the historical understanding of the Gospels and the problem of the proper exegesis of the Sermon on the Mount. This will not be done with the presupposition that still defines Windisch's work, according to which historical exegesis can be separated from the appropriation of its results. The exegetical history of the Sermon on the Mount in recent years has shown that such a separation has not been possible in any generation and, indeed, would not even be desirable. It is rather a matter of allowing room for the particularity of the text. This will make apparent not only the gulf that separates the Sermon on the Mount from our situation, but also the fact that the message of the Preacher has unmistakable significance for our time.

Comparison with the ethical tradition of the rest of the New Testament will confirm the uniqueness of the Sermon on the Mount. The unconditional demands it makes are not limited by reflection on the relationship of an ethical requirement to the motivation for that requirement, as occurs in the letters of Paul and in the Johannine writings. Moreover, the Sermon comprises many layers of tradition. In its present form, it can only be understood in connection with the theology of the Evangelist Matthew, but its core reaches back to the

7

proclamation of Jesus of Nazareth. In what follows, this thesis will be substantiated as we look at individual passages. In the process the theological richness of the Sermon on the Mount will come to light with its complexity of tradition and religious history, and it will become evident that today as well as then the Sermon on the Mount lays a claim not only on the Christian community, but also on humanity as a whole.

Concerning the origin of this book, I must report that the problems of Sermon on the Mount exegesis have drawn me under their spell ever since the preliminary work on my redaction-historical examination of Matthew, *Der Weg der Gerechtigkeit*. They have been treated again and again in lectures and seminars and have found expression in a number of articles. These reflections are incorporated here without being expressly noted in every case. My earlier conception of Matthew's theology has not basically changed, yet I believe I have made some progress on the question of the authentic Jesus tradition in the sense of a clearer understanding of the connection—but also the distance—that exists between the final form of the Sermon on the Mount in Matthew's Gospel and the primitive tradition going back to Jesus.

The reader may become acquainted with this by reading the final chapter, "Outlook," which might well function as an introduction to the book. This translation is based on the second German edition. I would like to express my gratitude to Dr. O. C. Dean, Jr., for his very careful work and for his proofreading of the quotations.

Göttingen, August 1987   Georg Strecker

Abbreviations

In addition to the abbreviations found on the standard list of the *Journal of Biblical Literature*, the following are used in this volume:

BDR   F. Blass, A. Debrunner, and F. Rehkopf, *Grammatik des neutestamentlichen Griechisch* (Göttingen: Vandenhoeck & Ruprecht, 1976)

EK   *Evangelische Kommentare*

EWNT   *Exegetisches Wörterbuch zum Neuen Testament*, ed. Horst R. Balz and Gerhard Schneider (Stuttgart: Kohlhammer, 1980-83)

FS   Festschrift

FzB   Forschung zur Bibel

GTA   Göttinger Theologische Arbeiten

KEK   Kritisch-exegetischer Kommentar über das Neue Testament (= MeyerK)

KNT   Kommentare zum Neuen Testament, ed. T. Zahn, 18 vols. (Leipzig, 1903–)

ÖTK   Ökumenisher Taschenbuch-Kommentar

TEH   Theologische Existenz heute

TRE   *Theologische Realenzyklopädie*, ed. Krause, Müller, et al. (Berlin, 1976–)

1 Introduction

1.1 Literary-Analytical Presuppositions

No proper exegesis of the Sermon on the Mount can ignore the results of more than two hundred years of historical-critical research into the New Testament. One of these results is the determination that the Sermon on the Mount in the First Gospel is not a speech made by Jesus but the literary work of the Evangelist Matthew, for between the historical Jesus and the composition of the New Testament Gospels there is a broad domain of oral and written tradition within the early Christian communities. Here, under the changing conditions of community thought and life, the gospel of Jesus was interpreted, and the binding order for these communities was established with reference to the authority of the risen Christ. This tendency can be seen in the two source documents, which—as the overwhelming majority of research assumes and will also be presupposed in this volume—were used by Matthew and Luke: the Gospel of Mark as the oldest of the New Testament Gospels and the collection of sayings that is called the Q source (= Q).

Around the year A.D. 70, the Evangelist Mark presented the life and message of Jesus in the form of a biographical outline interpreted according to the history of salvation. Though his work was available to his fellow Evangelists Matthew and Luke, presumably in a slightly modified recension (Deutero-Mark), Mark's influence on the Sermon on the Mount is, nevertheless, relatively small,[1] since he passed on primarily narrative material and not sayings. By contrast, the basic content of Matthew 5-7 can be traced back to the Q source, as a comparison with the Lukan parallel, the Sermon on the Plain of Luke 6:20-49, will demonstrate. Not only the framework (setting and epilogue) and the basic elements of the composition, but also above all the essential units of tradition in

11

the Sermon on the Mount (the beatitudes, the commandment to love one's enemy, the Golden Rule, the closing parables, and more) are passed on by Matthew and Luke. If we compare the outlines of the Sermon on the Mount and the Sermon on the Plain, the far-reaching correspondences will become clear.

Matthew	Luke	
5:1-2	6:12, 20a	setting
5:3-4, 6, 11-12	6:20b-23	beatitudes
5:39b-40, 42-48, 7:12	6:27-36	love of enemy, Golden Rule
7:1-5	6:37a, 38c, 41-42	on judging
7:16-21a	6:43-46	on good and bad trees
7:24-27	6:47-49	closing parables
7:28	7:1a	epilogue

These correspondences are not coincidental, nor are they to be explained by the underlying common oral tradition. Rather, they presuppose Q as a written source document in the Greek language, which can be reconstructed from the transmitted material common to Matthew and Luke but not Mark. The Q source document may have begun with the description of John the Baptist's appearance (Matt 3:7-12 par.) and ended with the parable of the Talents (Matt 25:14-30 par.). Even if Q offers no account of the passion or resurrection, the parallel arrangement in Matthew and Luke suggests, nonetheless, a chronological outline. It contains a preponderance of aphoristic material of wisdom and apocalyptic origin, which was subject to various Palestinian-Jewish Christian and Hellenistic-Gentile Christian influences.[2] The often assumed but not unmistakable time of composition, between A.D. 50 and 70, implies that the Q source was constantly changed in the course of being transmitted. Thus even the comparison between the Gospels of Matthew and Luke is not sufficient to reconstruct its actual extent. We can presume— and this thesis will be further substantiated in what follows— that Matthew and Luke did not use one and the same Q document, but each had as a source a different copy of Q (Q[Matt] or Q[Luke]). The special material that Matthew and Luke transmit independently of each other, which has no parallels in the Gospel tradition, can in part be traced back to the distinct compositions of Q^{Matt} and Q^{Luke}. Such differences prevent us from achieving a purely synchronic exegesis of the Sermon on the Mount and all the more from reaching back immediately from the text of the Sermon on the Mount to the historical Jesus, circumventing source-critical findings in the process. On the contrary, it can be shown that the layers of tradition are manifold, that many of the developmental tendencies that characterize Matthew's Gospel belong to pre-Matthean tradition, and that the way "back to Jesus" cannot be traveled without taking into account the various layers of tradition that are united in one text.

On the question of what criteria are to be applied in order to infer the proclamation of the historical Jesus, two distinguishing traits named by Rudolf Bultmann are often discussed. According to them, one may claim for the historical Jesus those statements in the Jesus tradition that (1) are not derivable from Judaism and (2) cannot be traced back to the post-Easter community.[3] To be sure, it can be objected that the application of this differentiating criterion isolates the words of Jesus from their Jewish environment as well as from the early Christian community, and also that it amounts to a reduction process that does not allow statements of the historical Jesus containing Jewish concepts to be put forward as genuine. The named criterion, however, is to be questioned above all because it presupposes a prior understanding both of Judaism at the time of Jesus and of the post-Easter church, which as such must be open to debate.

In the following pages, it will be shown that out of the literary analysis of the texts of the Sermon on the Mount we may lift up a further characteristic that can correct or expand the one just mentioned. If we begin with the fact of the stratified tradition of a text, we can apply to it the image of the growth rings of a tree. The older a unit of text is, the more it is surrounded and even overgrown with secondary traditional material. Even if the law of increasing text expansion is not the only applicable form-historical rule, the growth criterion still provides an important viewpoint for lifting up the original Jesus material, especially when it becomes apparent that this material occurs in more or less disconnected sayings and that the attached secondary bits of text were not handed down independently. In this case the underlying primary nucleus can, with relative certainty, be recovered as the starting point of tradition-historical development. From here we reach the conclusion that statements especially critical of the law and ethical radicalisms in the mouth of Jesus belong to the primitive tradition of the Sermon on the Mount and were increasingly superimposed with secondary tradition and thus adapted to the situation of the early Christian communities.

The last stage of the tradition-historical development is represented by the Evangelist Matthew, the "redactor" of the First Gospel. He composed his work perhaps in the next to the last decade of the first century in a Greek-speaking community, presumably in Syria. He not only wrote under the influence of Mark's Gospel and the sayings source (Q^{Matt}), but also used isolated special material. Above all, however, the traditions available to him were determined by the lively oral tradition of his community. Even if Matthew did not write the history of Jesus Christ—as it was occasionally assumed—as a "handbook for congregational leaders," he still had in mind, in any case, the worship and catechetical instruction of a community that had to orient itself anew in a situation of expanding time and an expanding church, a community that based its faith and its order on the life and teachings of the earthly Jesus, whom it addressed and awaited as the exalted and coming Lord.[4]

Although the Gospel of Matthew follows the outline of both Mark's Gospel and the Q source, its structure is especially characterized by five composed speeches, the first of which is the Sermon on the Mount. As the literary composition of the Evangelist Matthew, it reflects the conceptual structure of his theology, which is clearly expressed in the organization of the speech. The caesuras are recognizable in the theme statement with its demand for a righteousness that is to be more in evidence than that of the scribes and Pharisees (5:20), in the demand for perfection that closes the series of antitheses (5:48), and especially in the Golden Rule, which—as the sum of the law and the prophets and as a variation of the commandment of love—summarizes the Sermon on the Mount (7:12). Thus we have the following outline:

	5:1-2	The Setting
I.	5:3-20	The Opening
II.	A. 5:21-48	The Antitheses
	B. 6:1-18	Almsgiving, Praying, and Fasting
	C. 6:19-7:12	Individual Directives (wealth, anxiety, judging, prayer)
III.	7:13-27	Closing Admonitions and Parables
	7:28-29	Epilogue

1.2 Types of Exegesis of the Sermon on the Mount

Aukrust, T. "Bergpredigt II: Ethisch." *TRE* 5:618-22. 1980.

Barth, G. "Bergpredigt I: Im Neuen Testament." *TRE* 5:611-18. 1980.

Berner, U. *Die Bergpredigt: Rezeption und Auslegung im 20. Jahrhundert*, 2nd ed. GTA 12. 1983.

Beyschlag, K. "Zur Geschichte der Bergpredigt in der Alten Kirche." *ZTK* 74 (1977): 291-322.

Bornkamm, G. *Jesus von Nazareth* (1956), 12th ed. (1980), 195-98; English translation (1960).

Fascher, E. "Bergpredigt II: Auslegungsgeschichtlich." *RGG* 1 (3rd ed. 1957), 1050-53.

Kantzenbach, F. W. *Die Bergpredigt: Annäherung, Wirkungsgeschichte.* 1982.

Kissinger, W. S. *The Sermon on the Mount: A History of Interpretation and Bibliography.* Metuchen, N.J.: Scarecrow Press, 1975.

1. The Sermon on the Mount as Law and Gospel (the Pauline-Lutheran type of exegesis)

In his writings, the Reformer Martin Luther often mentioned and interpreted the Sermon on the Mount—for example, in his weekly sermons.[1] His statements moved in two directions. On the one hand, he turned against the Roman Catholic exegesis of Scholasticism, which differentiated between *praecepta* and *consilia*. In this view Jesus did not intend to teach *praecepta*, that is, generally binding commandments to be kept by every Christian. His aim was rather to set up *consilia*, that is, "evangelical advice," which was not generally binding but was reserved for a class with a special perfection, for example, the monastics. Luther rejected this distinction.[2] The gospel of justification by faith was valid for all Christians and not merely for a privileged class within Christianity. Thus Jesus' Sermon on the Mount is also generally binding and addressed to all.[3] Luther's second exegetical direction addressed the fanatics who understood the Sermon on the Mount as normative law. For Luther the acceptance of the wording of the Sermon on the Mount as binding law included the danger that law and gospel would be confused with each other and there would be no distinction between secular and spiritual realms.[4] On the contrary, says Luther, the Sermon on the Mount is the law of Christ that leads people to the knowledge of sin.[5] Here the Reformer stands in the tradition of Paul (Rom 1:18ff.) and Augustine, who taught the total fallenness of humanity in consequence of sin.[6] Thus the law of Christ, which is expressed in the Sermon on the Mount, accuses humankind, because it remains unfulfilled. It cannot establish the righteousness of humanity before God.[7]

Yet the Sermon on the Mount in Luther's interpretation is not just the accusing law that points to sin (*usus theologicus* or *elenchticus legis*); it is also *gospel*. This is especially true of the beatitudes (5:3-12). When Christ "does not press but in a friendly way entices and speaks: 'Blessed are the poor,' and so forth," it is the comfort of God.[8] Such "evangelical" exegesis of the Sermon on the Mount can likewise lay claim to the position of Pauline theology (cf. Gal 5:25; Rom 12:1ff.).

When Sermon on the Mount exegesis in recent times appeals to Luther, it often attaches itself to only one of the two indicated possibilities: either to the gospel character of the Sermon on the Mount, through which one distinguishes between gift and duty or between indicative and imperative,[9] or to the legal character of the Sermon on the Mount, through which the accused is to be found guilty of sin.[10] In accordance with the last named interpretation, the Sermon on the Mount contains the absolute demands of Jesus. Since these remain unrealized, the Sermon on the Mount can awaken the knowledge of sin.[11]

2. The Sermon on the Mount as Realizable Demand (the fanatical type of exegesis)

Of greater significance for a topical interpretation in the present day is this type of exegesis, whose image in history has fluctuated.[12] The term *fanatic (Schwärmer)* does not necessarily mean something negative; the German word comes from beekeeping and designates people who swarm around like bees, are found in many places, and are distinguished by such wandering from the settled population. After the Reformation, however, the reproach of fanaticism was especially linked with the Anabaptists, who, on the authority of the Sermon on the Mount, rejected oaths and military service and interpreted the commandment to love one's enemies literally and radically. They were encountered by the Swiss Reformers: "They cling to the letter but do not interpret it according to what is needed."[13]

Thus this exegetical direction means that Jesus' demands in the Sermon on the Mount must be fulfilled literally and also on principle are to be fulfilled literally. A significant example for the present age is the Russian writer Leo Tolstoy (1828-1910).[14] He raised against the Christian church the reproach that it has weakened the demands of Jesus and made them ineffective. For him the key sentence of the Sermon on the Mount is Matt 5:39 ("do not resist one who is evil"), that is, the demand of powerlessness. With recognition of the commandments of the Sermon on the Mount, thought Tolstoy, would come paradisiacal conditions on the earth. This is a resurrection of the old fanatical viewpoint against which Luther formulated his teaching of the two authorities. Here the total fallenness of humanity under sin is not taken into account, nor does Paul's radical critique of the law have any influence on this interpretation. Yet it should be recognized that this view takes up the concern of Matthew, for whom it was a matter of the fulfillment of concrete commandments and the realization of the righteousness demanded by Jesus.

Of the same exegetical type, Leonhard Ragaz (1868-1945) is to be counted as a representative of the Religious Socialists. He subscribes to Marxist class-warfare thinking and transforms it within a Christian framework. The Jesus of the Sermon on the Mount becomes counsel for the oppressed and those deprived of their rights. He calls into question the existing state order. Jesus' Sermon on the Mount "is the unheard message of world revolution through God. . . . It stands back when Christianity reigns; it steps forward when Christ and the kingdom of God break through."[15] Only this can be the foundation for building a new community.[16]

The politician Friedrich Naumann (1860-1919) interpreted

the Sermon on the Mount in a different way. Originally a Protestant pastor, Naumann believed that, starting from "Jesus' standpoint," one could promote a "Christian economic order." A trip to Palestine in 1898 produced a fundamental change in his theology. He realized that Jesus was something other than "the helper who sees all kinds of human needs."[17] Jesus had apparently not wanted to transform the social and economic conditions of his land. Tolstoy's way, the application of Jesus' Sermon on the Mount to political relationships, was not practical. There are things, says Naumann, that elude Christian regulation.

3. The Sermon on the Mount as an Ethic of Attitude (the liberal type of exegesis)

If one is convinced of the unrealizability of Jesus' Sermon on the Mount,[18] the unavoidable conclusion seems to be that it is not to be adopted as an ethic of action but at best is to be interpreted for the present within the framework of an ethic of attitude. The outstanding representative of this liberal position is the Marburg systematic theologian Wilhelm Herrmann (1846-1922). In his work *Die sittlichen Weisungen Jesu* [the ethical instructions of Jesus], he pursues the idea that the commandments of the Sermon on the Mount may be understood, not literally, but only as an appeal to the conscience. They call for the "inner obedience of those who are free."[19] It is a question of the founding of a new consciousness, not of real action.[20]

Also beginning with the unrealizability of Jesus' demands in the Sermon on the Mount is the important Strasbourg New Testament scholar Heinrich Julius Holtzmann (1832-1910). He explicitly professes the "understandable and useful key word *Gesinnungsethik* ('ethic of attitude')," which finds itself "in contrast with the demand that presses for obedience in relation to the letter"; for "not only the generally accepted, but almost any sound exegesis [knows] that those extreme and excessive sounding demands of the Sermon on the Mount become understandable and obeyable only on the assumption of the principle of the ethic of attitude";[21] indeed, "the attitude of the heart that characterizes a member of the kingdom is at the same time the condition for entrance into the kingdom."[22]

4. The Religious-Historical Horizon of the Sermon on the Mount (the historical type of exegesis)

The end of the nineteenth century was the great era of the history of religion school, which included the Göttingen New Testament scholars Wilhelm Heitmüller, William Wrede, and Wilhelm Bousset. Historical interpretation dominated, and special significance was given to the quest for the historical Jesus and to the position of Christianity within the religious history of late antiquity. One result was the discovery that the New Testament stands on a broad horizon of ancient religious movements. Although important, Judaism is not the only source for understanding the New Testament, and the history of religion school determined correctly that this Judaism appeared in many shades.[23]

The Göttingen (and later Heidelberg) scholar Johannes Weiss (1863-1914) is of significance because he, in disagreement with his father-in-law Albrecht Ritschl,[24] emphasized the strangeness of Jesus' proclamation.[25] If Ritschl understood the kingdom of God as "the spiritual and moral task of humankind gathered in Christian communion,"[26] then appropriate to this conception, of course, was a supernatural excellence of the "moral forms of community";[27] yet it remained bound, nevertheless, to the goal of the inner realization of the kingdom of God. In contrast to this, Weiss worked out the eschatological-apocalyptic horizon of Jesus' proclamation: the kingdom of God occurs at the end of the world, as already taught by apocalyptic Judaism. Only on the basis of this expectation are the demands of Jesus to be understood. The Sermon on the Mount is not the prescription for a moral community established for the long term: it is not for the church; it is rather the watchword of the few who stand under the imprint of the end of the world.[28]

This eschatological understanding of Jesus was presented even more thoroughly by Albert Schweitzer (1875-1965).[29] In his view, Jesus' proclamation is fundamentally aimed at the future revelation of the Son of man, at the inbreaking of God's kingdom, which needs no moral standard but rather brings in a supramoral condition of perfection. Jesus' ethical demand can be termed an "interim ethic"—not so much to identify a temporal boundary as to characterize the fact that Jesus' ethic was determined by the expectation of the kingdom of God. "As penitence in anticipation of the kingdom of God, even the ethic of the Sermon on the Mount is equivalent to an interim ethic."[30]

It was the concern of Paul Billerbeck (1853-1932) to work out the Sermon on the Mount's connection not only with apocalyptic Judaism but also with rabbinic Judaism.[31] No less decisively, Gerhard Kittel (1888-1948), the founder of the *Theological Dictionary of the New Testament*, established the close relationship between Jesus' demands in the Sermon on the Mount and ancient Judaism. There is no single demand of Jesus for which one can make the claim that as an individual demand it is simply unique within the context of Judaism. The special nature of Jesus' demand lies in his claim that the kingdom of God is present in his person.[32] This claim leads to the recognition of one's own involvement, so that, in consonance with Luther's type of exegesis, the Sermon on the Mount becomes a mirror of sin.

More recently, William D. Davies (b. 1911) has stressed that the Sermon on the Mount is closely connected with Judaism. He asserts that Matthew's Gospel can be interpreted on the basis of a confrontation with the rabbinical school at Jamnia. The Sermon on the Mount is the Christian answer to the revival of Jewish theology after A.D. 70.[33]

A genuine, if later, spokesman of the history of religion school—and also a representative of liberal theology—is Hans Windisch (1881-1935, lastly in Halle). The subtitle of his monograph,[34] "A Contribution to the Historical Understanding of the Gospels and to the Problem of Correct Exegesis," shows that Windisch is dealing critically with dialectical theology's interpretation of the Sermon on the Mount. He wants to pursue historical and theological exegesis and at the same time clearly separate the two from each other.[35] One might object, in regard to Windisch, that it is not possible to hold fast to the ideal of an absolute objectivity of historical criticism; yet in a thoroughgoing historical exegesis, he calls attention to the different, strange nature of the text of the Sermon on the Mount. In his view, eschatology and wisdom teaching are the two main components of Jesus' Sermon on the Mount. Jesus is teacher and prophet, the one sent by God, whose demands are to be literally understood and fulfilled.

5. The Interpretation of the Sermon on the Mount under the Influence of Dialectical Theology

Vis-à-vis the purely historical approach, dialectical theology brought about a historical turning point with the commentary on Romans of Karl Barth (1886-1968).[36] Also connected with dialectical theology are the names Friedrich Gogarten, Rudolf Bultmann, and Eduard Thurneysen. As much as these theologians in the first half of the twentieth century embodied various traditions—from the Calvinist and Lutheran Reformations and Protestant orthodoxy through Kierkegaard to liberal theology—they held nonetheless a relatively unified view in exegesis. They are united on the point that interpretation of the Bible may not be carried on under the historical viewpoint alone: the theological meaning of the text must also be drawn in. While the historical work may not be neglected, one must forgo a "presuppositionless exegesis" and focus on the personal involvement of the individual. Thus, Bultmann wrote his *Theology of the New Testament* with the presupposition that its books have something to say to the people of today.[37]

Also in his book *Jesus*, Rudolf Bultmann (1884-1976) is concerned with the Sermon on the Mount. For him, in contrast to his teacher Wilhelm Herrmann, it is a question not only of the Jesus' demand of a right attitude, but also of the actual assertion that Jesus links with the demand: he means the whole person, not just a part such as an attitude or a deed. Jesus' demand is a radical call to decision; it requires a response to the claim of God; it demands radical obedience. This is realized in the fulfillment of the commandment of love, and concrete instructions are no longer necessary.[38]

Günther Bornkamm (b. 1905) adopts a similar standpoint in his *Jesus of Nazareth*.[39] For him also, Jesus' demand is a radical one; it lays claim to the whole person and demands the eschatological orientation of human existence. The Sermon on the Mount is the "exhortation to the disciples of Jesus to establish in the midst of the world the signs of God's lordship and his righteousness."[40]

Eduard Thurneysen (1887-1974) attempts to work out the theological meaning of the Sermon on the Mount in a different way.[41] His intention is to interpret the Sermon on the Mount christologically, but not in a historical sense. The speech is bound to the person of Jesus in the sense that the Christ who lives today is the one who speaks to us through the Sermon on the Mount. It is the living word of Christ, and it must be read basically as the word of grace, that is, as the word that concerns nothing other than the fulfillment of God's law, which occurs in Christ for us.[42] Jesus brings the new righteousness, because he takes our place and fulfills for us the law that he proclaims in the Sermon on the Mount. This is the gospel in the law of the Sermon on the Mount. The required obedience is an obedience that is realized on the basis of the Christ event and at the same time is already fulfilled because of grace through Christ as the resurrected One. From here on, the demand of the Sermon on the Mount gives way to the christological confession. There is no doubt that in this interpretation great weight has been given to the Pauline-Augustinian doctrine of grace.

Various phases of Sermon on the Mount interpretation are incorporated in Dietrich Bonhoeffer (1906-45), who saw himself, among other things, as a follower of Karl Barth. The relevance of the Sermon on the Mount was demonstrated for him in his disagreement with the dictators of the Third Reich, which he sealed with his death in the concentration camp at Flossenbürg on 9 April 1945. His book *Nachfolge (The Cost of Discipleship)* is based on the lectures he gave in 1935 at the Finkenwalde seminary. Discipleship is life without compromise,[43] which was practiced exemplarily—but in its exclusivity also problematically—by early Christian monasticism.[44] Accordingly, what is at stake in the Sermon on the Mount is not just the concept *faith*, but also the keeping of the law. In another place Bonhoeffer says, "The truth of the church for the present day is revealed when it preaches and does the Sermon on the Mount"[45]—and this in commitment to the person of Jesus Christ. An individualistic privatization of the Sermon on the Mount is excluded here, as is any fanatical ethic of the law that sees itself as an interpretation of the Sermon on the Mount.

6. *The Peace Movement and the Sermon on the Mount*

In the past peace initiatives, movements for nonviolent resistence, and pacifist groups have cited the Sermon on the Mount. Along with Tolstoy, one could name Mahatma Gandhi (1869-1948)[46] and Martin Luther King (1929-68).[47]

In more recent times, faced with excessive atomic armament and the fundamental problem of a "just war," Helmut Gollwitzer (b. 1908) in particular, appealing to the fifth thesis of the Barmen Declaration,[48] has inquired about the limits of the power monopoly granted to the state. According to him, the Sermon on the Mount is also, in Luther's sense, the great primer for shaping—in view of the inbreaking dominion of God—"a power-free brotherhood and at the same time the cooperation of Christians in a world ordered by power structures."[49] In this the unity of the biblical canon comes into play when Gollwitzer asserts: "As the Torah is directed toward the entire life of the nation, toward the social behavior of the people of Israel . . . so also is Jesus' sermon. . . . Promises as well as imperatives are aimed at a new social behavior, that is, not so much at introspection in the court of conscience (Luther) as rather at brotherly behavior in service of the neighbor in distress (Matt 25:37ff.)."[50] This aspect of the Sermon on the Mount has been understood "more in accordance with the text" by the social and religious opposition movements—from the Waldensians to the Religious Socialists—than by the large churches.[51]

The same exegetical direction is found in the assertions of the retired Berlin bishop Kurt Scharf (b. 1902), who designates the Sermon on the Mount a "government declaration of Jesus," which encompasses all areas of life.[52] He draws from that the conclusion that what matters for the congregation as the body of Christ is the unconditional "yes to political servanthood" and to the political mandate of the church.[53]

By contrast, professional politicians are not the only ones to hold the view that the Sermon on the Mount concerns only the private life of the Christian and is not to be interpreted in a socio-political fashion; its limit is reached where people bear responsibility for others.[54] In fact, there is scarcely a realm of New Testament exegesis in which the danger of erroneous interpretations is so great as in the area of actualizing the Sermon on the Mount. Before its meaning is translated into the present, we must hear its original statement. In the process we will find opening up, precisely in the strangeness of this text that belongs to the past, not only an unmistakable identity, but also a specific relevance for today.

2 Exegesis

2.1 5:1-2 The Setting

Foerster, W. ὄρος, *TDNT*.
Kleine, H. ὄρος, *EWNT* 2:1304-7.
Lange, J. *Das Erscheinen des Auferstandenen im Evangelium nach Matthäus*. FzB 11 (1973), 393-404.
Mánek, J. "On the Mount—On the Plain (Matt 5:1–Luke 6:17)." *NovT* 9 (1967): 124-31.
Schmauch, W. *Orte der Offenbarung und der Offenbarungsort im Neuen Testament*. 1956.

[1]*Seeing the crowds, he went up on the mountain, and when he sat down his disciples came to him.* [2]*And he opened his mouth and taught them, saying:*

Comparison with Luke shows that Matthew linked Jesus' speech with the mountain setting.[1] Only superficially does this naming of the setting have a parallel in Luke 6:12, where the ὄρος is mentioned as Jesus' place of prayer. Nonetheless in the Lukan presentation, this "mountain" is the place where twelve disciples are called to be apostles (Luke 6:13-16).[2] Thus only Matthew localizes Jesus' speech to the mountain.[3]

In Mark, the term ὄρος designates a mountain or mountains into which Jesus withdraws for prayer (Mark 6:46 par. Matt 14:23). Mark 9:2 (par. Matt 17:1) shows Jesus with three disciples on the mount of transfiguration. According to Mark 3:13, Jesus calls the twelve on a mountain (cf. Luke 6:12-13). In Mark's Gospel, it is above all a matter of a place of Jesus' revelation.[4] The concept *mountain* signalizes that here is a suitable place for an epiphanous event! Here God's revelation makes itself known! Here Jesus appears as the revealer! So also says Matt 15:29: the sick are healed by Jesus on a mountain. And according to 28:16, the resurrected One appears to his disciples on a mountain in Galilee.[5]

As these comparisons make clear, the mountain motif in our

passage is not set up as a parallel to Sinai as the mountain of the old covenant and the law of Moses. Jesus does not appear as the "new Moses."[6] Nor can other observations named in this connection—for example, the comparison of the five Matthean speeches with the five books of the Pentateuch—support such an analogy. Jesus appears, rather, as the Lord and Son of God whose post-Easter majesty is reflected in his teaching; for Jesus is presented as the one who teaches. His sitting is the typical posture of a teacher among Jews and Greeks.[7] The teaching of Jesus on the mountain means: in his speech divine epiphany occurs. This teaching is eschatological revelation.

Who are the hearers of the Sermon on the Mount? According to Luke 6:20, Jesus directs his eyes toward his disciples. Yet the content of the Sermon on the Plain shows that these are not the only listeners presupposed. The woes of the Sermon on the Plain are aimed at the rich and satisfied. The reference is not to the disciples but to a larger circle than is represented by Jesus' followers. This is confirmed by Luke 7:1 ("After he had ended all his sayings in the hearing of the people . . ."): the closing of the Sermon on the Plain presupposes disciples and people as listeners. The same conclusion can be drawn from the preceding section, which reports an influx of "a great multitude of people from all Judea and Jerusalem and the seacoast of Tyre and Sidon" (Luke 6:17).

The idea that disciples and people are the hearers of Jesus' speech was probably already asserted by the Q source,[8] for on this point Matthew agrees basically with Luke. Faced with the influx of the crowd of people, Jesus climbed the mountain. This is not to be understood as flight, as if he wanted to escape from the throng; Jesus moves onto the mountain, rather, in order to be visible and audible to the people when he speaks. The disciples approach him and form, as it were, an inner circle vis-à-vis the outer one of the multitude.[9] Thus, as opposed to Luke, Matthew distinguishes between the μαθηταί, who in general are identical with the twelve disciples,[10] and the ὄχλοι, Jesus' listeners, who stream to him mostly from Jewish territory (8:1, 18; 23:1). They experienced not only the speech, but also the deeds of Jesus and applauded them (9:8; 15:31). As such an applauding chorus, the multitude of people is also present for the Sermon on the Mount, as can be concluded from the redactionally formed closing verses, 7:28-29. Here, the people are distinguished from the official representatives of Judaism. Not until the passion of Jesus are the high priests and elders united with the entire multitude: "all the people" joined in the call for crucifixion (27:25). Even the disciples are drawn into the human failure.[11] Since Matthew has the Sermon on the Mount spoken to the disciples and to the people, Jesus' speech is not directed at only an esoteric group, say, at the circle of twelve disciples as a model of monastic asceticism and conduct of life. On the contrary, Jesus' demand excludes no one: those who belong to him and those who do not belong to him are all addressed in the Sermon on the Mount!

Since the disciples of Jesus are addressed as the inner circle of hearers, it is clear that Jesus was not presenting general, secular information. The solemn introduction also shows this: "And he opened his mouth and taught them, saying. . . ." Here the language of the Greek Bible (LXX) is used (cf. Dan 10:16; Job 3:1). The dependence on the Septuagint as the holy book of the church means that this speech is raised above the secular world. This comes above all through the person of the speaker. The Sermon on the Mount cannot be properly understood apart from the person of Jesus. Its interpretation cannot ignore the fact that Jesus as the teacher of the Sermon on the Mount is at the same time the eschatological Lord and Son of God, the revealer of God's will, as he is presented by the prologue of Matthew's Gospel (1:18ff.) and also by his shout of joy and redemption (11:25-30). This teacher is not simply comparable to a Jewish scribe. His teaching contains an eschatological call to decision, for it is expressed with divine ἐξουσία ('authority'—7:29). It points ahead to the *eschaton* and through teaching makes it present. Therefore, the ethical admonition of Jesus in the Sermon on the Mount is an eschatological demand.

2.2 5:3-20 The Opening of the Sermon on the Mount

The following part of Jesus' speech divides into three subsections: the beatitudes (5:3-12), the nature of discipleship

(5:13-16), and the new righteousness (5:17-20). This division answers at the same time the question of the theme of the Sermon on the Mount, which is given in verse 20 with the key word δικαιοσύνη ('righteousness'). The concept of righteousness is mentioned already in the beatitudes (5:6, 10), and it is taken up again in the second and third parts of the Sermon on the Mount (6:1, 33).

Accordingly, verse 20 not only is the heading of the six antitheses (5:21-48), but also names the decisive key word for the body of the Sermon on the Mount, which reaches its high point in 7:12.[12] After the announcement of the theme in verse 20 comes the first main section, the antitheses (5:21-48). Then follow the second main part, the instructions on almsgiving, praying, and fasting (6:1-18), and the third section, the individual directives, which are closed by the summarizing "Golden Rule" (6:19-7:12). In the closing section warnings and parables call Jesus' hearers to decision (7:13-27). The epilogue marks the end of the speech and the response of the people (7:28-29).

2.2.1   5:3-12   The Beatitudes

Best, E. "Matthew V.3." *NTS* 7 (1960-61): 255-58.

Betz, H. D. "Die Makarismen der Bergpredigt (Matthäus 5:3-12)." *ZTK* 75 (1978): 3-19.

Braumann, G. "Zum traditionsgeschichtlichen Problem der Seligpreisungen Mt V.3-12." *NovT* 4 (1960): 253-60.

Brown, R. E. "The Beatitudes According to Luke." In idem, *New Testament Essays*, 334-41. New York, 1965.

Dupont, J. "Les πτωχοὶ τῷ πνεύματι de Matthieu 5,3 et les עֲנָוֵי רוּחַ de Qumrân." In *Neutestamentliche Aufsätze*, FS J. Schmid, edited by J. Blinzler et al., 53-64. 1963.

———. *Les Béatitudes*, 3 vols. Paris, 1958, 1969, 1973.

Frankemölle, H. "Die Makarismen (Mt 5, 1-12; Lk 6,20-23)." *BZ* n.s. 15 (1971): 52-75.

Guelich, R. A. "The Matthean Beatitudes: 'Entrance Requirements' or Eschatological Blessings?" *JBL* 95 (1976): 415-34.

Heinrich, R. "Gott – rücksichtslos der Gott der Armen. Leben mit Matthäus 5, Vers 3." In Moltmann, *Nachfolge und Bergpredigt*.

Kähler, C. "Biblische Makarismen." Diss., Jena, 1974. Also *TLZ* 101 (1976): 77-80.

Kieffer, R. "Weisheit und Segen als Grundmotive der Seligpreisungen bei Matthäus und Lukas." In *Theologie aus dem Norden*, edited by A. Fuchs, 29-43. SNTU 2. 1976.

Koch, K. *Was ist Formgeschichte?* 3d ed. (1974), 7-9, 36-37, 50-55, 74-78.

Lapide, P., and C. F. von Weizsäcker, *Die Seligpreisungen*. 1980.

Légasse, S. "Les pauvres en esprit et les 'volontaires' de Qumran." *NTS* 8 (1961-62): 336-45.

McEleney, N. J. "The Beatitudes of the Sermon on the Mount/Plain." *CBQ* 43 (1981): 1-13.

Michaelis, C. "Die π-Alliteration der Subjektsworte der ersten vier Seligprei-sungen in Mt V.3-6 und ihre Bedeutung für den Aufbau der Seligpreisun-gen bei Mt, Lk und in Q." *NovT* 10 (1968): 148-61.

Schweizer, E. "Formgeschichtliches zu den Seligpreisungen." In idem, *Matthäus und seine Gemeinde*, 69-77. SBS 71. 1974.

Steck, O. H. *Israel und das gewaltsame Geschick der Propheten*, 20-26. WMANT 23. 1967.

Strecker, G. "Die Makarismen der Bergpredigt." *NTS* 17 (1970-71): 255-75. (=*Eschaton und Historie*, 108-31.)

Trilling, W. "Heilsverheissung und Lebenslehre des Jüngers (Mt 5,3-12)." In idem, *Christusverkündigung in den synoptischen Evangelien*, 64-85. Biblische Handbibliothek 4. 1969.

Walter, N. "Die Bearbeitung der Seligpreisungen durch Matthäus." *SE* 4, (TU 102, 1968): 246-58.

Windisch, H. "Friedensbringer – Gottessöhne." *ZNW* 24 (1925): 240-60.

Zimmerli, W. "Die Seligpreisingen der Bergpredigt und das Alte Testament." In *Donum Gentilicium*, FS D. Daube, edited by E. Bammel et al., 8-26. Oxford, 1978.

Matthew 5	Luke 6
[3]Blessed are the poor in spirit, for theirs is the kingdom of heaven.	*[20b]Blessed are you poor, for yours is the kingdom of God.*
[4]Blessed are those who mourn, for they shall be comforted.	*[21b]Blessed are you that weep now, for you shall laugh.*
[5]Blessed are the meek, for they shall inherit the earth.	
[6]Blessed are those who hunger and thirst for righteousness, for they shall be satisfied.	*[21a]Blessed are you that hunger now, for you shall be satisfied.*
[7]Blessed are the merciful, for they shall obtain mercy.	
[8]Blessed are the pure in heart, for they shall see God.	
[9]Blessed are the peacemakers, for they shall be called sons of God.	
[10]Blessed are those who are persecuted for righteousness' sake, for theirs is the kingdom of heaven.	

[11]Blessed are you when men revile you and persecute you and utter all kinds of evil against you falsely on my account. [12]Rejoice and be glad, for your reward is great in heaven, for so men persecuted the prophets who were before you.

[22]Blessed are you when men hate you, and when they exclude you and revile you, and cast your name as evil, on account of the Son of man! [23]Rejoice in that day, and leap for joy, for behold, your reward is great in heaven; for so their fathers did to the prophets.

The Sermon on the Mount begins with a series of beatitudes, a characteristic style form that is authenticated both in Greek and in Old Testament-Jewish literature.[13] They are the positive counterpart of cries of woe (e.g., Luke 6:24-26) or words of damnation (Rev 21:8; cf. 22:14-15), and in the New Testament, in agreement with non-Christian tradition, are recognized by the preposed predicate μακάριος or μακάριοι ("blessed"). The predicate appears in second or third person but can be missing altogether. Frequently a condition for a beatitude is given in a following statement. It can also be expressed in the form of a relative clause. Sometimes a beatitude is defined by the deed-result schema and is thereby ethically oriented.[14] The New Testament beatitudes are predominantly associated with admonition and spoken to the congregation as warnings. In addition, beatitudes can also have a paracletic sense and thus announce comfort. This is demonstrated by the tradition-historical analysis of Matthew's series of beatitudes.

The oldest accessible version results from a comparison with Luke 6:20b-23. This tradition goes back to the Q model that Luke and Matthew together presuppose (Matt 5:3-4, 6). It comprises, first, three like-formed beatitudes, namely, the blessing of the poor, those who hunger, and those who mourn (Matt 5:4; contrast Luke 6:21b: "weep"). The form of these beatitudes is determined and set apart from the remaining beatitudes by the alliteration of the Greek π.[15] Coming later as a unit likewise common to Matthew and Luke is the beatitude of the persecuted (Matt 5:11-12; Luke 6:22-23). It contains the announcement that the sufferers have the promise of God's kingdom. Such a message corresponds to the picture that the Q source paints of Jesus as the friend of the tax collectors and sinners (Matt 11:19, par. Luke 7:34).

If the Q tradition is defined by the triad of like-formed beatitudes, then in the foregoing Matthean version another trio is recognizable. The beatitudes of the merciful, the pure in heart, and the peacemakers (vv. 7-9) form an originally independent unit. They were presumably contained in the Q^Matt text, together with the beatitude of the meek (v. 5), which was possibly added to the joining of the two triads to make a total of seven.[16] From this we can presuppose for Q^Matt seven like-formed beatitudes (vv. 3-9). The number seven also has a special meaning in the (pre-)Matthean tradition (1:1ff.: genealogy of Jesus; 6:9ff.: Lord's Prayer; 23:13ff.: cries of woe). In verses 5:7-9, ethical beatitudes expand the original tradition. Beside the blessing of the sufferers comes now the blessing of the doers of the word. The demand is not for passivity but for the active behavior of people: for deeds of forebearance, mercy, purity, and peacemaking.

Matthew placed these mutually conflicting arrangements of the two traditional units of beatitudes to fit his conception. Comparison with the Lukan parallel shows that the text in verses 3 and 6 was redactionally altered, and verse 10 was added by Matthew.[17] In this way the first Evangelist impressed an ethical intention even on the originally paracletic beatitudes, as detailed exegesis can demonstrate.

The disagreement is on the question of which principle of composition Matthew followed. Since the eight like-formed beatitudes are placed together in verses 3-10, then it seems obvious to subdivide this section into two strophes of four members each (thus Schniewind, *Matthäus* 40; Grundmann, *Matthäus* 199). Accordingly, A. Schlatter (*Der Evangelist Matthäus*, 137) carried out a differentiation of content in which he asserted that in the first strophe Jesus addressed the "burden that humanity bears" (vv. 3-6) and in the second strophe refers "to the way that people act" (vv. 7-10). Yet this distinction leaves verses 11-12 unconsidered and underestimates Matthew's ethical intention, which expresses itself already in the first beatitudes. It is more likely that for Matthew the principle of the number three, which had especially shaped the tradition, was also asserted in the nine beatitudes of his text.[18]

5:3. The word μακάριος can have the general meaning of "blessed, happy, fortunate." In this unspecific sense, the word is found in the New Testament (Acts 26:2) and also in the Jewish wisdom literature (e.g., Sir 25:8-9). Since Jesus appears in the Sermon on the Mount as teacher, the general, wisdom signification can be applied to the Matthean series of beatitudes. This would turn our text into wisdom teaching and Jesus into a wisdom teacher. Besides this secular meaning, however, the word also has an eschatological sense in the New Testament. It introduces the salutation that promises eschatological salvation (e.g., Luke 10:23-24) and is to be translated as "salvation/grace to . . . " or the traditional "blessed are. . . ." The wisdom and eschatological meanings have import for our text. In Matthew's Gospel, wisdom teaching can be expressed as eschatological proclamation with an eschatological claim. Conversely, eschatological assertions appear in the form of wisdom instruction. Jesus is the teacher who speaks with eschatological authority (cf. 7:29).

The eschatological orientation becomes clear in the second clause; βασιλεία τῶν οὐρανῶν ('kingdom of heaven') in Matthew is the typical expression for God's dominion or the kingdom of God. Although the Evangelist can speak of the present kingdom of God (e.g., 12:28), in the Sermon on the Mount this concept appears exclusively in the future sense. The second clause of the beatitudes, which is introduced by ὅτι ('for'), gives reasons out of the apocalyptic future. This is demonstrated by the following future verb form.[19] The second clause of the beatitudes contains a promise that pledges future, eschatological salvation.

Following tradition, Luke has the first beatitude addressed to the πτωχοί ('poor'). This direction was originally intended in the material sense, and in Luke's Gospel it still is. The promise applies to those who are poor in earthly goods. God's pledge is given, not to the rich, but to the have-nots. Consequently, in the Lukan version a (presumably pre-Lukan) cry of woe against the rich is appended (6:24). In Old Testament-Jewish literature, to be sure, wealth and poverty were already concepts filled not only with economic but also with theological content. Jewish wisdom writing teaches that wealth and sin are closely tied together, and possessions and the striving for possessions lead into sin (Prov 15:16-17; Sir 20:21). Conversely, God's devotion is specifically for the poor: Yahweh will lift up the poor (Ps 113:7-8). In his Gospel, Luke describes how wealth places itself as an insurmountable barrier between the rich person and God (e.g., 12:13-21; 16:19-31). As wealth and distance from God are identical, so also are poverty and nearness to God. The have-not has nothing to rely on; he is dependent on divine grace alone.[20] In the Jewish tradition the poor are also the godly (Pss. Sol. 5:2; 10:6; 15:1; 1 Enoch 94:8; 97:8-9), therefore, it is understandable that the Jewish Christians of the second century assumed the name *ebyonim* ('the poor'), originally a title of honor, which with the church fathers became a term for Jewish-Christian heretics.[21]

Matthew expanded the first beatitude with the addition of τῷ πνεύματι ('in the spirit'). Even in Luther's translation ("Selig sind die da geistlich arm sind"—"Blessed are those who are spiritually poor"), this expression does not refer to the Spirit of God. The promise is not addressed to those who lack the gift of God's Spirit, nor is poverty to be understood in an ideal, religious sense. On the contrary, Matthew's intention is to fill the concept of poverty with a different content. Πνεῦμα means human, not divine, spirit (thus also 26:41; 27:50). The dative is a dative of reference. The poverty refers to the human spirit as the location of insight, feeling, and will.[22] Thus it is no longer connected with goods and possessions, but rather confronts the high self-estimation of the Pharisees and scribes, as presented in 6:2 and 23:1ff.[23] The encouragement is for the people with low self-esteem, those who are humble. Thus have many church fathers interpreted this verse.[24] It addresses the attitude of *humilitas*, as the Matthean Jesus also teaches it elsewhere.[25]

The pre-Matthean beatitude is substantially changed by Matthew's redactional intrusion. He does not combine the theological with the anthropological meaning of the concept *spirit*; it is not his intention to equate the willful human spirit with the Holy Spirit given by God,[26] but rather to emphasize straightaway that the promise is not granted to those who are poor in possessions but to those who are not proud and who count themselves among the lowly. The original literal sense of poverty is thus interpreted in a spiritual and, at the same time, ethical fashion. The War Scroll from Qumrân also interprets the concept of poverty in such a spiritual and ethical sense.[27] The Jesus of the Sermon on the Mount speaks, accordingly, to people who are content, who know their limits and turn that knowledge into appropriate behavior. He sets up norms that are obligatory for the lives of his followers. He demands that they realize this very attitude. And he gives the reason, stated in the second clause, that the pledge of the future kingdom of heaven is only for the humble.

From here on the beatitudes can be compared with the cultic list of virtues of the Old Testament. They name the conditions that must be fulfilled in order to gain entrance to the holy of holies.[28] Jesus, of course, teaches not cultic but eschatological virtues. They refer to entrance not into the earthly temple but into the kingdom of God. It is thus a matter of entrance requirements for admittance to the βασιλεία τῶν οὐρανῶν.[28a]

As entrance requirement for the kingdom of God, the first beatitude formulates an indirect demand. Admittance to the *eschaton* is linked to the requirement of being poor in spirit. Luke, in agreement with the Q tradition, understands the beatitude differently. His beatitude makes a paradoxical assertion: in contrast to the desperate situation of the poor, they are given possession of the hope of the divine dominion. Theirs is the Paraclete, Jesus' salvation-filled consolation. The beatitude in Matthew, on the other hand, has an aim that is not primarily indicative but imperative. He summons the hearers to something they do not possess as yet, but through their actions are supposed to realize. Thus, according to Matthew's understanding, the beatitudes are ethical demands. And one cannot escape this conclusion by saying that it is not to be interpreted without the person who is speaking here; for the Matthean Jesus is not understood in the Pauline sense as the one who vicariously fulfills God's righteousness for human-kind or who out of grace reveals the righteousness of faith. His divine majesty is rather the majesty of the Lawgiver.[29] The Sermon on the Mount is the law of the Lord. The Jesus of the Sermon on the Mount does not distinguish in the Pauline sense between gift and duty, between indicative and imperative. He does not teach an opposition of law and gospel and does not know justification *sola gratia*, but rather obligates his followers to the demand that is unconditional because it is eschatologi-cally motivated. Those who follow him are sent on their way. Without deriving any claim from it, they hear and do what they are commanded, because they trust the word of the *Kyrios*.

Therefore, even on the level of the Matthean redaction, the law of the *Kyrios* includes consolation. The paracletic element of the Matthean beatitudes consists in the fact that the kingdom of God is promised as the result of the demanded action. The comfort contained in the demand is based on the future, for which salvation is pledged to the hearers. And it is based on the person of the Preacher on the mount, who speaks with eschatological authority (7:29). His demands are distinguished from similar or like-sounding ethical instructions by their eschatological foundation. His promise is that of the Son of man and Judge of the world. It defines even now the being and doing of his followers. In the hearing and doing of the eschatological demand, the Jesus community is sure of the future. In contrast to the Lutheran tradition, Matthew does not place the law before the gospel; and different from the theology of Karl Barth, the gospel is not put before the law. On the contrary, law and gospel are united. Indicative and imperative do not stand opposed to each other, but rather the eschatological-ethical demand of Jesus has the character of evangelical consolation, and the gospel—the liberating and comforting devotion of God toward humanity—occurs as the teaching and demanding message of Jesus. The law of the Preacher on the mount is the salvation-filled instruction of God.

5:4. In distinction to Matthew's "those who mourn," Luke 6:21*b* speaks of "you that weep"; they are promised that they "shall laugh." The opposition of laughing and weeping occurs also in the woe of Luke 6:25, and it is conceivable that Luke found it present in his copy of Q (Q^{Luke}) and on that basis changed the language of the second beatitude. This is supported by the fact that Luke 6:25 attests the verb πενθεῖν ('mourn') and accordingly presupposes Matt 5:4. Moreover, the arrangement of the woes of Luke 6:24-26 follows the order of beatitudes in Q. Thus the noun παράκλησις (verse 24, 'consolation') picks up the future passive παρακληθήσονται (Matt 5:4, 'they shall be comforted'). The beatitude of the mourning, therefore, came in third place in the Q order of beatitudes (Luke 6:21*b*). Matthew, to be sure, is closer to the original version in content, if not in composition. Already in Q, those who mourn were given the pledge that they "shall be comforted." Thus there is general agreement with the orientation of the Q series of beatitudes, according to which those who suffer need will be given comfort. Isa 61:2 is also applicable to this exegesis: in the year of the Lord's favor the prophet is to "comfort all who mourn."[30]

In the Matthean understanding, the paracletic element is included as a matter of course.[31] It is not, to be sure, the intention of the Matthean series of beatitudes only to grant comfort, but rather to provoke an ethical attitude that includes the eschatological promise. In particular, it is uncertain what the expression πενθοῦντες refers to concretely: to grief over the present eon,[32] which at the same time evokes a distance between the mourner and the world? Or is it a question of penitent grief, say, in the sense of the apocalyptic tradition of the Testaments of the Twelve Patriarchs?[33] The latter would include the idea that those grieving over sin are at the same time supposed to stand away from the sin and overcome it. It is also conceivable, however, that Matthew understands *mourn* in the sense of abasing oneself. Thus, Jas 4:9 attests the imperative "Mourn!" beside "Be wretched!" in addressing sinners, who are thereby called to penitence and humility before God. In any case, the Preacher on the mount is also speaking at this point to people who are ready to let him show them the way. In discipleship to Christ, grief has an eschatological promise. The passive of the eschatological future speaks of God's action, which will be revealed at the end of the world but is already happening in the present. The pledge is thus not different in content from that of the first beatitude (verse 3*b*). As in the following one, the salvation of God's dominion is promised.

5:5. As already demonstrated, the beatitude of the meek does not belong to the primitive tradition. No parallel exists in Luke's Gospel. The adjective πραΰς is a favorite Matthean word, so it may be presumed that this beatitude was composed by Matthew.[34] Yet this assumption cannot be otherwise confirmed in terms of either language or content. Moreover, this verse stands out from the series of beatitudes because it amounts to an almost literal quotation from the Septuagint (Ps 36:11 LXX). Perhaps it was assumed into the list of beatitudes in a second stage of pre-Matthean tradition (Q^Matt) in order to fill out the number of seven beatitudes (verses 3-9). The Evangelist can identify with the beatitude's assertion. In 21:5 he cites the prophetic word of Zech 9:9. Jesus is the meek king

of the end time, who enters his city riding on an ass. Also in
11:29 Jesus is portrayed as the one who is "gentle" and "lowly
in heart." This signifies that Jesus, the already present and at
the same time expected king of the end time, has in his person
realized meekness and humility and in this respect is a model
for the community. Thus, the third beatitude is not trying to
describe a condition, for example, weakness[35] or a "depressed
state," in which what matters is "recognizing God's great and
gracious will."[36] It contains, rather, an indirect summons to
active deeds that fulfill the new law of Christ: active dedication
to the high goal of meekness, friendliness, and gentleness—
deeds that are determined not by anger, brutality, or enmity,
but entirely by goodness.[37]

For these active deeds, the Preacher on the mount pledges
paradoxically what worldly activity can generally achieve only
through force and through the use of political and economic
power: inheritance of the land. Although with this expression
the psalmist designated the promised land of Israel, Matthew
cannot emulate such a conception. It goes without saying that
for the community of the first Evangelist the "land" is not
identical with Palestine (as in Gen 15:7; Deut 4:38), nor is it a
question of a realistic conception of the coming kingdom of
Zion.[38] Instead, Matthew spiritualizes the traditional view.[39]
The promised legacy of the land is the participation in the
coming kingdom of God, which is invisible and not at one's
disposal and yet present in Jesus Christ.

5:6. The interpretation of verse 6 is disputed.[40] When
compared with Luke, the understanding of the Evangelist
Matthew stands out from the pre-Matthean tradition. Luke
6:21*a* attests a shorter version that goes back to the common Q
tradition. Here the hungering are promised salvation. Luke
introduced the little word νῦν ('now') in order to make clear the
reference to the present. Like the Q model before him, he has
this beatitude directed toward those who find themselves in
basic material need, who do not have the necessities of life and
do not know how their hunger can be stilled. Jesus grants them
satisfaction. He gives them a pledge that goes against human
expectation. The promised satisfaction is not of this world, but
will be fulfilled in the kingdom of God. Jesus announces that
the grace of the Judge of the world is certain for those who

hunger. He reaches beyond the material plight. The hunger of
humanity anticipates the end. It opens up another dimension:
that of the kingdom of God. This comfort, says Jesus, is more
than any social program can provide. It is meant for the whole
person and lasts beyond the coming and going of the world.

Such is the report of the Q tradition. With the addition of a
few words Matthew changed this original meaning. He inserts
"for righteousness" and perhaps even "and thirst." Now the
hunger of Jesus' hearers is no longer understood in the material
sense; he directs his attention, not toward earthly food, but
toward "righteousness." The originally concrete, realistic understanding of hunger and thirst has been spiritualized.[41]

What does *righteousness* mean in the Matthean understanding? The first Evangelist employs the concept δικαιοσύνη
seven times, of which five are in the Sermon on the Mount
(3:15; 5:6, 10, 20; 6:1, 33; 21:32). With the exception of 6:33,
where the Matthean mode of expression is determined by the
inherited context,[42] all of the occurrences are construed in an
anthropological, not theological, fashion; the word designates
the righteousness of people, a human attitude that is supposed
to be realized through active deeds (cf. esp. 5:20 and 6:1).[43]

This interpretation is apparently contradicted by the phrase
hunger and thirst, which seems to express a passivity; thus,
righteousness would have to designate the gift of God to
humankind and not a human ethical attitude. Do hunger and
thirst thus characterize in the figurative sense a human longing
that could be stilled only from outside, say through the gift of
righteousness presented by God? Significant for this understanding is the pre-Matthean version of the verse, which
indisputably means a condition of dependence, a passive
attitude. Nevertheless, because of the Matthean understanding of righteousness, it can be established that hunger and
thirst designate an active, energetic longing, a decisive effort
toward the realization of righteousness. With the adoption of
this view, the picture of hunger and thirst is ethicized. It urges
a decisive ethical initiative that stakes everything on realizing
righteousness here and now.[44]

The hearers of the Sermon on the Mount are thus exhorted
to do righteousness, and indeed not just a part of righteousness. It is significant that the concept is constructed with the
article: it is the whole of righteousness that is demanded! At

this point one can translate with C. F. von Weizsäcker: "Blessed are those who hunger and thirst to be righteous, for they shall be satisfied."[45] The beatitude presents the followers of Jesus with the goal of wanting to be righteous.

The conceptions of the righteous and of righteousness that are present on the religious-historical landscape are quite diverse. What is meant here cannot be derived in a one-sided way, say, from the Hebrew Bible or from the ethics of Plato or Aristotle. It is problematic to base the Old Testament idea on the concept of Yahweh's צדקה (zedakah), for example by equating the righteousness of Yahweh with compassion (thus Lapide-Weizsäcker, Seligpreisungen, 72, 74). In the Old Testament understanding, Yahweh can also appear as a jealous, angry God, who punishes sin, exercises retribution, and exhorts to the execution of his ban. Whoever sets himself against the will of Yahweh becomes guilty vis-à-vis Yahweh and is unrighteous (cf. 1 Sam 15). Righteousness in the Old Testament as well as the New is what corresponds to the will of God (τὸ θέλημα τοῦ θεοῦ: Mark 3:35; 1 Pet 4:2). But while in the Old Testament even a holy war can be commanded by God, this idea would be unthinkable in the Sermon on the Mount. The will of God is thus interpreted differently at various times and in various situations; it is not a timeless reality but one that is related to the situation. On the basis of Plato's philosophy, righteousness can be defined in a formal sense. According to this definition, one is righteous if one does what one has to do (Lapide-Weizsäcker, Seligpreisungen, 73). This is required here of the followers of Jesus, and in what follows, he details what makes up the content of the demanded righteousness.

The second clause of the beatitude remains in the picture and has not been changed by Matthew. Being "satisfied" circumscribes with the passivum divinum the action of God. It means the same thing that is asserted by the other second clauses: the pledge of the kingdom of heaven. It is valid for those who strive unremittingly for the realization of righteousness.[46] Again Matthew has spiritualized and at the same time ethicized his source.

5:7. Verse 7 begins the second trio of beatitudes (vv. 7-9) that Matthew presumably likewise adopted from the Q tradition (Q^Matt), which originally speaks not of passivity, but of the activity of people. Thus, here the eschatological promise is made exclusively and originally to an ethical attitude. In addition to this instance, the term ἐλεήμων ('merciful, having mercy') appears in the New Testament only in Heb 2:15 (of

Christ as the heavenly high priest). The translation in English is the same as for οἰκτίρμων (cf. Luke 6:36). H. Cremer distinguishes between the two terms: οἰκτίρμων refers to (merciful) human feeling, while ἐλέμων indicates the "attitude and action" of mercy.[46a] If this is presupposed here, then the word ἐλεήμων was consciously chosen in order to demand compassionate action and not just a merciful feeling. The demand of mercy does not distinguish this beatitude from the ethics of Judaism. The tractate Šabbat says, "Whoever has mercy on people will receive mercy from heaven; whoever does not have mercy on people will not receive mercy from heaven."[47] The demand of mercy acquired a firm position in early Christian admonition.[48] In our text, the announcement of the coming kingdom of heaven is already linked with the idea of judgment. In the final judgment, the Judge of the world will show mercy to the people who exercised mercy in their time. For the present the demand is made to be merciful. This is what Jesus demands of his hearers. The "virtue" of mercy characterizes discipleship to Jesus, just as the doers of mercy are true followers of Jesus (cf. Matt 25:31-46). Merciful action requires human initiative without any reservations; it realizes the demand for unlimited love. Such undivided action is the mark of the perfect person (cf. 5:48). If this beatitude can be designated a "statement of divine right,"[49] then this means that it brings to expression the unconditionality of the demanding will of God.

5:8. The beatitude of those who are "pure in heart" adopts an Old Testament formulation. In Pss 24:4 and 73:1 (MT) the pious who are conscious of their innocence before God are called ברי לבב (*bare lebab*) = καθαροὶ τῇ καρδίᾳ (LXX). The dative is to be understood as dative of reference. In Hebrew the heart is the seat of the will. Accordingly, in 1 Tim 1:5 the "pure heart" can be placed parallel to the "good conscience." Pure in heart is the one who has a good conscience and harbors no evil intention. In other words, this beatitude is for those who choose the good and perfect as their life's goal. In the language of Matthew this means that the person with a pure heart is the one who fulfills the demand of righteousness; such a person stands before God spotless, without sin.[50]

The demand of purity is turned indirectly against the attitude of the Pharisees, who are pictured as the antitype in Matthew's Gospel. According to 23:25-26, the Pharisees cleanse only the outside of the cup and the plate, but the inside is full of robbery and impurity. They are admonished to cleanse first the inside of the cup, "so that" the outside may also be clean. This admonition was already a part of the Q source and there too had an antipharisaical pointedness (cf. Luke 11:39-42). The attitude of Pharisaism, based on cultic ceremonial legalism, is rejected as something external. What matters in Matthew (as in Q before him) is the inside of the cup, that is, having the person himself become clean. The particle ἵνα ('so that') means that the will of the pure individual is also supposed to determine his outward appearance. In contrast to the "hypocrisy" of the Pharisees, therefore, Jesus' demand requires agreement between inner and outer attitude. Both must be spotless. The ritual, legalistic obligation of Pharisaism is thereby lifted, because it holds to the external. In such an opposition, Matthew can join with the cult critique of the Old Testament (e.g., Amos 5:21-25). Yet in the realm of Gentile Christianity (as also in Acts 7:2-52, esp. vv. 42ff.), the Old Testament-Jewish ritual legalism is given a fundamentally negative valuation. Matthew does not "rejudaize" Mark's Gospel but, like the other Evangelists, faces the Jewish tradition in a way that is open and at the same time critical. On the one hand, the Old Testament-Jewish conceptual world is adopted; on the other, Jesus' critique and intensification of the Torah is passed on slightly modified (5:21-48). The repudiation in 15:20 is characteristic of the position of the first Evangelist on the Jewish purity law, as is the fundamental alternative: "I desire mercy, and not sacrifice" (9:13; 12:7; cf. Hos 6:6).[51]

Such an unconditional requirement is followed by the promise "they shall see God." In the Old Testament *seeing God* is a cultic concept. Whoever goes up to the temple seeks the face of God (Ps 24:6). Seeing God is reported of Moses and the elders on Sinai[52] and especially of the prophets in connection with visions at their calling.[53] For the Greeks seeing is the highest form of knowledge and mediates the relationship with God.[54] Here also, it may lie thus in the background and signify no difference from the Old Testament or from Hellenism. Yet for Matthew, it is not a question of the knowledge of God or of an ecstatic, mystical seeing of God, but of a meeting with God that will occur in the end time and is characteristic of the kingdom. This is attested also by the pre-Pauline agape hymn: "Now we see in a mirror dimly, but then face to face" (1 Cor 13:12). To the people of a pure heart is promised the gift of communion with God.

5:9. The same pledge is given to the εἰρηνοποιοί (= εἰρήνην ποιοῦντες), the 'peacemakers.' Again through a beatitude a demand is made. The admonition of peacemaking can be similarly expressed in Jewish apocalyptic. Thus 2 Enoch contains a beatitude for the peacemaker or preserver of peace: "Blessed is the one who walks in peace; cursed is the one who disturbs the peace" (52:11-12). Rabbinical literature praises the godly of the Old Testament who served peace.[55] *Shalom* is contained in the (peace) greeting of the Old Testament[56] and was already used in this sense by the Assyrians and Syrians. The concept of peace and peacemaking is part of the expectation of the time of salvation; therefore, the Hebrew שלום (*shalom*) can be translated both with *peace* as well as with *salvation*.[57]

The commandment to practice peace assumed an important place in early Christian admonition. Matthew himself gives an example in 5:23-24: the duty of reconciliation, of peacemaking, is a central Christian commandment, if not a Christian virtue. So admonishes Christ in Mark: "Be at peace with one another."[58] And in the Epistle of James, righteousness and peace are expected from those who make peace.[59] Thus, the New Testament writings know no limitation on the duty of peace.

The peace-loving are granted the promise. The words of the second clause (v. 9*b*) are found in Hos 2:1 LXX (ἐκεῖ κληθήσονται υἱοὶ θεοῦ ζῶντος 'There they will be called the sons of the living God'). There the promise of divine sonship is tied to the expectation of the reuniting of the northern and southern kingdoms. The *passivum divinum* makes it known that the establishment of this kingdom of peace will be accomplished through the action of Yahweh. The concept of divine sonship has an important function in connection with the idea of the royal Davidic dynasty. It asserts that the king of Israel is "adopted" or "legitimized" as son by Yahweh.[60] In the Jewish wisdom literature the righteous are designated "sons of God" (Wis 2:13, 18). Something similar is found in Greek and Hellenistic literature.[61] When Luther's translation of our verse chooses the phrase "Kinder Gottes" ('children of God'),[62] this would presuppose as Greek text τέκνα θεοῦ. In truth, the verse has the adult sons in mind (so also Gal 4:4-5). Thus, it is supposed to represent the relationship of humankind to the

Ground of all being. Whoever is "God's son" has come to the reality of his existence. Thus, in terms of the future and eschatology, it is asserted as promise. Although the sphere of Old Testament-Jewish tradition is thereby not yet abandoned, this pledge gains its proper place through the fact that the Preacher on the mount, who pronounces this promise, is himself the "Son of God" (cf. Matt 1:18-2:23). The peacemakers are pledged the essence that Jesus embodies as the Son of God.

5:10. The tradition of the seven beatitudes that Matthew found before him as a unit in his copy of Q reaches up to this point. In content verse 10 agrees largely with verses 11-12. The reason ἕνεκεν δικαιοσύνης ('for righteousness sake') anticipates the parallel assertion in verse 11 (ἕνεκεν ἐμοῦ 'for my sake'). The second clause (v. 10*b*) repeats verse 3*b*. *Righteousness* has already been recognized as a favorite Matthean word.[63] The entire verse was composed by Matthew. It concludes the series of third person beatitudes. Although there are eight of these beatitudes, Matthew is not concerned with a twofold division,[64] but with an appeal to an attitude that reflects the essence of discipleship to Jesus.

In this verse the situation of the Matthean community becomes visible. The congregation lives in persecution, as is also attested in the second part of the mission speech (10:17ff). It is significant that the promise is not for the persecuted in general, but for those who are persecuted "for righteousness' sake." Presumably, it is not unimportant that the article is missing.[65] Accordingly, the difference from verse 6 is intentional: persecution burst in on the Christian community not because of discipleship to Christ (*the* righteousness); rather, the beatitude relates specifically to an attitude that can be termed righteous and as such represents the reason for persecution. The *conditio sine qua non* of this beatitude is thus a human ethical attitude. This is also expressed in verse 11 with the word ψευδόμενοι ('falsely') and is assumed by 1 Pet 3:14, where our verse is apparently presupposed. Ethical reflection leads to a differentiation. There are persecutions—for example, actions of the state—which are lawful, because they proceed on the basis of law and justice. When, however, the Christian community is patently subjected unjustly to official

compulsory measures and such interference is even carried
out on account of a legitimate activity, then the promise takes
effect. Such persecution can confirm the certainty of faith.
Thus, the beatitude contains encouragement for the hearers
who find themselves in the persecution situation. At the same
time it expresses a demand; it is a question of not leaving the
standard of righteousness out of consideration when under
persecution, of proving oneself among the δίκαιοι; for the
pledge of the kingdom of heaven is for the "righteous."

5:11-12. Finally comes the most extensive beatitude in this
collection; it comprises verses 11-12.[66] In the Q level common
to Matthew and Luke, it was already composed in the second
person plural, as is made clear by the break between third and
second person (v. 10 versus v. 11) and by the parallel in Luke
6:22-23. Even if this tradition is old, it still does not belong to
the oldest Jesus tradition. For it is different from the terse
beatitudes of Luke 6:20-21 par., in that these verses are
executed in a relatively broad way and reflect the persecution
situation of the community—a *vaticinium ex eventu* that
compares the fate of the persecuted Christians with the
prophets of the old covenant.[67]

According to Luke 6:22, the persecution is connected with
the relationship of the synagogue to the Christian congregation. While the oldest congregation in Jerusalem sought to
hold fast to the original bond of unity between synagogue and
church, it is broken here; and it is not the Christians but the
Jews who are presented as the cause. The persecutors confront
the Christians with hate and apply synagogal disciplinary
measures against them. Ἀφορίζειν amounts to 'excommuni-
cate' and is thus identical with ἀποσυνάγωγος εἶναι (John 9:22;
12:42; 16:2). The expression ἐκβάλλειν τὸ ὄνομα is also to be
understood in this way: it is not just a matter of reviling but of
casting out. The word ὄνομα can refer to the name "Christian"
(cf. 1 Pet 4:16) or to the personal name of individual Christians
through whom the bearer of this name is represented. The
Christians are declared "unpersons" and excluded from the
synagogue because they belong to the Son of man. If the Christ
title points to the apocalyptic horizon and implies an
announcement of judgment, then this is picked up in the
following verse 23 with the indication of a μισθός ('reward').

The calamity-filled history of the Jews, who had persecuted the prophets, is contrasted with the salvation-filled future of the Christian community.[68] Luke 6:22-23 is an early document of the dispute between church and synagogue. The parallel between the persecuted Christians and the prophets of the old covenant makes known that the community not only understood itself as followers of the Old Testament prophets but also claimed for itself possession of God's Spirit.

In Matt 5:11, the Lukan parallel appears shortened. Missing are the concrete details on "excommunication" and "exclusion." It speaks only in general of "reviling" and "persecuting." Here a change in the congregational situation is recognizable. Matthew is writing in Gentile territory; his congregation is predominantly composed of Gentile Christians. The persecutions come, accordingly, not primarily from the Jews, but from Gentile compatriots.[69] Although Matthew also reflects synagogal persecution in 10:17 (deliverance to the councils, flogging in "their synagogues"), he continues in 10:18, "You will be dragged before governors and kings for my sake, to bear testimony before them and the Gentiles." The church of Matthew has a universal expanse and appears with a universal claim (cf. 28:16-20). Therefore, the persecution of this church is also not to be restricted to a special area, such as the Jewish disagreements. The persecution terminology also has a broad scope: ὀνειδίζειν designates the (public) reviling and cursing; διώκειν in Matthew is an often employed technical term for 'persecute the Christian community' (5:10-12; 10:23; 23:34 par.). Verse 11c refers to vile gossip. Comparison with the Lukan parallel shows that here it is not a question of synagogal use of force. Matthew makes the addition of ψευδόμενοι, which characterizes such gossip. A few manuscripts omit this expression,[70] perhaps because of the idea that evil gossip "for Jesus' sake" is, in any case, identical to "lies." Yet Matthew thinks juridically: the subject of this beatitude is not just any evil gossip that is occasioned by the community's being Christian; there are Christians who, under the pretext of Christian concern, abuse the reputation of the community. Only in a case where the hostile attacks are false, unfounded, and thus deceitful, can the persecuted be certain of the pledge of salvation.

The persecution occurs "on my account" because the

Christians belong to Jesus Christ and confess Christ as their
Lord. When Luke, on the other hand, reports "on account of
the Son of man," he thus represents the older Q version. In
other places also, Matthew replaces the concept "Son of man"
with the personal pronoun (cf. 16:21). Rather than depriving
Jesus of the title "Son of man," this substitution makes very
clear a personal relationship with Jesus Christ as the Lord of
the community. In place of the personal pronoun, Codex D
(Bezae Cantabrigiensis) and the Itala read ἕκενεν δικαιοσύνης
('on account of righteousness'). In view of its weak attestation,
this variant is secondary. In substance it is an assimilation to
verse 10*a*, which correctly repeats Matthew's view: in verse 10
the persecution occurs "for righteousness' sake" versus here
"on account of me" (that is, for Jesus' sake). The reason for
persecution can be the one as well as the other. Thus, the
person of Jesus is very closely related to righteousness. As the
teacher of righteousness, he points to the "way of righteousness" (21:32). Since his appearance is defined by righteousness, the cause of persecution can be adherence to the person
of Jesus as well as the attitude of righteousness. Both times it is
a question of the same goal: the community that knows itself
called by the word of Jesus is set on the way of righteousness.

According to the usual style of a beatitude, μακάριοι comes
in predicate-first position. Generally, if the predicate is to be
expanded, then it is indicated as here in the second person
plural (ἐστέ 'you are'). Then follows the subject, the listeners,
who in our passage are circumscribed by the conditional clause
(ὅταν 'when'). The beatitude ends with a substantiating clause
that is found in verse 12 (ὅτι 'for'). This second statement is
introduced with a cry of jubilation: "Rejoice and be glad." The
two expressions are related in content and go back to the Q
source.[71] According to the Old Testament-prophetic view, the
eschatological time of salvation will be fulfilled with joy and
gladness (Joel 2:21). In the beginning of his Gospel, Matthew
speaks of the joy that comes over the Magi from the East when
they see the star of Bethlehem (2:10). This is the joy of the
messianic time that breaks forth with the birth of Jesus as the
Son of God. In our text—as in the Sermon on the Mount
generally—attention is directed toward the future. The
persecuted are promised the heavenly μισθός ('reward'). The
eschaton stands ready for those who suffer for the Lord. For all

who must bear it, persecution is a meaningful happening because of the goal toward which the community is moving. Thus, eschatological joy can be the very mark of the suffering community (cf. Phil 1:18; 2:17-18; 1 Pet 1:8; 4:13; and elsewhere). The conferences of the early Christian community, as reported by Luke, were characterized by eschatological jubilation (Acts 2:46). The same is expected for the glorious end time, for the marriage of the Lamb, of which the Revelation of John speaks.[72] The community under persecution did not realize such joy in spite of suffering: they rejoiced in suffering,[73] for their suffering contained the certainty of reward.

The word μισθός in Matthew's Gospel is a technical term for the heavenly reward beyond this world.

The idea of reward stems from Judaism. The Old Testament prophets teach a double retribution of God: the coming punishment but also preservation in the judgment. The Old Testament-Jewish wisdom literature—to which there are close parallels especially in the monitory passages of the New Testament—teach an inner-world compensation: whoever does good for a poor person will be repaid by Yahweh for his good deed (Prov 19:17). Thus, the teaching of wisdom seeks to introduce a person to the idea that through the doing of good he will also experience good in his life. Jewish apocalyptic had in mind especially the future heavenly reward that the pious would receive in the last judgment: "everlasting life" (Dan 12:2). Rabbinical theology was especially concerned with the size of the reward. By keeping the commandments of the law, the godly earn the wages that are reckoned to them according to their achievements. The reward in the coming world corresponds to a person's achievement during his earthly life (cf. Str-B 1:231-32; 4:484-500).

Matthew does not present a calculation of the reward in the world to come. He does not take part in the rabbinical discussion but reflects prerabbinical views. Therefore, he also does not determine casuistically which human achievements must go with the future reward. The godly, however, can count on a heavenly reward. The proper behavior of the Christian in the world is motivated on this basis (6:1ff.; cf. Rev 22:12). Matthew mentions the idea that the heavenly reward is like a treasure that is laid up in heaven (6:20 par. Luke 12:33). The sufferings of the persecuted will be reminted, as it were, into this treasure. In later Jewish Christianity the Holy Spirit, who is received at baptism, has the duty of bearing the good works of the baptized up to heaven (Ps Clem Hom 18). From this point it is not far to the ecclesiastical doctrine of *thesaurus spiritualis* as it is found in medieval Scholasticism.[74]

In any case, the seeds of such ecclesiastical calculation and administration of reward are found in New Testament thought. Of course, the Evangelist is not morally suspect because of his conception of reward. He stands here in the sphere of influence of his Jewish environment. A depreciation of the idea of reward, such as occurs in idealistic thinking, is foreign to him. On the other hand, it cannot be disputed that the idea of reward plays no small role in the theology of Matthew. Even if it must be questioned critically, the concept he is trying to express here still remains important. Matthew is saying that the endurance of suffering is meaningful. God acknowledges as his own those who endure torment for the sake of Christ. This is reason enough for joy and exultation in a world that, on its own, has no access to such joy.

Persecution places the Christian community in company with the Old Testament prophets. The Old Testament knows of the persecutions of Elijah (1 Kings 19) and Jeremiah (Jer 37:11ff. and elsewhere). In later legend these stories were expanded through martyrologies and other reports of the persecution and death of Old Testament prophets. The Old Testament-Jewish traditions attach themselves thereby to the idea of the violent fate of the prophets, which was developed in Deuteronomic theology.[75] Such tradition is also presupposed by Matt 23:29ff. The Christian community learned for themselves the fate of the prophets. The phrase "who were before you"[76] designates the followers of Jesus as followers of the prophets. As the unspecific *persecute* (vv. 10-11) makes clear, Matthew is thinking not only of Christian prophets but of all community members as followers of Jesus. If they are compared to prophets, this means that they have a mission to fulfill. Like the prophets of the old covenant, they have received a divine commission. That is why the redactor Matthew, in contrast to the original Q composition, has included the images of salt, light, and a city on a hill.

2.2.2 5:13-16 The Nature of Discipleship

Berger, P. R. "Die Stadt auf dem Berg." In *Wort in der Zeit*, FS K. H. Renstorf, edited by W. Haubeck and M. Bachmann, 82-85. Leiden, 1980.

Campbell, K. M. "The New Jerusalem in Matthew 5:14." *SJT* 31 (1978): 335-63.

Cullmann, O. "Das Gleichnis vom Salz." In idem, *Vorträge und Aufsätze*, edited by K. Fröhlich, 192-201. 1966.

Hahn, F. "Die Worte vom Licht, Lk 11:33-36." In *Orientierung an Jesus*, FS J. Schmid, edited by P. Hoffmann et al., 107-38. 1973.

Jeremias, J. "Die Lampe unter dem Scheffel." *ZNW* 39 (1940/41): 237-40. (= *Abba*, 99-102.)

Krämer, M. "Ihr seid das Salz der Erde. . . . Ihr seid das Licht der Welt." *MTZ* 28 (1977): 133-57.

Rad, G. von. "Die Stadt auf dem Berge." *EvT* 8 (1948/49): 439-47. (= *Gesammelte Studien zum Alten Testament*, 214-24. TBü 8. 1958.)

Schnackenburg, R. "Ihr seid das Salz der Erde, das Licht der Welt." (On Matt 5:13-16.) In idem, *Schriften zum Neuen Testament*, 177-200. 1971.

Schneider, G. "Das Bildwort von der Lampe." *ZNW* 61 (1970): 183-209.

Souček, J. B. "Salz der Erde und Licht der Welt." *TZ* 19 (1963): 169-79.

Steinhauser. *Doppelbildworte*, 327-83.

¹³You are the salt of the earth; but if salt has lost its taste, how shall its saltness be restored? It is no longer good for anything except to be thrown out and trodden under foot by men.

¹⁴You are the light of the world. A city set on a hill cannot be hid.

¹⁵Nor do men light a lamp and put it under a bushel, but on a stand, and it gives light to all in the house. ¹⁶Let your light so shine before men, that they may see your good works and give glory to your Father who is in heaven.

As synoptic comparison shows, this section goes back to isolated words of Jesus in the primitive tradition. Thus Mark 9:50 identifies verse 13 as an originally independent saying. The parallel in Luke 14:34-35 indicates, however, that this passage was already present in Q in expanded form. Also verse 15, through its parallel Luke 11:33, is attested for the Q tradition. In this case there is a double tradition (cf. Mark 4:21 par. Luke 8:16). The text on the light of the world and the city on a hill (v. 14) seems to be an addition, whose unskilled placement points, nonetheless, to a pre-Matthean origin. Verse 16, on the other hand, is a redactional formation. The language is Matthean.⁷⁷ This verse brings the application of the foregoing images and at the same time provides transition to what follows.

In terms of form history, verses 13-15 deal with image sayings. An abstract truth is poured into the form of an image. Originally, the third person was appropriate to such image sayings. The Evangelist probably introduced the second person as an accommodation to what precedes and in preparation for what follows. Jesus is speaking to his hearers: not only to his twelve disciples but to his followers in all times, as the closing chorus of the Sermon on the Mount makes clear

(7:28-29). If the images of salt and light are related to Jesus' teaching in Mark and Luke, in Matthew they illustrate the nature of discipleship. This indicative—the description of the state of discipleship—is not to be separated from the imperative. Like the foregoing beatitudes, these verses also contain admonition. Being salt and light expresses the duty of discipleship.

5:13. According to rabbinical teaching, salt cannot lose its power to season.[78] When Mark 9:50 mentions the saltness of salt, it expresses thereby an impossibility: either salt is salt or it is not! There is no other alternative. The Markan parallel attests an αὐτό as direct object: "How will you season *it*?" If the same pronoun were added to our verse, the statement would be identical with the Markan text. Yet we must still go from the given wording and translate it, "How will you salt?" (RSV: "How shall its saltness be restored?") The image is defined by the intended content. The question is, if salt has become unusable,[79] then what is there to salt with? The answer: nothing! Salt that has become unusable can only be thrown away. This description of the nature of discipleship states unmetaphorically both an assertion and an admonition. In their listening to the word of Jesus, in their doing of righteousness, the disciples are for the world what salt is for eating: a necessary, indispensable component. The word γῆ ('earth') has the meaning of κόσμος ('human world'; so also 18:7; cf. Gen 11:1 LXX). Matthew's community stands under the commission to evangelize all nations (28:16-20). The matter of being disciples is decided by the carrying out of this mission assignment![80]

5:14. The expression φῶς τοῦ κόσμου ('light of the world') also designates the disciples of Jesus in the broadest sense of the word. Thus, the Johannine Jesus claims it for himself (John 8:12). The servant of Yahweh was earlier called the "light to the nations" (Isa 42:6). And in Matthew's Gospel, Jesus can relate to himself Isaiah's words about the light coming on in the darkness (4:15-16; cf. Isa. 9:1-2). In regard to discipleship, the expression means that radiating is an essential part of being a disciple.[81] Light cannot be perceived apart from its function of shining. Only its radiation makes it light. The anthropological application of this expression is also utilized monitorily elsewhere in the New Testament (Rom 2:19; Phil 2:15). Verse 14a anticipates verse 16; here the missionary task of the community of Jesus Christ is already asserted.

That discipleship to Jesus cannot be lived in a corner and that the Matthean Jesus does not bring esoteric instruction— these ideas also come from the image saying of the city on a hill. The older exegesis derived it from a secular proverb expressing a general truth that meant something like: whatever is outstanding in the world will also find its proper recognition. G. von Rad discovered here an apocalyptic motif, according to which it is a question of Zion, the city on the hill of salvation. It is the goal of the final pilgrimage of the nations.[82] Matthew understands it as an image that should be interpreted not apocalyptically but monitorily and ethically: by their righteousness, the disciples are lifted up out of the world. They are separated from others by Jesus' eschatological demand. Since Jesus has given them his law, their consciences are sharpened. They are called to responsible action. No one can relieve them of this duty.

5:15. The image sayings of the city on a hill and the lampstand are also connected in the Gospel of Thomas (Gos. Thom. 32, 33). This could be an indication that Matthew found this connection in his Q tradition. Nevertheless, the Gospel of Thomas is a gnostic reworking of the synoptic Gospels, and thus essentially of importance only for the history of interpretation.[83]

Here we have two image sayings, of which the second, of course, is shaped in more detail,[84] but corresponds to the first in the content of its statement. The word λύχνος designates an oil lamp, an oil container with a wick, without a base or stand. The burning lamp is placed under a μόδιος.[85] Luther translated this word with *Scheffel* ('bushel'), which was taken from the peasant life of his time and on the basis of this verse has attained proverbial status in German. According to Jeremias, there is a contrast between the "bushel," to which he ascribes the function of extinguishing light, and the lighting of the lamp.[86] Thus, for Matthew it has a good sense:[87] as the light is extinguished, or at least is not equal to its task, when one puts it under a bushel, so also discipleship loses its meaning when it is not active. The essence of the disciple consists in his activity; being and action are inseparable from each other.

The only point of lighting a lamp is to let it shine. For this purpose it needs a lampstand (λυχνία). From this position the lamp can fulfill it function. Only Matthew emphasizes that it shines for "all" in the house (cf. Luke 11:33: those who enter see the light). Is it presupposed that a Palestinian house consisted of only one room? This, however, would have made the express emphasis of πᾶσιν ('all') unnecessary. Matthew lifts up consciously the universality of the light's radiation. The intended content fits into the image and is expressed even more clearly in the following Matthean verse.

5:16. The particle οὕτως ('so') refers back to the foregoing and connects the image with the application that now follows.[88] Inherent in the nature of salt is the fact that it salts; in the nature of a city on the hill, that it cannot be hid; in the nature of light, that it shines. Likewise, inherent in the nature of discipleship are καλὰ ἔργα ('good works').[89] Thus, Matthew does not distinguish between the light that is the community as such, and the one that it should let shine;[90] he does not differentiate between gift and duty. Rather, the application is supposed to make clear that the church must be visible in its appearance.[91] *Ecclesia visibilis* for Matthew means that the Christian community must match Jesus' demand through its initiative toward righteousness among the people. Only thus can it make its claim of being the "light of the world"—but not as a possession that it has at its disposal: the quality of being light is put on the line anew every day, and it must be attained anew every day.

Verse 16 is, accordingly, the interpretation and application of verses 13-15. Discipleship takes place in the concrete realm of human reality. The required "good works" are to be accomplished in service to humanity. Yet the final goal of following Jesus is not humankind—not the neighbor and, of course, even less one's own self—but "your Father who is in heaven." The deeds of Jesus' disciples glorify, not the doers (this is made clear in the antipharisaical discussion of 6:1ff.), but the one who gave the promise of sonship (5:9).

As a redactional verse, verse 16 has special importance. It leads not only verses 13-15, but also the preceding series of beatitudes (vv. 3-12), to a climax and confirms that the whole opening of the Sermon on the Mount has a monitory cutting edge. This is made clear by the second person plural (ὑμεῖς: v. 13), which dominates the presentation right up to the end of the Sermon on the Mount. In content the demand for "good works" anticipates the fundamental assertion of verse 20. At this point it is no longer so important whether verse 16 or verse 20 is called the theme of the Sermon on the Mount.[92] Both verses emphasize that the nature of discipleship consists, not in hearing the words of the Preacher on the mount, but in the connection between hearing and doing. Everything is focused on the deed of discipleship.

2.2.3   5:17-20   The New Righteousness

Arens, E. *The* HΛΘON-*Sayings in the Synoptic Tradition.* Orbis Biblicus et Orientalis 10. 1976.

Banks, R. "Matthew's Understanding of the Law: Authenticity and Interpretation in Matthew 5:17-20." *JBL* 93 (1974): 226-42.

Barth, G. "Das Gesetzesverständnis des Evangelisten Matthäus." In G. Bornkamm et al., *Überlieferung und Auslegung im Matthäusevangelium*, 7th ed., 54-154. WMANT 1. 1975.

Betz, H. D. "Die hermeneutischen Prinzipien in der Bergpredigt (Mt 5:17-20)." In *Verifikationen*, FS G. Ebeling, edited by E. Jüngel et al., 27-41. 1982.

Broer, I. *Freiheit vom Gesetz und Radikalisierung des Gesetzes*, 11-74, 123-30. SBS 98. 1980.

Giesen, H. *Christliches Handeln: Eine redaktionskritische Untersuchung zum δικαιοσύνη-Begriff im Matthäus-Evangelium.* 1982.

Harder, G. "Jesus und das Gesetz (Matthäus 5,17-20)." In *Antijudaismus im Neuen Testament?* edited by W. P. Eckert et al., 105-18. 1967.

Heubült, C. "Mt 5,17-20: Ein Beitrag zur Theologie des Evangelisten Matthäus." *ZNW* 71 (1980): 143-49.

Hübner. *Gesetz*, 15-39.

Ljungman, H. *Das Gesetz erfüllen.* Lunds Univ. Årsskr. n.s. 50. 1954.

Luz, U. "Die Erfüllung des Gesetzes bei Matthäus (Mt 5,17-20)." *ZTK* 75 (1978): 398-435.

Marguerat. *Judgment*, 110-41.

Meier, J. P. *Law and History in Matthew's Gospel*, 41-124. AnBib 71. 1976.

Sand. *Gesetz*, 33-39, 183-87, 203.

Schweizer, E. "Matth. 5,17-20: Anmerkungen zum Gesetzesverständnis des Matthäus." In idem, *Neotestamentica*, 399-406. 1963.

———. "Noch einmal Mt 5,17-20." In idem, *Matthäus und seine Gemeinde*, 78-85.

Trilling. *Das wahre Israel*, 167-86.

[17]*Think not that I have come to abolish the law and the prophets; I have come not to abolish them but to fulfill them.* [18]*For truly, I say to*

you, till heaven and earth pass away, not an iota, not a dot, will pass from the law until all is accomplished. ¹⁹Whoever then relaxes one of the least of these commandments and teaches men so, shall be called least in the kingdom of heaven; but he who does them and teaches them shall be called great in the kingdom of heaven. ²⁰For I tell you, unless your righteousness exceeds that of the scribes and Pharisees, you will never enter the kingdom of heaven.

As the conclusion and climax of the opening of the Sermon on the Mount, verses 17-20 show especially strong evidence of redactional intrusion. Both verse 17 and verse 20 were composed by Matthew, as can be argued on linguistic grounds,[95] but one must also deal with Matthean influence in verses 18-19.

The transition from verse 16 to verse 17 is easily achieved. The demand for good works (v. 16) is nothing other than the obligation to "the law and the prophets," which Jesus does not want to abolish but to fulfill. The proper attitude of Jesus' disciples is obedience to the Torah. The law of the Lord and the Torah of the Old Testament are not in contradiction with each other; both express the eschatological demand whose fulfillment characterizes discipleship to Jesus Christ.

5:17. With the phrase μὴ νομίσητε ('think not'), the Evangelist takes up a formulation that also appears in 10:34 and there, too, introduces an ἦλθον saying from Jesus ("Think not that I have come to bring peace . . ."). Although such "I-have-come" sayings are formulations of the community, they hark back thereby to the mission of Jesus Christ that has already occurred. In our passage a misunderstanding of Jesus' appearance is warded off by taking a position against the view that Jesus wanted to abolish the law and the prophets. Νόμος ἢ προφῆται ('law *or* prophets' in some translations) is a frequent combination in Matthew and corresponds to νόμος καὶ προθῆται ('law and prophets': 7:12; 22:40; also in Greek-speaking Judaism: 2 Macc 15:9; 4 Macc 18:10). This expression designates the whole Old Testament. Basically, it can be used in two respects: (1) in regard to the history of revelation (thus 11:13 par. Luke 16:16, a pre-Matthean formulation that relates the whole Old Testament as prophecy to the Christ event), and (2) ethically and nomologically, in that

the Old Testament is understood as the obligatory demand of
God. This is the Matthean intention in 7:12 and 22:40 and is
also to be presupposed here. Jesus speaks against the
supposition that he intended to revoke the law as the
demanding will of God. With this assertion, were Matthew and
his community in disagreement with an antagonistic group of
antinomians? Is this statement put in the mouth of Jesus in
order to refute the opposing view that he himself had spoken
out for the abolishing of the Old Testament? The problem of
antinomian opponents of Matthew has been frequently
overestimated.[94] In our text it can be clearly established that
Matthew is rejecting only a theoretical possibility and does not
have concrete adversaries in mind. So much can be gained
from the introductory "think not," for in the parallel text of
10:34, it is not a matter of a concrete polemic. The Evangelist
presents a declaration of principle that places Jesus unequivo-
cally on the side of the Old Testament Torah and is obligatory
for all followers of Jesus.

The verbs $\kappa\alpha\tau\alpha\lambda\acute{\upsilon}\epsilon\iota\nu$ and $\pi\lambda\eta\rho o\hat{\upsilon}\nu$ are, accordingly, related
to the Old Testament law; they express two mutually exclusive
possibilities: (1) to 'abolish' or 'repeal' a law, or (2) to "fill up the
measure" (thus 23:32), that is, 'affirm,' 'confirm,' or 'realize.'
$\pi\lambda\eta\rho o\hat{\upsilon}\nu$ (literally, 'make full, fulfill') is a favorite Matthean
word and often asserts the fulfillment of Old Testament
promise, as in the introduction of the quotations Jesus reflects
upon. It also occurs, however, in the sense 'to realize a
requirement of the law' (thus 3:15, redactionally). Thus, the
Matthean Jesus stands in a basically positive relationship to the
Torah; he affirms the Old Testament law and "fulfills" it in his
exemplary appearance. In this passage, nevertheless, the verb
fulfill is not primarily related to Jesus' action, but to his
teaching.[95] For verse 19 also speaks of teaching, and the
following text (vv. 20ff.), as well as the general situation of the
Sermon on the Mount, presents Jesus as teacher. His
proclamation means that he, as God's ambassador, "brings to
full measure"—that is, confirms in their real meaning—the law
and the prophets. The Old Testament Torah in itself does not
carry its own validity, but needs realizing fulfillment and
authorizing confirmation through Jesus Christ. Hence the
verb $\pi\lambda\eta\rho o\hat{\upsilon}\nu$ also contains a critical element. By no means

does the Preacher on the mount simply repeat the Old Testament Torah in his teaching; he also, however, does not bring a new law that replaces the Old Testament. Rather, he "fulfills" or "realizes" the will of God expressed in the Old Testament. By power of his authority, Jesus, as God's ambassador, reveals the intended meaning of the Old Testament Torah and thus leads it to its actualization (cf. 19:8).

5:18. In a solemn "truly" statement, Jesus professes the validity of the law. Verse 18 goes back to pre-Matthean tradition (Q), as revealed by the parallel Luke 16:17. The question in dispute is the form of the pre-Matthean model. From the synoptic tradition K. Berger and U. Luz reconstruct the sequence of an ἀμήν statement: ἀμήν . . . οὐ μή . . . ἕως ('truly . . . not . . . until'; thus also Mark 9:1; 13:30; 14:25; Matt 10:23). This would mean that the first ἕως (RSV: "till") clause is a Matthean formation.[96] Yet speaking against this suggestion is the fact that Luke 16:17 attests the content of the first ἕως clause as pre-Matthean and belonging to the Q source. On the basis of the Q tradition, the secondary intrusions can be recognized: verse 18a (ἀμήν) and verse 18d (second ἕως clause). Hence, in his source Matthew found an old saying, which was perhaps originally composed in Aramaic and which asserted the absolute validity of the law. It is possible that this Jewish-Christian saying had already experienced changes in Q[Matt] (vis-à-vis Luke 16:17). In any case, its meaning is clear. Not even the iota as the smallest letter in the Hebrew alphabet nor even a dot, the little point that distinguishes one letter from another or is added as ornamentation, shall pass away. The whole Torah will endure!

Thus affirms the first ἕως clause. No limitation of the Torah is thereby asserted, for example, saying that it is valid until the end of the world but not beyond—that would contradict the Jewish teaching of the eternity of the Torah and in the Matthean sense would unjustly distinguish between the period of validity of the Old Testament law and the words of Jesus (cf. 24:35). Verse 18b is, rather, to be understood as a circumlocution for "never," as indeed in the popular understanding heaven and earth are eternal, and their end is not imaginable. By means of the introduction,[97] Matthew stressed the validity of the Old Testament Torah, and the final clause also emphasizes this aspect of the assertion.[98] Ἔως ('until') has a sense of finality. The law cannot and may not pass away, so that everything it demands will be realized. Thus γένηται ('is accomplished') is not to be interpreted in terms of revelation history—as if to expess the purpose that the salvation-historical will of God might come into fulfillment[99]—but has instead an ethical meaning. This is in accordance with the overall understanding of the concept of law in Matthew's Gospel[100] and is not in contradiction with the statement that the whole requirement of the law must be met. In the Matthean formulation of the saying, the stress falls, rather, on the unconditional validity of the Torah. To be sure, the word πάντα ('all') requires interpretation. This will come from the antitheses (5:21ff.). Matthew does not think that Jesus and his followers cling slavishly to the wording of the Old Testament law. By virtue of his authority as the Son of God (1:18ff.) Jesus stands, not under, but over the Torah. At this point the interpretation of the Evangelist is different from that of the Jewish-Christian community, out of which this saying probably came, for it hung on to every detail of the Old Testament-Jewish Torah in order to preserve the connection with the synagogue through faithfulness to the Old Testament law. Such a pre-Matthean Jewish-Christian position stood implicitly, and in part explicitly, in contrast to the preaching of Paul and also of the Gentile-Christian church, in which Jesus Christ was proclaimed as not only the fulfillment but also the end of the law of Moses.[101]

5:19. The following verse also has as its theme the validity of the law. It belongs to Matthew's special material. Matthean intrusions are not out of the question,[102] but on the basis of the content, this saying is of pre-Matthean origin.[103] At the same time the question remains open as to whether it belongs to the Q^Matt source, perhaps already linked to verse 18, or whether the Evangelist found it before him as an isolated, individual saying. In any case, according to the structure it involves a casuistic legal statement (the ὃς ἐάν construction: "if anyone . . ."). E. Käsemann understands it as one of the statements of holy law, in which eschatological law was spoken through early Christian prophets, that is, as a legal saying of the early Christian community which was founded on the prospect of the *eschaton*.[104] Without doubt the pre-Matthean version reflected Jewish Christian legal debates. The phrase "the least of these commandments" implies the idea of great, important commandments. In the background stands the rabbinical distinction between, on the one hand, small and light, that is, insignificant commandments and, on the other hand, great and heavy, that is, important commandments. Thus, in the Torah 613 individual statutes (מצווח *mitzwoth*) were counted, comprising 248 commandments and 365 prohibitions. Light commandments included the statutes that made only minor demands; conversely, major demands were linked with heavy commandments.[105] The distinction was left to interpretation and was subject to controversy. Even light commandments were obligatory, although Jewish practice often decided in a way different from rabbinical theory.

What was originally intended by the distinction between small and great commandments in the *pre-Matthean* tradition of the saying? E. Schweizer suggests the apostolic decree (Acts 15:20, 28-29; 21:25) that was discussed in the Syrian church.[106] According to this judgment, the Gentile Christians, in distinction to the Jewish Christians, were required to observe minimal demands, namely, abstinence "from what has been sacrificed to idols and from blood and from what is strangled and from unchastity" (Acts 15:29). Were these demands supposed to have been designated great commandments, in contrast to which other, specifically Jewish commandments could assume less importance? Yet one would expect the commandments of Judaism to be called the important ones. Moreover, apart from Acts and the Pseudo-Clementines, the validity of the apostolic decree is as good as unattested in the ancient church.

It is more probable that the "least" commandments refer to the Christian debates that are known through Paul as well as Mark (7:1ff.) and Acts. Although the validity of the Jewish ceremonial law was problematic, the Jewish cultic laws could be defined as little commandments. Accordingly, the community that created this saying stands on the threshold between Jewish and Gentile Christianity. They accept it when Gentile Christians "relax" the ceremonial commandments (λύειν 'to loose' as opposed to καταλύειν 'to abolish'), but fundamentally they themselves hold fast to the Torah. Whoever evades the

requirements of the Jewish ceremonial law will be called
ἐλάχιστος ('least') in the kingdom of heaven. Here as in verse
19a the superlative form has the meaning of the elative ('very
small').[107] The person concerned will not be excluded from the
kingdom of heaven,[108] but he will have to be satisfied with a
small, modest place; for it is an old rabbinical view that the
kingdom of heaven is characterized by a rank order.[109] This
view lies in the background of several passages in Matthew's
Gospel (18:4; 11:11; 19:28; 20:23). In relation to the
pre-Matthean tradition of verse 18, the Jewish Christian
community assumes a tolerant attitude, according to verse 19.
Not every detail of the Old Testament law is binding: for the
sake of the unity of the church, obedience to the Torah can be
qualified. In spite of different valuations of the Old Testament
law, Jewish and Gentile Christians can live together and
practice ecclesiastical fellowship. Nevertheless, it is clear that
the bearers of this word have not given up their Jewish
Christian position of faithfulness to the law.

What caused Matthew to quote this saying largely unchanged? Is it the Evangelist's intention not to do away with
parts of the Torah but only to put them aside from case to case
when they fall into conflict with the central commandment of
love?[110] With this assumption, however, how can the "very
small" commandments be more closely defined? Matthew
knows no casuistic ethic oriented toward the commandment of
love. Nor does he hold the position of the Jewish-Christian
tradition with its qualified affirmation of the Jewish ceremonial legal system. The reason for adopting this saying is indicated
in the last half of the verse. The doing and teaching of the
commandments of the Torah bring with them the promise of
the coming kingdom of heaven. Thus, they agree with the
fundamental affirmation of the Old Testament law in this
context, even if here Matthew does not preclude—and in the
foregoing already points to—the idea that the affirmation of
the law is tied to the interpretation of the Son of God, who
announces the approaching reign of God in power.[111]

5:20. As the justifying γάρ ('for') shows, verse 20 is composed
as the conclusion to the preceding words. Here, as the
vocabulary reveals, Matthew is speaking. The introduction,
λέγω γὰρ ὑμῖν ('for I tell you'), recalls the redactional

introduction to verse 18 (cf. 18:10, redactional?). Matthean is
the concept of "righteousness" and also the statement on
entrance into the kingdom of heaven (cf. 18:3 par.; also 7:21,
redactional).

With this verse, Matthew closes off the discussion by giving a
justification for the previous section. The affirmation of the
law and the prophets by Jesus (v. 17), the absolute validity of
the Torah (v. 18), the unity of doing and teaching (v. 19)—all
of this has its ultimate reason in the fact that only righteousness
can smooth one's entrance into the kingdom of heaven. At the
same time, the way is thereby prepared for the following
passage. This does not mean that verse 20 provides transition
from one understanding of the law to another.[112] What is at
stake for Matthew, rather, is the one assertion that Jesus' legal
demand stands on the foundation of the Old Testament
Torah, but discovers it in its true meaning. Speaking for the
unity of this section with the larger context is the fact that
Matthew's ethic was motivated—not exclusively, to be sure, but
still to a considerable degree—by the eschatological future.
Hence in the summation of 4:17, Jesus is presented as a
preacher who announces the nearness of the kingdom of
heaven. What is true for the proclamation of Jesus is also true
for the followers of Jesus who meet his demand. Their actions
are directed toward the *eschaton*, which has already come near
in the person of Jesus.

The required attitude measures itself antitypically against
the image of the scribes and Pharisees. The scribes were the
representatives of the Jewish rabbinate; they transmitted
binding interpretation of the Torah. The Pharisees, on the
other hand, were a religious party that had great influence in
the political life of first-century Judaism. They linked the
written Torah with the oral tradition, and in the process
showed themselves more flexible than the Sadducees, who
represented the more conservative element in Judaism.[113] In
Mark (7:1, 5), the Pharisees and scribes are the theological
representatives of Judaism at the time of Jesus. The mention
of both groups together involves a lack of precision; in truth
one cannot differentiate stringently between scribes and
Pharisees; both Sadducee scribes and Pharisee scribes are
attested (cf. Mark 2:16). Thus, Matthew does not reflect a
historically faithful picture. In terms of content also, he

records the attitude of the rabbis at the time of Jesus. They are not presented in their own self-understanding but are polemicized. Matthew does not find himself in dispute with the Judaism of his time; he strives in his Gospel rather to present the life of Jesus as a previous event lying in the past. Accordingly, the scribes and Pharisees named here belong primarily to the time of Jesus. They are not presented in historically true fashion, but are schematized; they are drawn as an antitype. Against this background Matthew presents the right Christian attitude as it is demanded by Jesus.

The expression περισσεύσῃ . . . πλεῖον is a pleonasm; it indicates 'being more amply present,' the quantitative more. In the background may lie the Jewish view that at the final judgment a settling of accounts will take place. The saying means that at that time the good deeds of Jesus' disciples should exist in ampler quantity and show a surplus vis-à-vis the Pharisees. Although the scribes and Pharisees are seen as the antitype of right Christian behavior, one must not ask what measure of righteousness the Evangelist accords the representatives of Judaism. In our text, it is not a question of granting them a tiny remnant of righteousness; the emphasis, rather, lies one-sidedly and exclusively on the monitory assertion: your righteousness is to be considerably different from the attitude of the scribes and Pharisees!

The concept of the quantitative increase in righteousness makes clear that the attitude of Jesus' followers is not an abstraction and is not resident in an extrahuman realm. In regard to the substance of the Christian concept of righteousness, it agrees largely with the Jewish and pagan ideas of righteousness. The special nature of the Christian ethic is not to be demonstrated through a different kind of ethical content. The following antitheses will show that the ethical demands of Jesus are built on what is given.[114] As in the proclamation, in the ethic of Jesus and the Christian community there is the possibility and the necessity of linkage. Here is the real basis for Christian attention to the world. Whatever is "good" in the Jewish and pagan spheres can and should also be recognized in the Christian community. This will emerge from what follows (6:1ff.). Of course, what is at stake for Matthew, in contrast to his pagan and Jewish surroundings, is an augmentation: Christian behavior is supposed to be marked by a περισσόν ('more': cf. 5:47). The goal of Jesus' followers is perfection (5:48). The comprehensive fulfillment of the requirement of righteousness is also demanded at the end of the Sermon on the Mount (7:12). If the righteousness of Jesus' followers is the realization of the will of God expressed in the Old Testament law and in the prophets (5:17-19), thus it is also identical, in the Matthean view, with love of God and neighbor; this is articulated in various ways and appears more than once as the summary of the requirements of the law and the prophets (7:12; 22:40).

The connection with the commandment of love announces that the distinct nature of the righteousness of Jesus' disciples is not simply to be measured quantitatively; rather it is also qualitatively a different and therefore a new righteousness. It alone opens the entrance to the *basileia;* only this righteousness has the pledge that the kingdom of heaven belongs to it. The qualitative difference in this righteousness is based on the fact that it is an eschatological phenomenon, however much it must be manifested here and now. Above all, however, the qualitative difference is based on the person who makes the demand of righteousness. The Preacher on the mount is the *Kyrios*-Son of God who teaches with eschatological power; he is the crucified and resurrected one, the present Lord of his community. His demand is unmistakably bound to his person and his claim. Thus, it is the christological dimension that makes the required attitude of righteousness new, different, and better.

2.3 5:21-48 The Antitheses

Broer, I. "Die Antithesen und der Evangelist Matthäus." *BZ* n.s. 19 (1975): 50-63.

———. *Freiheit vom Gesetz und Radikalisierung des Gesetzes,* 75-113, 123-30. SBS 98. 1980.

Descamps, A. "Essai d'interprétation de Mt. 5,17-48." *SE* 1 (TU 73, 1959): 156-73.

Dietzfelbinger, C. *Die Antithesen der Bergpredigt.* TEH 186. 1975.

———. "Die Antithesen der Bergpredigt im Verständnis des Matthäus." *ZNW* 70 (1979): 1-15.

Guelich, R. "The Antitheses of Matthew V. 21-48: Traditional and/or Redactional?" *NTS* 22 (1976): 444-57.

Hasler, V. "Das Herzstück der Bergpredigt. Zum Verständnis der Antithesen in Matth. 5,21-48." *TZ* 15 (1959): 90-106.

Hübner. *Gesetz,* 40-112, 230-36.

Lohse, E. "Ich aber sage euch." In *Der Ruf Jesu und die Antwort der Gemeinde*, FS J. Jeremias, edited by E. Lohse et al., 189-203. 1970. (= idem, *Die Einheit des Neuen Testaments*, 73-87. 1973.)

Marguerat. *Jugement*, 142-67.

Meier, J. P. *Law and History in Matthew's Gospel*, 125-61. AnBib 71. 1976.

Strecker, G. "Die Antithesen der Bergpredigt (Mt. 5,21-48 par)." *ZNW* 69 (1978): 36-72.

Suggs, M. J. "The Antitheses as Redactional Products." In *Jesus Christus in Historie und Theologie*, FS H. Conzelmann, edited by G. Strecker, 433-44. 1975.

In the next section, Matthew reports six antitheses, and thus adopts a figure of speech coined in the Jewish tradition. It is characterized by a thesis, in which a statement of dogma is cited, and an antithesis, in which the cited doctrinal view is contradicted. The introduction of the thesis, in its most detailed form, reads ἠκούσατε ὅτι ἐρρέθη τοῖς ἀρχαίοις ('you have heard that it was said to men of old'—vv. 21, 33). This introduction can be shortened to a simple ἐρρέθη δέ ('it was also said'—v. 31). It is generally followed by an Old Testament quotation. In each case the antithesis is introduced by ἐγὼ δὲ λέγω ὑμῖν ('but I say to you') and contains a statement of Jesus critical of the Torah. In it the Torah commandment or prohibition previously cited is radicalized or revoked. In every case the antithesis brings a new directive and articulates the law of the Lord.

E. Lohse has demonstrated that the antithetical way of speaking is a form of argumentation of the rabbinate or, more precisely, of the Tannaitic scribes. In connection with scribal discussions, a reigning doctrinal view is contradicted with the words "but I say to you."[1] Thus, the Jesus of the Sermon on the Mount adopts a known rabbinical form of expression and thereby makes himself known as "teacher." It is also true that the content of the antitheses is to a great extent attested in the Jewish ethical tradition. On the other hand, Jesus is not comparable to a Jewish rabbi. The Jewish scribes do not oppose the Mosaic law directly but confront various Torah interpretations with each other. Jesus, however, stands at a distance from the law of Moses. The Kyrios stands over the Torah; his authority makes it possible to be critical of the Torah, which leads even to dissolving individual commandments and setting up new instructions.

In the investigation of the primitive tradition, we must

distinguish between the antithetical framework and the substance of the antitheses. In the Lukan Sermon on the Plain, the only parallel is in 6:27-36 (cf. Matt 5:39*b*-48). This means that in the Q tradition common to Matthew and Luke, there was no antithetical formulation.[2] The substance of the fifth and sixth antitheses, however, is no doubt attested here for Q. Also for the third antithesis (Matt 5:31-32) one can infer the Q tradition, although here a parallel is offered not only by Luke 16:18 but also by Mark 10:11-12 (par. Matt 19:9).

At this point one must, with M. J. Suggs and I. Broer, ask whether the antithetical framework was created by the redactor Matthew. For this presumption one must maintain that a comparable antithetical tradition cannot be demonstrated in the New Testament and that the first, second, and fourth antitheses are attested only in Matthew's Gospel, and thus belong to Matthew's special material. It is more likely that the antitheses themselves were present in the special Matthean material in Q^Matt. This would suit the conservatism of the first Evangelist, who also in other cases does not work independently from tradition.[3] Moreover, we can determine the order of the three antitheses that come from the special material. The thesis of each cites a prohibition from the Decalogue: number one, the fifth commandment; number two, the sixth; and number four, the eighth. This allows the presumption that Matthew had this series of three antitheses before him as a unit in his copy of Q. The number three also shaped the pre-Matthean tradition elsewhere (cf., e.g., 6:1-18). Through the composition of three more antitheses the Evangelist expanded the series to two times three (equals six) antitheses.

Accordingly, tradition-historical differentiation produces the following picture:

Q^Matt	Matt-Luke
1. Vv. 21-26: On Killing (fifth commandment)	
2. Vv. 27-30: On Adultery (sixth commandment)	

3. Vv. 31-32 par. Luke 16:18
(Mark 10:11-12 par. Matt
19:9): On Divorce

4. Vv. 33-37: On Oaths
(eighth com-
mandment)

5. Vv. 38-42 par. Luke 6:29-
30: On Retaliation

6. Vv. 43-48 par. Luke 6:27-
28, 32-36: On Love of
Enemy

The redactional division of the series of antitheses is
indicated by πάλιν ('again') in verse 33a. This word separates
the third from the fourth antithesis. Matthew seems to want
consciously to separate an initial group of three from a second
group. Only the first and the fourth antitheses begin with a
detailed introduction, and the form of the first group of three
is different from the second in that the antithesis of each
begins with πᾶς ('every one'). In terms of content, one must
distinguish between the first three and the last three, that is,
between relations with fellow Christians (intracommunity
problems) and relations with non-Christians (extended-
community ethics).

2.3.1   5:21-26   The First Antithesis: On Killing

Guelich, R. A. "Mt 5:22: Its Meaning and Integrity." ZNW 64 (1973): 39-52.
Jeremias, J. " 'Lass allda deine Gabe' (Mt 5,23f)." ZNW 36 (1937): 150-54.
  (=Abba, 103-7.)
Merklein. Gottesherrschaft, 260-62.
Weise, M. "Mt 5,21f—ein Zeugnis sakraler Rechtssprechung in der
  Urgemeinde." ZNW 49 (1958): 116-23.
Zeller. Mahnsprüche, 62-67.

*21You have heard that it was said to men of old, "You shall not kill;
and whoever kills shall be liable to judgment." 22But I say to you that
everyone who is angry with his brother shall be liable to the council, and
whoever says "You fool!" shall be liable to the hell of fire. 23So if you are
offering your gift at the altar, and there remember that your brother has
something against you, 24leave your gift there before the altar and go;*

first be reconciled to your brother, and then come and offer your gift.
*²⁵Make friends quickly with your accuser, while you are going with him
to court, lest your accuser hand you over to the judge, and the judge to
the guard, and you be put in prison; ²⁶truly, I say to you, you will never
get out till you have paid the last penny.*

5:21-22a. There are good reasons to assume that the primitive
form of the antitheses lies in verses 21-22a, 27-28, and 33-34a,
and that it goes back to the historical Jesus.[4] These verses
express a prominent eschatological claim, which, of course,
should not be called "messianic,"[5] but which reveals the
self-consciousness of a prophet of the end time. Jesus pits his
authority against that of Moses! Accordingly, the ἀρχαῖοι
('men of old') are, first of all, the members of the Sinai
generation, including Moses and Aaron. Other exegesis
speaks more generally of the "earlier generations."[6] In any
case, this phrase refers to the guarantors of the Jewish legal
tradition, which was still valid in the time of Jesus. Ἠκούσατε
("you have heard") presupposes that the cited statement goes
back to oral tradition. Hence, the antithetical statement
concerns contemporary Judaism as well as the Torah, the root
of Jewish tradition.

When the Torah of Moses says in the Decalogue, "You shall
not kill" (Exod 20:13; Deut 5:17), it threatens the murderer
with judgment. According to general view κρίσις is identical
with a Jewish court of justice, the Court of the Twenty-three.[7]
According to other interpretation, the word designates the
death penalty that is imposed on a murderer.[8] Yet in this
case such a meaning could only be used figuratively in the
following antithesis. In keeping with his proclamation of the
kingdom of God, Jesus is thinking of the final judgment (thus
also Matt 10:15; 12:41-42). It happens with the coming of
God's kingdom (Matt 19:28 par.) and concerns the wrong-
doer.[9]

Against the statement of Old Testament-Jewish law and its
threat of judgment, Jesus sets his own law: not just murder but
even anger makes one subject to judgment! With this the
meaning of the Old Testament prohibition changes. Not only
(treacherous) murder is placed under Jesus' verdict, but also
anything that can harm one's neighbor.[10] Jesus' new commandment, which apparently ended originally with this short

antithesis (v. 22*a*), concerns relations with one's fellow human beings. The word ἀδελφός means (Jewish) fellow countryman and only in later tradition was interpreted as brother in the Christian faith.

Thus, Jesus gives a new directive that radicalizes the prohibition of the Torah. At this point he has still not left the realm of Judaism. The idea that anger is reprehensible is common property in Jewish ethics.[11] To this extent Jesus appears as the teacher of a Jewish wisdom that is specifically accented by a future-eschatological perspective not found in the Jewish wisdom literature. It would thus be in agreement with other wisdom-like sayings of Jesus, and at this point the interpretation of liberal theology would gain arguments for declaring the ethic of the Sermon on the Mount an "ethic of attitude" that must be understood as a summons to a proper inner spirit. Accordingly, Jesus would have exhorted his hearers to the moral attitude that he himself exemplarily realized by practicing love, not anger, and by forgiving his enemies.

Yet such an association with Jewish wisdom fails to appreciate the dynamics of Jesus' sermon. Jesus measured the representatives of Old Testament-Jewish tradition by their own behavior. They can base their moral decorum on the literal wording of the law of Moses, but Jesus maintains that the law goes deeper; it condemns not only the evil deed but also thoughts and feelings. Before this unconditionality of the law's demand, Jesus' hearers can only confess their failure and guilt; they know that they have indeed observed the literal but not the real meaning of the Mosaic law. Jesus' critique of the Torah is thus a critique of the Torah believers. Their good conscience is called into question. If even anger makes one guilty and delivers a person up to the devastating judgment of God, then who can stand? At this point the theological significance of the law comes to expression. The idea that Jesus knew and taught the devastating power of the law agrees with the fact that he, like John the Baptist, called people to repentance. The unrepentant cities are subject to judgment (11:20). "Here is something greater than Jonah," who with his call could, nevertheless, move the inhabitants of Nineveh to repentance (12:41). The historical Jesus is not only the friend of the sinner and the tax collector; he is also the preacher of judgment. This agrees with his announcement of the coming reign of God, for this reign will bring grace and judgment!

5:22b-c. Even the early community tried to escape such an uncompromising call to repentance. An attempt to dull its dynamic cutting edge is seen in the second stage of this saying's tradition, which now, in the form of a climax, connects ethical failings with their punishments. As the starting point in this intensification, anger is seen as only an inner evil and is covered by the lowest punishment: in contrast to the meaning of κρίσις in Jesus' proclamation, here it means the local court. More serious is the insulting of a brother as a fellow Christian. Whoever says "Raca" ('dummy') to his brother will be liable to the Sanhedrin, the high council, as the supreme Jewish court of justice. But whoever calls his brother a μωρέ ('fool') is subject to hellfire. The two terms of abuse may also involve an intensification in that *Raca* declares one incapable of interpersonal relations while *fool* means that a person is incapable of relating to God, that is, disobedient, godless. In any case it is clear that here is the voice of the Palestinian community, which is subject to the Jewish court system and familiar with the Semitic conceptual world.[12] It creates a casuistic justice, just as the relative clauses show juridical style. Although the lines of verse 22b-c represent an old accretion that was secondarily connected to the original antithesis, the latter itself can be dated before the early community. The expansion means that the original saying of Jesus was subject to an augmentation process: it is interpreted in an ethicizing fashion. The community adapted Jesus' word to its situation, and for itself derived from his call to repentance a wisdom-like, ethical directive.[13]

5:23-24. The following two verses are presumably from an originally independent source. They contain a community rule,[14] which Matthew perhaps found already in this location. The connector οὖν ('so') indicates that a conclusion is to be drawn from the preceding text. The directive on proper relations with one's Christian brother is followed here by an example from the practice of making an offering. It contains a warning: reconciliation comes before cultic practice! According to juridical understanding, both reconciliation and the presentation of an offering are the subjects of obligatory commandments. Moreover, reconciliation is identical not only with pardoning but also with making good.[15] This obligatory commandment is placed over against the cult: more correctly, worship that is pleasing to God can only come from a reconciled person! Such a Jewish-rabbinical ordering of worship is here acknowledged and tied to the admonition to be reconciled. This community rule presupposes the existence of the second temple and an unbroken relationship to the cult of offering in the early Christian community in Jerusalem. This is the way Matthew found it, but he himself lived in the time after the destruction of the temple and after the end of the Jerusalem cult of offering. For him this piece of tradition is important because it illustrates the admonition to reconciliation. This admonition also affects what follows.

5:25-26. The next verses—"a parable developed from an image saying"[16]—are attested by Luke 12:57-59 and thereby identified as part of the Q tradition. The central assertion was originally eschatological. The point of the "crisis parable"[17] is the announcement of judgment: it is imminent! Whoever is delivered to the judge shall not escape punishment. This is the basis for the admonition to be reconciled with one's trial adversary. Luke has made this future-eschatological point clear, for the context (Luke 12:49ff) deals with signs of the end. The same orientation is found in the Q source, for the closing ἕως . . . ἀποδῷς ('till you have paid'—v. 26; Luke 12:59) is also found in the future-eschatological parables (cf. Matt 18:30, 34).

Thus, the Evangelist Matthew found the future-eschatological parable of crisis already in the tradition, and he gave it a double interpretation. (1) The expression ἴσθι εὐνοῶν has the meaning 'make friends'; it picks up the foregoing διαλλάγηθι ('be reconciled') in verse 24. Matthew breaks through the visual image of a court trial. Instead of the concrete ἀπαλλάχθαι (Luke 12:58: "be delivered from" your adversary, KJV), the expression *make friends* no longer refers only to one's behavior in the trial; rather, the object of the warning is reconciliation in general. (2) The image of the trial is also clearly superseded at another point. If Luke 12:58 speaks of going to the ἄρχων ('magistrate'), Matthew speaks of the ὁδός in the absolute sense.

This word no longer has the concrete meaning of the 'way' to the courthouse but the general sense of 'life's way.' The original concept is spiritualized and related to one's life as a whole. This is underlined by the particle ἕως ὅτου ('while'). Matthew is thinking of the time span of human life. While one lives, one has the possibility of reconciling oneself with an adversary. In accord with the present composition, this means with fellow Christians, even if in the wider context it is clear that the Sermon on the Mount reaches beyond the level of disciples and includes the people. Here a rule of life is established which—without detriment to its primary association with community reality—has the rank of a general maxim that concerns Christians and non-Christians alike.

The fact that Matthew is thinking about the duration of human life makes it clear that there is no immediate, absolute expectation of the Parousia. The originally urgent, near-expectation that governed the early community has been dispelled. Nevertheless, Matthew still has the *eschaton* in view; the threat of judgment is retained (v. 26). The context also contains this idea in various terminology (v. 20: entrance into the kingdom of heaven; v. 22: the hell of fire; vv. 29-30: *gehenna*). The introductory *amen* ('truly') emphasizes the absolute nature of the threat of judgment.

Furthermore, it is, of course, no accident that in verse 25 Matthew, unlike Luke, does not read πράκτορι ('court official'), but ὑπηρέτῃ ('servant'). The parable is interpreted in allegorical fashion. The "servant" designates the angel of the final judgment, and the angels have a special duty at the close of the age (13:41-42, 49-50).

Thus, the redactor Matthew has consciously reworked his tradition and given it the stamp of his own theology. On one hand, he historicizes his material: influenced by a new situation, namely, the delay of the Parousia, he now includes the span of human life. As long as a person is alive, there is still the possibility of reconciliation. It behooves one to use it! On the other hand, the future-eschatological goal has not been lost, but even strengthened by allegorically interpreting the figure of the servant of the court as the angel of judgment. The eschatological perspective defines ethical behavior! The eschatological virtue of reconciliation is not removed from this tension. It is perceived in a community that discovers history as the place of its activity, as more clearly expressed in the missionary commandment of the resurrected One (28:16-20). In the concrete realm of history, it is necessary to hear the word of the Lord. As the Preacher on the mount, he gives proper instruction for the life of the individual as well as for the ordering of the community as a whole. This has already been said in the beatitudes. The requirement of reconciliation concretizes the beatitude of the meek (v. 5) and that of the peacemakers (v. 9). The focus is on interpersonal relationships. Thus, like the community before him, Matthew is removed temporally and materially from Jesus' apodictic call to repentance. He sees the necessities of community organization. Hence, he is at pains to assure that the community of Christ does not lose its identity in the course of time. Therefore, he offers practical instruction.

2.3.2   5:27-30   The Second Antithesis: On Adultery

Haacker, K. "Der Rechtssatz Jesu zum Thema Ehebruch (Mt 5,28)." *BZ* n.s. 21 (1977): 113-16.
Merklein. *Gottesherrschaft*, 262-65.
Niederwimmer, K. *Askese und Mysterium*, 24ff. FRLANT 113. 1975.
See also under 5:31-32.

[27]You have heard that it was said, "You shall not commit adultery." [28]But I say to you that every one who looks at a woman lustfully has already committed adultery with her in his heart. [29]If your right eye causes you to sin, pluck it out and throw it away; it is better that you lose one of your members than that your whole body be thrown into hell. [30]And if your right hand causes you to sin, cut it off and throw it away; it is better that you lose one of your members than that your whole body go into hell.

5:27-28. Formally, the second antithesis differs from the first in its shortened introduction. The express mention of the "men of old" is missing; also there is no indication of the punishment that requites the violation of this Old Testament prohibition.[18] Nonetheless, the parallelism with the first antithesis is apparent. Here, too, it is a question of an instruction regarding the Old Testament Torah—more precisely, the sixth commandment of the Decalogue (Exod

20:13; Deut 5:17)—which was handed down by the oral tradition of Judaism. Presumably, it originally followed the earliest version of the first antithesis, for it concerns the following commandment in the Decalogue.

The foundation for this thesis is the Jewish marriage law. The verb μοιχεύειν means 'to make an adulteress';[19] it presupposes the patriarchal structure of society in the ancient Orient. The man who seduces the wife of another man destroys her marriage, not his own. He is fundamentally entitled to have more than one wife (Deut 21:15ff.). Thus, this Old Testament-Jewish legal practice rests on the viewpoint of polygamy; therefore, a wife cannot call her husband to account because of a marriage violation.

This position is not challenged by Jesus: it is presupposed in the counterthesis when not just the deed, but also the longing look is considered destructive of marriage. Even the man, says Jesus, who looks lustfully at the wife of another destroys her marriage. The man is thus addressed as the responsible perpetrator, even if the legal offense of adultery relates only to the wife. Likewise, in Jesus' assertion that the lustful look counts as adultery, he is in agreement with Jewish teaching.[20] Nevertheless, the counterthesis goes beyond the realm of Old Testament and contemporary Judaism. Here, Jesus expresses his authority, which stands over the Torah. His claim is based on the coming reign of God, which has approached in his person. The eschatological justice that Jesus establishes is not oriented toward the world; it is defined by the coming reign of God. The nearing of God's kingdom excludes all casuistry and demands the total human being. It discloses the fractured nature of human existence because it lays claim to the whole of a person's being. Here there is nothing that one can place between oneself and God.

Presumably the addendum ἐν τῇ καρδίᾳ goes back to Matthew. The heart is the seat of human will (5:8; Luke 21:4; 2 Cor 9:7). Not only the deed of the sinful look, but also the perverted will of an individual is the object of Jesus' judgment saying. For the Christian who is summoned to obedience of the absolute will of God, it is not enough to refrain from something. It is crucial that outward action and inner direction of the will agree. Jesus demands wholeness and undividedness, that is, human perfection (5:48). This means overcoming the pharisaical hypocrisy that is characterized by the contradiction between a seemingly faultless outward appearance and a wrong inner direction of the will (6:1ff.).

5:29-30. Appended as a further unit of tradition is the double saying of the offense of the right eye and the right hand. This saying is also presented in 18:8-9 (par. Mark 9:43-48).[21] In addition to the Markan witness, we have here a second influential line of tradition, presumably Q^Matt; thus, it is conceivable that the Evangelist found the sayings already in this location. In terms of content, the connection is based on the linking of βλέπων (v. 28: 'looking') and ὀφθαλμός (v. 29: 'eye'). This tradition is based on Palestinian origins, as shown by the Semitic choice of words, which can also be demonstrated in the parallels Mark 9:43-48 and Matt 18:8-9.[22] The two Greek versions, which are accordingly to be traced back to a common Hebraic or Aramaic foundation, were taken over, essentially unchanged by Matthew. Only the addenda ὁ δεξιός/ἡ δεξιά ('right') may come from him as a clarification.[23]

Both sayings make the same assertion. In Mark they come in the context of giving offense and make clear a radical either-or. Faced with the threat of judgment, external wholeness is unimportant if it includes becoming fuel for "the unqenchable fire." It is an unconditional demand for a decision that has radical consequences. Following his source, Matthew relates this to the example of the lustful look that causes adultery. The radical nature of the demand for decision is then intensified: even if the (more valuable) right hand gives offense, its loss weighs little vis-à-vis the threat of judgment that will affect the whole person. Σῶμα ('body') characterizes a human being comprehensively as an earthly, personal being. The parallel 18:8-9 speaks of only two members. By contrast the totality of the individual is emphasized here. The proper ethical behavior is demanded of the whole person. The aspect of apocalyptic judgment—which may have been contained already in Jesus' original saying—is spelled out. The image is completely permeated with the content.

2.3.3 5:31-32 The Third Antithesis: On Divorce

Baltensweiler, H. "Die Ehebruchklauseln bei Matthäus." *TZ* 15 (1959): 340-56.
———. *Die Ehe im Neuen Testament,* 87-102. ATANT 52. 1967.

Bauer, J. B. "Bemerkungen zu den matthäischen Unzuchtklauseln (Mt 5,32; 19,9)." In *Begegnung mit dem Wort*, FS H. Zimmermann, edited by J. Zmijewski and E. Nellessen, 23-33. BBB 53. 1980.

Bonsirven, J. *Le divorce dans le Nouveau Testament*. 1948.

Dupont, J. *Mariage et divorce dans l'Évangile: Matthieu 19,3-12 et parallèles*. Bruges, 1959.

Fitzmyer, J. A. "The Matthean Divorce Texts and Some New Palestinian Evidence." *TS* 37 (1976): 197-226.

Greeven, H. "Ehe nach dem Neuen Testament." In *Theologie der Ehe*, edited by G. Krems and R. Mumm, 37-79. 1969.

Lohfink, G. "Jesus und die Ehescheidung. Zur Gattung und Sprachintention von Mt 5,32." In *Biblische Randbemerkungen*, FS R. Schnackenburg, edited by H. Merklein and J. Lange, 2d ed., 207-17. 1974.

Moignt, J. "Ehescheidung 'auf Grund von Unzucht' (Matth 5,32/19,9)." In *Wie unauflöslich ist die Ehe?* edited by J. David and F. Schmalz, 178-222. 1969.

Nembach, U. "Ehescheidung nach alttestamentlichem und jüdischem Recht." *TZ* 26 (1970): 161-71.

Niederwimmer, K. *Askese und Mysterium*, 13-24. FRLANT 113. 1975.

Rordorf, W. "Marriage in the New Testament and in the Early Church." *JEH* 20 (1969): 193-210.

Sand, A. "Die Unzuchtsklausel in Mt 5,31-32 und 19,3-9." *MTZ* 20 (1969): 118-29.

Schaller, B. "Die Sprüche über Ehescheidung und Wiederheirat in der synoptischen Überlieferung." In *Der Ruf Jesu und die Antwort der Gemeinde*, FS J. Jeremias, 226-46. 1970.

Schnackenburg, R. "Die Ehe nach dem Neuen Testament" (1969). In *Schriften zum Neuen Testament*, 414-34. 1971.

Schneider, G. "Jesu Worte über die Ehescheidung in der Überlieferung des Neuen Testaments." *TTZ* 80 (1971): 65-87.

Schürmann, H. "Neutestamentliche Marginalien zur Frage nach der Institutionalität, Unauflösbarkeit und Sakramentalität der Ehe." In *Kirche und Bibel*, FS E. Schick, edited by A. Winter et al., 409-30 (bibl.). 1979.

———. "Die Verbindlichkeit konkreter sittlicher Normen nach dem NT, bedacht am Beispiel des Ehescheidungsverbotes und im Licht des Liebesgebotes." In *Sittliche Normen: Zum Problem ihrer allgemeinen und unwandelbaren Geltung*, edited by W. Kerber, 107-23. 1982.

[31]*It was also said, "Whoever divorces his wife, let him give her a certificate of divorce."* [32]*But I say to you that every one who divorces his wife, except on the ground of unchastity, makes her an adulteress; and whoever marries a divorced woman commits adultery.*

5:31. With the third antithesis, Matthew continues the previously announced theme. If in the foregoing section adultery and the sixth commandment of the Decalogue were sharpened antithetically by also placing the lustful look under the prohibition, now the radical nature of Jesus' ethical demand is related to divorce. Thus, both antitheses concern the relationship of a person to marriage and especially that of the Christian husband to the wife.

In form this antithesis is different from the two preceding ones. It cites, not a prohibition of the Decalogue, but an Old Testament commandment. Against this thesis a new and different commandment is juxtaposed. In content verse 31 goes back to Deut. 24:1, 3, according to which the husband is entitled to send his wife away through a bill of divorce if he finds in her a πρᾶγμα ἄσχημον (= ערות דבר‎ *arwat dabar*). The sense of this expression has often been discussed in rabbinic scribal scholarship. Rabbi Hillel understood it as "any shameful affair." According to this, all kinds of offenses are recognized as grounds for divorce; for example, the husband can separate himself from his wife if she lets the food burn.[24] Rabbi Shammai, however, limited the concept and understood it as "a certain shameful matter."[25]

Matthew cited the thesis, not out of the Old Testament, but on the basis of Christian tradition, as it is also found in Mark 10:11.[26] Here the Jewish marriage law is properly addressed. According to it, divorce is largely placed at the discretion of the husband. The primary goal is hardly the "protection of the wife,"[27] but rather the establishment of the right of the Israelite husband, through which, of course, its limits are also recognizable.

5:32. Jesus' counterthesis expresses the viewpoint of the community. Here Matthew follows the Q tradition when, as already in verse 31, he understands ἀπολύειν as a technical term for 'dismiss from the marriage.'[28] Nonetheless, he changes this tradition when he introduces verse 32*b* with the particle of a conditional relative clause (ὅς ἐάν 'whoever') and thereby assimilates it to verse 31. In this way the form of a casuistic legal statement is more clearly accentuated.

Also introduced secondarily is the expression παρεκτὸς λόγου πορνείας ('except on the ground of unchastity'). Similarly, we find μὴ ἐπὶ πορνείᾳ ('except for unchastity'), in 19:9, where without doubt the redactor Matthew has introduced it into the Markan antecedent. In the present passage one can ask whether Matthew himself inserted the addendum or found it already in this environment. In any case, the stipulation characterizes the position of Matthew and also that of his community on the marriage law. It is closer to the interpretation of Rabbi Shammai than to that of Rabbi

Hillel and may have been thus influenced. In early Christian tradition, πορνεία can have the general meaning of 'fornication,' but here it refers to the unfaithfulness of the wife.[29] Hence the word can be equated with the usual linguistic usage of μοιχεία ('adultery').[30]

What does such a modification say about the marriage law practice of Matthew and his community? Behind the Evangelist is a multistage tradition-historical development that begins with Jesus' absolute prohibition of divorce (1 Cor 7:10-11*; Mark 10:2-9*).[31] This prohibition belongs to the realm of Jesus' ethical radicalisms—for example, the first and second antitheses—and is to be considered like them: an instruction that is based on the nearness of God's dominion; it confronts one with the claim of the *eschaton* and calls one to repentance. This absolute demand is not suited to regulating human life; rather, it calls fundamentally into question the law's function of constituting community life.

The next stage is noted in Mark 10:11-12 par. Luke 16:18. Here it is not divorce alone but divorce and remarriage that are prohibited. Taken together they are equivalent to adultery.[32] The divorce stipulation in Matthew stands at the end of this tradition-historical scale. It presupposes the early Christian discussion and interprets it in a specific sense. The adverb παρεκτός does not have an inclusive meaning ('even in the case of')[33] but an exclusive one ('except in the case of'). The originally strict regulation is thereby softened. An exception is allowed in which divorce and remarriage are permitted. The early Christian regulation does not cover the situation of marital unfaithfulness. In harmony with his community tradition, Matthew lays down a practical instruction, with whose help the current problems of order can be resolved.

With this divorce stipulation, Matthew and his community apparently adopted the interpretation of Rabbi Shammai. Yet the rabbinical rule begins fundamentally with the possibility of divorce, as this is indeed expressly conceded in Deuteronomy 24. By contrast, the New Testament conception is defined by Jesus' absolute prohibition of divorce. The exception stipulated in Matthew's Gospel does not basically rescind the prohibition of divorce, even though it adapts it to the necessities of the community situation.

How is this rule related to the Old Testament? There is no

disputing the fact that Jesus' absolute prohibition of divorce stands in opposition to the regulation of Deuteronomy 24. This is expressly confirmed by Mark 10:2ff. par., where Jesus calls the Torah commandment on divorce a concession by Moses, for "from the beginning it was not so" (Matt 19:8). Here the order of creation stands in opposition to the Mosaic Torah. Jesus' critique of the Torah leads thus to the dissolution of the Torah commandment. This is based by the supreme authority of Jesus. Vis-à-vis the Torah as the prevailing law of Judaism, Jesus represents the holy will of God; vis-à-vis the justice of the world, he represents the demand of the kingdom of God. Nevertheless, it is not a question of Jesus wanting to establish a new justice in the worldly sense or a new legal order. His message calls attention, rather, to the fragility and relativity of the prevailing legal arrangements.

Even on Matthew's level the difference from Deuteronomy 24 is indisputable. In contrast to the law of Moses, but in agreement with early Christian tradition, the first Evangelist begins with the fundamental indissolubility of marriage. Only one exception is granted in that, analogous to the rule of Rabbi Shammai, Deut 24:1, 3 is relatively narrowly interpreted. Regarding the problem of remarriage, a man is not permitted to marry a divorced woman, and this accords with the rigorous early Christian ethic. Also, the separated Christian man may not remarry, since his marriage is still considered valid (cf. Matt 19:9)—this in clear contrast to Deuteronomy (24:2), where even the divorced woman is expressly permitted to remarry.[34]

Thus, as much as the Jewish scribal tradition may have influenced the Matthean version of the third antithesis, the Matthean Jesus formulates here his own law. He thereby proves himself as the fulfiller of "the law and the prophets" and as the proclaimer of the demanding will of God laid down in the Old Testament. In contrast to the historical Jesus, the Preacher on the mount stands, in the Matthean understanding, on the ground of the given and the possible. The sharpening of the Torah and practicability are not in opposition to each other, but bind themselves to an eschatological demand that is issued in the name of the Lord to the community and to the world.

2.3.4   5:33-37   The Fourth Antithesis: On Oaths

Bauernfeind, O. *Eid und Frieden*, 91-142. Forschungen zur Kirchen- und Geistesgeschichte n.s. 2. 1956.

———. "Der Eid in der Sicht des Neuen Testaments." In *Eid. Gewissen. Treupflicht*, edited by H. Bethke, 79-112. 1965.

Dautzenberg, G. "Ist das Schwurverbot Mt 5,33-37; Jak 5,12 ein Beispiel für die Torakritik Jesu?" *BZ* n.s. 25 (1981): 47-66.

———. "Eid IV: Neues Testament." *TRE* 9:379-82.

Klauser, T. "Beteuerung. *RAC* 2:219-24.

Kutsch, E. "Eure Rede aber sei ja ja, nein nein." *EvT* 20 (1960): 206-18.

Merklein. *Gottesherrschaft*, 265-67.

Minear, P. S. "Yes or No: The Demand for Honesty in the Early Church." *NovT* 13 (1971): 1-13.

Schneider, J. ὀμνύω. *TDNT* 5:176-85.

Stählin, G. "Zum Gebrauch von Beteuerungsformeln im Neuen Testament. *NovT* 5 (1962): 115-43.

Zeller. *Mahnsprüche*, 124-26.

Cf. also the commentaries on James 5:12 (e.g., M. Dibelius, KEK 15, 1964; F. Mussner, HTKNT 13/1, 1967).

[33]Again you have heard that it was said to the men of old, "You shall not swear falsely, but shall perform to the Lord what you have sworn." [34]But I say to you, Do not swear at all, either by heaven, for it is the throne of God, [35]or by the earth, for it is his footstool, or by Jerusalem, for it is the city of the great King. [36]And do not swear by your head, for you cannot make one hair white or black. [37]Let what you say be simply "Yes" or "No"; anything more than this comes from evil.

5:33. With the fourth antithesis, Matthew begins the second trio of verses 21-48. The caesura is clearly marked by πάλιν ('again'). Only in verse 21 is the introduction as detailed as here: "Again you have heard that it was said to the men of old." The third antithesis has already shown that the Evangelist does not always cite the underlying Old Testament text, but reaches back instead to early Christian oral tradition for the formulation of the thesis. In any case, the fact that oral tradition is also the basis of the fourth thesis is confirmed by the word ἠκούσατε ('you have heard'). This explains why the exact wording cannot be documented in the Old Testament. If one presupposes that the pre-Matthean order of antitheses follows the structure of the Decalogue, then at this point the most probable reference is to the eighth commandment (Exod 20:16; Deut 5:20: "You shall not bear false witness against your neighbor").[35]

One can also think of other Old Testament texts. For example, the prohibition of perjury, that is, swearing falsely in God's name, is expressed in Exod 20:7 (Lev 19:12). The admonition to honor one's oaths is attested in the content of Ps 50:14 (MT = 49:14 LXX); it relates to vows (promissory, in distinction to assertive swearing); there also, in the expression ἀπόδος τῷ ὑψίστῳ τὰς εὐχάς σου ('fulfill your vows to the most high'), the verb ἀποδίδωμι actually means 'pay'—in the figurative sense, 'fulfill, keep' (also Num 30:3; Deut 23:21).[36]

In the ancient view an oath was sworn by a higher power, whose retribution a person invoked if the obligation of the oath was not met. This is also attested in the Old Testament. Yahweh is the defender of oaths; he punishes perjury and demands that vows made in his name be kept (Lev 6:1ff.; Ezek 16:59; Zech 8:17).

5:34a. The citing of an Old Testament prohibition places the fourth antithesis in the pre-Matthean series of the first and second antitheses. Here also a shorter version can be inferred as the primitive tradition. It would comprise verses 33-34a, and thus contain in Jesus' counterthesis an absolute prohibition against oaths.[37] At this point Jas 5:12 offers an important parallel in which the prohibition occurs in an imperative form (μὴ ὀμνύετε 'do not swear').[38] Presumably Jas 5:12 goes back to a parallel tradition, which has, to be sure, no longer preserved the old antithetical form but in other respects is older than the Matthean version.

The uniqueness of Jesus' prohibition of swearing becomes visible against its religious-historical background. In ancient Judaism as well as in Greece and in Hellenism, the oath is a largely uncontroversially practiced custom.[39] On the other hand, the ancient literature advises against swearing irresponsibly. The Hellenistic Jew Philo in particular recommends discretion in appealing to God as a witness to oaths.[40] Yet an absolute prohibition against oaths is attested only for Jesus. His prohibition of swearing (v. 34a) uncovers the untruthfulness of humanity, but without being expanded with an admonition to speak truthfully. In this it is in harmony with the other ethical radicalisms of Jesus. Like them it is based on the announcement of the coming of God's reign and on Jesus' eschatological authority. Jesus demands radical repentance: whoever is open to the unconditional, original will of God

needs no oath, even if it is allowed in the Torah. Here, too,
Jesus finds himself in opposition to the Old Testament and to a
practice of oaths based on the Old Testament. The law of the
old order falls to pieces when the unconditional, true will of
God is brought to bear.[41] On the basis of this text, the practice
of oaths in every human society must be questioned as to
whether it leaves room for such unconditionality.

5:34b-35. The parallel in James 5:12 makes it clear that the
following verses also belong to the pre-Matthean tradition.
They show that even Jesus' prohibition against oaths was
subject to a growth process, namely, by secondary expansion
through the listing of examples from Jewish and pagan
practice. For the first three examples an Old Testament basis
can be demonstrated. The oath by heaven and by the earth is
rejected with a reference to Isa 66:1. The oath by Jerusalem is
dismissed with an allusion to Ps 47:3 (LXX). Behind these
oaths is the Jewish-rabbinical teaching that the direct naming
of God could be avoided through such circumlocutions. By
contrast the counterthesis says that even such circumlocutions
insult the majesty of God, for ultimately they represent God.

5:36. The last example, the oath by one's own head, is not only
attested in the Jewish environment, but also was in use in
Greek and Roman swearing practice. Hence, this example of
swearing by one's own head may be a secondary accretion from
the Hellenistic-Christian community. This oath is dismissed
here, not as in the preceding examples with the statement that
even thereby the appeal is ultimately to God, but with the
assertion that a human being has no power over himself or
herself. Even if one swears by one's self or by a part of one's
body, one is a dependent being, entirely reliant on God's action
and creative power. Thus, even the oath by one's head is
revealed as an attempt to place God, the Creator, at one's
disposal.

The four cited examples are intended to say that any oath,
even if it avoids an immediate reference to God, violates God's
sovereignty. Every oath reduces God's omnipotence to an
object of human manipulation. Such an assertion is a logical
extrapolation of Jesus' absolute prohibition of oaths. Yet here
is a step in theological reflection that has gained some distance

from the call to repentance of the historical Jesus. At this level of tradition we no longer have just proclamation but also argumentation.

5:37. The closing verse is attested in James 5:12 by a parallel that calls for unqualified, truthful speech. The yes is supposed to be identical with yes, and the no with no.[42] The unconditional demand for truthful speech is conceivable as the conclusion of the pre-Matthean antithesis. It belongs to the last pre-Matthean stage in the process of expansion of the original antithesis. Jesus' prohibition of oaths is thus interpreted as the ethical demand for truthfulness. This admonition was concluded with an allusion to the last judgment. The commandment of truthful speech requires an attitude that allows one to survive the final judgment.

Matthew changed his source in two respects. (1) The article was removed, so that it reads ναὶ ναί, οὔ οὔ ('yes yes, no no'). This passes on a formula that was probably already used in that form in the Matthean community. The double negation or affirmation is attested in Jewish literature as a formula of solemn declaration (thus 2 Enoch 49:1: "When the truth is not among the people, then they may swear with the word 'yes, yes'; but when thus, 'no, no' . . ."). With the citing of this formula, the Evangelist's community avoided having to violate Jesus' prohibition against oaths, since it is a question of a formula, not for an oath, but for a solemn declaration. On the other hand, truthful speech may be thereby strengthened, as that may have been necessary, say, in judicial investigations (cf. Matt 18:17; 1 Cor 6:2). Even to a greater extent than was the case in the preredactional tradition, Matthew adapted the Jesus tradition to the requirements of the community life of his time and in part revoked Jesus' prohibition of oaths.[43]

(2) The addendum τὸ δὲ περισσὸν τούτων ἐκ τοῦ πονηροῦ ἐστιν ('anything more than this comes from evil') comes from Matthew; this is shown by the favored Matthean words περισσόν ('more') and πονηροῦ ('evil'). A minimal formula is to be used, but not a word that goes further and approaches the Jewish or pagan oath. In taking up the practice of his community, Matthew validates the traditional material and adapts it to the judicial necessities of community life. The

instruction has changed from Jesus' prohibition of oaths to a substitute oath.[44]

2.3.5   5:38-42   The Fifth Antithesis: On Retaliation

Fiebig, P. "ἀγγαρεύω." *ZNW* 18 (1917/18): 64-72.
Rausch, J. "The Principle of Nonresistance and Love of Enemy in Mt 5:38-48." *CBQ* 28 (1966): 31-41.
Schottroff, L. "Gewaltverzicht und Feindesliebe in der urchristlichen Jesustradition. Mt. 5,38-48; Lk 6,27-36." In *Jesus Christus in Historie und Theologie*, FS H. Conzelmann, edited by G. Strecker, 197-221. 1975.
Theissen, G. "Gewaltverzicht und Feindesliebe (Mt 5,38-48/Lk 6,27-38) und deren sozialgeschichtlicher Hintergrund." In idem, *Studien zur Soziologie des Urchristentums*, 160-97. WUNT 19. 1979.
Zeller. Mahnsprüche, 55-60.
See also below under 5:43-48.

Matthew 5	Luke 6
38You have heard that it was said, "An eye for an eye and a tooth for a tooth."	
39But I say to you, Do not resist one who is evil. But if any one strikes you on the right cheek, turn to him the other also;	*29To him who strikes you on the cheek, offer the other also; and from him who takes away your cloak do not withhold your coat as well.*
40and if any one would sue you and take your coat, let him have your cloak as well;	
41and if any one forces you to go one mile, go with him two miles.	
42Give to him who begs from you, and do not refuse him who would borrow from you.	*30Give to every one who begs from you and of him who takes away your goods, do not ask them again.*

As a comparison with Luke 6:27-36 will make clear, the content of the fifth and sixth antitheses goes back to the Q tradition, yet it was not formed antithetically in that tradition. In all probability the redactor Matthew created the antithetical formulation (vv. 38-39a, 43-44). From him also came the division of the originally unitary material into two parts, the antithesis on retaliation and the one on love of enemy, for in the Q source the two are not distinguished.

5:38. The thesis cites the Old Testament *ius talionis* from Exodus 21:24 (or from the literal parallels Lev 24:20; Deut 19:21). It is based on the LXX text, in which the accusatives ὀφθαλμόν ('eye') and ὀδόντα ('tooth') are explained by the fact that δώσει ('he shall give') is understood. The Old Testament background is that of the Israelite legal system. The principle of retaliation demands "life for life, eye for eye, tooth for tooth, hand for hand, foot for foot. . . ." The damage that a criminal causes is to be expiated by the perpetrator being inflicted with like damage. This legal maxim is set against a vengefulness blinded with rage. It is attested as early as the Codex Hammurabi, as well as in Greek, Roman, and rabbinical law. It is a question of an officially sanctioned regulation that cannot at all be understood as a call for taking the law into one's own hands—even if such a misunderstanding through our text seems to lie near at hand—since in what follows, personal modes of behavior come to expression.

5:39. The counterthesis was formed by Matthew himself. Πονηρός ('evil') is a favorite Matthean word. It designates the evil person (add: ἀνθρώπῳ), for it is picked up in the following clause with ὅστις ('whoever'). The infinitive μὴ ἀντιστῆναι ('do not resist') is modeled after the preceding infinitive μὴ ὀμόσαι ὅλως (v. 34: 'do not swear at all'). If the statement in 39*a* is accordingly to be traced back to the Evangelist, it still summarizes what is asserted in the next verses, following the Q tradition.

Against the legal commandment of the Torah, the Preacher on the mount places his own law: not retaliation but renunciation of revenge, not struggle with evil but submission to hostile power! This does not apply only to the community sphere (only the first three antitheses refer primarily to intracommunity relations), but to the personal life of the Christian in general. The admonition to renounce resistance may thus not be restricted to "resistance to judgment."[45] The Christian community is, rather, to take its Lord's demand seriously by not confronting a hostile neighbor with violence. Matthew is not thereby advising compliance vis-à-vis the power of evil. Like Jesus during his temptation (4:1-11), every Christian is, of course, supposed to resist the "tempter." As the communion of the "called," the church must present itself in ethical purity. This admonition is also supposed to help achieve that end.

In the context of the history of religion, the admonition to compliance is not a new commandment. Compliance and humility are also commended in the rabbinic literature as model attitudes.[46] Matthew goes beyond the rabbinic norm of behavior by setting the directive of compliance against the Old Testament-Jewish legal system. One is commanded, if need be, not to claim one's right but to renounce that right, in agreement with the German saying, "Better to suffer wrong than to do wrong" (cf. 1 Cor 6:1-8). In terms of content this directive is a variation of the foregoing admonitions to humility (v. 3), meekness (v. 5), peacemaking (v. 9), and readiness for reconciliation (vv. 22-25). Christian law is the law of love, which does not seek to prevail against the other person, but can even make room for an evil fellow human being. Even while being overcome by evil, even in defeat, believers know that they are borne by the agape of God.

The counterthesis of verse 39a stands at the beginning of a series of examples that are anticlimactically arranged. They form a downward sloping line from the greater evil to the lesser one: violent encounter, court trial, coercion, request. On this scale one could regard being harried by an evil fellow human being as the initial greatest evil. It is more probable, however, that this is a general statement that provides the basis for all of those that follow. Matthew wants to say: whenever anyone comes against you with evil intention, do not repay evil with evil, but show yourself to be Jesus' disciple; demonstrate an attitude of humble love and compliance.

This is clarified by the following anticlimactic series. The example of the slap of the hand on the cheek (v. 39b) is identified by Luke 6:29 as part of the Q tradition. Matthew adds τὴν δεξιάν ('right'). Here, it is not just a matter of a coincidental concretization (cf. 5:29-30; 6:3; Did. 1:4) but also of designating the special disgrace of a blow with the back of the hand.[47] The one struck is supposed to offer the other cheek also, as proof of unreserved compliance that seeks neither to

preserve one's own honor nor to maintain one's own position
of power.

5:40. In second place follows the suit over the χιτών, the
shirt-like undergarment that is worth less than the ἱμάτιον, the
outer garment. One is supposed to demonstrate one's
compliance by handing over one's cloak too. The reverse order
appears in the Gospel of Luke, who is thinking of a robber
(αἴροντος). When he snatches away the cloak, one should not
keep him from taking the undergarment, too. In both cases
Jesus' demand breaks every rule of good sense. The radical
nature of the demand for compliance is based on nothing
other than the nearness of the kingdom of God, which
demolishes all human certainties; before it nothing can
prevail, and every person appears naked and bare.

5:41. Presumably Matthew found the example of the coercion
already present in this location. The verb ἀγγαρεύειν is a
Persian loanword; originally it referred to the Persian courier
(ἄγγαρος) who had the right to demand and if need be to
compel forced labor and escort service. From this the verb
gained the meaning 'force' or 'coerce' (so also in 27:32 par.).
Faced with such compulsion to accompany, one is required to
go not only one mile but two. The Greek designation of the
distance measure[48] makes clear that this tradition grew up on
Hellenistic soil.

5:42. The final example, of asking and borrowing, is attested
for Q by Luke 6:30. In the second half of the verse, Luke
adopts the image of a robber. Even the return of stolen or
plundered goods should not be demanded. If this is a Lukan
expansion of the previous image, then Matthew, by contrast,
brings a more realistic statement: you shall not turn away from
one who wants to borrow from you![49] This admonition agrees
with the Matthean tendency to ethicize the traditional material
and to adapt it to the actual situation of the community. There
is no doubt that Matthew also understood the preceding
admonitions as instructions that were to be practiced in the
Christian community: compliance, humility, self-denial—
these are all components of the Christian attitude of greater
righteousness for which the followers of Jesus are supposed to

strive and which, so far as it lies within them, they seek to realize. In this way they are the "light of the world" and the "salt of the earth." Such a demand is not immanently based nor understood as a rule of common sense. It is not a maxim for governing the world—such a misunderstanding would lead to the reign of violence. Jesus' unconditional demand confronts the world, rather, with the question of whether it will let itself be changed for the better through an increase in compliance and nonviolence.

2.3.6 5:43-48 The Sixth Antithesis: On Love of Enemy

Bayer, O. "Sprachbewegung und Weltveränderung. Ein systematischer Versuch als Auslegung von Mt 5,43-48." *EvT* 35 (1975): 309-21.

Becker, J. "Feindesliebe—Nächstenliebe—Bruderliebe." *ZEE* 25 (1981): 5-18.

Huber, W. "Feindschaft und Feindesliebe." *ZEE* 26 (1982): 128-58.

Linton, O. "St. Matthew 5:43." *ST* 18 (1964): 66-79.

Lührmann, D. "Liebet eure Feinde (Lk 6,27-36/Mt 5,39-48)." *ZTK* 69 (1972): 412-38.

Moltmann, J. "Feindesliebe." *EK* 15 (1982): 503-5.

Piper, J. "Love your enemies." *SNTSMS* 38. 1974.

Reuter, H. R. "Liebet Eure Feinde!" *ZEE* 26 (1982): 159-87.

Seitz, O. J. F. "Love your Enemies." *NTS* 16 (1969/70): 39-54.

Unnik, W. C. van. "Die Motivierung der Feindesliebe in Lukas VI 32-35." *NovT* 8 (1966): 284-300. (= idem, *Sparsa Collecta* 1, NovTSup 29, 111-26. 1973.)

See also above under 5:38-42.

Delling, G. "τέλειος." *TDNT* 8:67-78.

Dupont, J. " 'Soyez parfaits' (Mt 5,48), 'soyez miséricordieux' (Lc 6,36)." In *Sacra Pagina* 2, edited by J. Coppens et al., 150-62. BETL 12/13. 1959.

Fuchs, E. "Die vollkommene Gewissheit. Zur Auslegung von Matthäus 5,48" (1954). In idem, *Zur Frage nach dem historischen Jesus*, 126-35. GAufs. 2. Tübingen, 1960.

Künzel. *Gemeindeverständnis*, 218-50.

Luck, U. *Die Vollkommenheitsforderung der Bergpredigt.* TEH 150. 1968.

Sabourin, L. "Why Is God called 'perfect' in Mt 5:48?" *BZ* 24 (1980): 266-68.

Schnackenburg, R. "Die Vollkommenheit des Christen nach Matthäus." In idem, *Christliche Existenz nach dem Neuen Testament* 1:131-55. 1967.

Yarnold, E. "Τέλειος in St. Matthew's Gospel." *SE* 4 (TU 102, 1968): 269-73.

Matthew 5	Luke 6
⁴³You have heard that it was said, 'You shall love your neighbor and hate your enemy.'	
⁴⁴But I say to you, Love your enemies	*²⁷But I say to you that hear, Love your enemies, do good to those who hate you,*

and pray for those who persecute you.

²⁸bless those who curse you, pray for those who abuse you.

⁴⁵so that you may be sons of your Father who is in heaven; for he makes his sun rise on the evil and on the good, and sends rain on the just and on the unjust.

³²If you love those who love you, what credit is that to you? For even sinners love those who love them.

⁴⁶For if you love those who love you, what reward have you? Do not even the tax collectors do the same?

⁴⁷And if you salute only your brethren, what more are you doing than others? Do not even the Gentiles do the same?

³³And if you do good to those who do good to you, what credit is that to you? For even sinners do the same.

³⁴And if you lend to those from whom you hope to receive, what credit is that to you? Even sinners lend to sinners, to receive as much again.

³⁵But love your enemies, and do good, and lend, expecting nothing in return; and your reward will be great, and you will be sons of the Most High; for he is kind to the ungrateful and the selfish.

⁴⁸You, therefore, must be perfect, as your heavenly Father is perfect.

³⁶Be merciful, even as your Father is merciful.

A synoptic comparison between the Lukan and Matthean versions[50] shows that Matthew reports the Q material more conservatively in terms of content, while the arrangement is, by and large, closer to the Q tradition in Luke. Only in Luke 6:32-35 do we find a "surplus" (vv. 27, 35: repetition of the love commandment). In Q the commandment to love one's enemy (Matt 5:44; Luke 6:27-28) is the compositional starting point; then follows a series of examples, which Matthew preposes in the fifth antithesis (5:39b-42 par. Luke 6:29-30) and Q brings to a close with the Golden Rule (7:12 par. Luke 6:31). This rule is elucidated by the example of the goodness of God (5:45 par. Luke 6:35b) and then that of the greeting (5:46-47 par. Luke 6:32-35a). The conclusion is formed by the exhortation to deeds of mercy (Luke 6:36 par. Matt 5:48).[51]

Matthew, on the other hand, formed two antitheses from the Q material. The redactional fifth antithesis is elucidated by examples that in Q, as just noted, originally followed the commandment to love one's enemy. In the formation of the sixth antithesis, Matthew takes up the remaining Q material. After the fundamental imperative (v. 44), he brings a final justification (v. 45), which is expanded with a double $\dot{\varepsilon}\dot{\alpha}\nu$ sentence (vv. 46-47). The summarizing imperative "Be perfect!" is a typical Matthean variation of the Q commandment of mercy (v. 48). Thus, if the Evangelist placed beside the commandment of unconditional compliance (v. 39a) the demand of radical love of enemy (v. 44), the two oppose each other only superficially as a passive and an active attitude; for the required compliance naturally requires decisive, self-conscious human behavior, just as, conversely, love for one's enemy and prayer for one's persecutor do not exclusively circumscribe an active mode of behavior (and certainly not an aggressive attitude), but include patience and endurance.

5:43. The thesis cites the Old Testament commandment to love one's neighbor (Lev 19:18), and indeed literally, according to the LXX, so that once again support is given to the presumption that the Evangelist Matthew gave antithetical form to the tradition. According to the Old Testament understanding, the love commandment refers to relations with one's fellow Israelites and not to the people's enemies. The expansion of the thesis through the commandment to hate your enemy is not attested in the Old Testament. Possibly, the redactor Matthew added it as a logical extension, perhaps adopting a Jewish catechetical rule, such as that passed down by the Qumran sect (1 QS I 3-4: God commanded "to love everything that he has chosen but to hate everything that he has rejected").[52] Matthew is trying to indicate here that the love commandment is expressed only in a limited way in Judaism. In his understanding, the verb $\mu\iota\sigma\varepsilon\hat{\iota}\nu$ has the literal meaning of 'to hate' and not only 'not to love.'[53] Matthew, to be sure, also knows the verb in the sense of 'not to love' or 'to reject,'[54] but he uses it predominantly in the unequivocal sense of 'to hate.'[55] Thus, as in verses 21b and 33b, the thesis is apparently expanded in order to fix the demand for love of neighbor in its literal sense and thereby to restrict it.[56] From the standpoint of the Evangelist, even the commandment to hate one's enemy has the task of polemically characterizing the Old Testament-Jewish position.

5:44. On the other hand, Jesus' counterthesis means not only that the will of God proclaimed by him requires love vis-à-vis one's neighbor and friend, but also that the commandment of love has validity vis-à-vis one's enemy. It is to be expressed thus in intercessory prayer; it applies to those who cover the followers of Jesus with curses.[57] If ἐχθρός is the (personal) enemy in the relations of everyday life (= *inimicus*),[58] then it is illuminating that the Greek word for an opponent in war or a state enemy (πολέμιος = *hostis*) does not occur in the New Testament. Nevertheless, this is not to say that Jesus' commandment consciously excludes the enemy in war. A specific stand on politically active persons is not intended. Jesus' demand is absolute and permits no restriction through any kind of reason of state. It says: whoever comes against you with hostile intent is supposed to encounter your love and intercession!

Jesus' demand for love of enemy is not based on human presuppositions. It refers neither to human rules of prudence nor to the stoic humanitarian ideal of a general love for humankind. Nor is the intention to restrict human aggressiveness by appealing to human rights. Jesus does not need to humanize human behavior illusorily; he can look at it realistically in relation to evil (cf. 6:13 par. Luke 11:4; Matt 5:39). As represented by the demand for love of enemy, the commandment of love is to be understood, not out of the human, but out of the divine realm: both friend and foe are nearing the coming kingdom of God. They will both have to answer for themselves before the supreme Judge. There is no escape! When this is known, one can disregard one's privileges, one's honor, and—more basically—oneself. Like oneself, one's fellow human beings—the pleasant and the unpleasant, those of good will as well as those of evil intent—can also be left to the judgment and grace of the universal Judge. Here is the unconditional solidarity of sinners before a judging God.

The commandment to love one's enemy is an example of the independence of Jesus' ethical radicalism both vis-à-vis his Jewish surroundings and in comparison with the Christian church. In this absolute orientation, the commandment is not attested in its religious-historical environment. Yet Jesus' position can be linked with Old Testament-Jewish and Greek-Hellenistic models. In Exod 23:4-5, one is required to give aid to an enemy in certain emergencies, and this was passed down and applied in the rabbinic literature.[59] The philosophy of the Stoics and Cynics includes the teaching that one is to love all people.[60] The wisdom literature of Judaism passes down the saying, "If your enemy is hungry, give him bread to eat; and if he is thirsty, give him water to drink" (Prov 25:21). Paul cites this in Romans 12:20 with the accompanying rationale: "For by so doing you will heap burning coals upon his head" (cf. Prov 25:22). The wisdom commandment to do good to one's enemy has divine reward in view. And the advice not to repay evil with evil (Rom 12:17)[61] also stands in a monitory-ethical environment and is rationally based.[62] Yet such apparent parallels have nothing to do with the radical call for repentance that characterizes the proclamation of Jesus.

The prayer for one's foes is also known in Jewish literature, although not in the Old Testament. There it is connected with the clear intention that the enemies should convert.[63] Such a definition of purpose is foreign to the absolute imperative of Jesus. According to early Christian tradition, Jesus on the cross (Luke 23:34) and the martyr Stephen before his death (Acts 7:60) prayed for their enemies without any utilitarian intention. Although this may have been stylized in the sense of Christian martyr-piety, and suffering and dying Christians are thereby exhorted to the imitation of Christ, this tradition reveals, nevertheless, an echo of Jesus' unconditional, purely eschatologically based demand to practice love of enemy.[64]

Matthew formulated the last antithesis with a view to the situation and the duties of his community. If in the Old Testament the "enemies" are identical with the opponents of the people of God, then the same is true for the new people of God. The phrase "your enemies" stands in parallel to "those who persecute you." Here as elsewhere in Matthew, the verb διώκειν is a technical term for the persecution of the Christian community. Thus the commandment of love and of intercessory prayer has as its object the persecutors of Christians. Similarly, the term *brethren* (v. 47) refers to fellow Christians (see also 18:15, 21; 23:8; 25:40; and elsewhere). Verses 10-12 have already shown that persecution marked the situation of the Matthean community. Faced with persecution and the experience of unwarranted suffering, the Christian community has its existence on the line. Will it allow the violence striking it to provoke it to hate and counterviolence, or is it capable of standing by the word of the Son of God and thereby holding fast to its calling? Will it allow itself to be bound by the usual, "normal" behavior in human society, or is it ready to renounce merely human reactions that are all too understandable and actively open itself to the goal of unbounded love and goodness? For the Evangelist, it is clear that the commandment of the Preacher on the mount has an unconditional validity and is to be accepted and realized in the world without any ifs or buts and also without any side glances toward potential positive or negative consequences.[65] Moreover, the following verses attempt to exhibit reasons that make it seem sensible to go farther on this already travelled path.

5:45. The image saying of the unconditional, universal goodness of God was independent in the primitive tradition. The *imitatio Dei* demanded there has parallels in the Jewish and in the Hellenistic-Roman spheres.[66] Seneca gives the advice, "When you imitate the gods . . . then give good also to the ungrateful, for the sun also rises over the criminals, and the ocean is open to the pirates" (de benef. IV 26). At this point the Stoic philosopher, of course, is thinking of the regular operation of nature, to which he is supposed to accommodate himself in his thinking and acting, in order to reach the ideal of a dispassionate, wise person. But the Q tradition of our saying is different: not an ideal of humankind but the unconditional demand of Jesus, not the regularity of nature but the self-identical action of the Creator, independent of human effort—this is what points to the foundation and the example for proper human endeavor. The introduction with ὅπως ('so that') marks the finality of the rationale. More clearly than in Luke (v. 35b: with a concluding καί 'and'), the goal and theme of human activity is expressed: sonship vis-à-vis the heavenly Father! The subjunctive γένησθε ('might become') designates not an evolution but perhaps a transformation into sons of God (cf. Mark 1:17; John 1:12). Thus a condition of divine sonship is not presupposed (cf. also 5:9). In content it corresponds to the future ἔσεσθε (Luke 6:35b) with the imperative meaning, 'you shall be.'[67] Although the goal of divine sonship for the followers of Jesus[68] is the object of promise (cf. 5:9; 13:38) and remains unrealized, it already defines present activity. God's being as "our Father, who art in heaven,"[69] motivates the behavior of the community. In his person, he realizes the highest commandment of love. He shows himself as caring Father. Through the sun he sends light and warmth, and through the rain he has the earth bring forth nourishment for humankind. His fatherly goodness is not directed according to good and evil, according to the worth and unworth of people.[70] God is benevolent without respect to persons. As the Creator, he supports everything created. Such unrestricted goodness must give rise to imitation. In like manner, the demanded realization of sonship in love vis-à-vis one's enemy may not inquire of the favorable or unfavorable nature of circumstances, but is supposed only to obey the commandment of love. The expected attitude is one that recognizes God's loving activity as model; it will be circumscribed in the following with the imperative: Be perfect! (v. 48).

5:46. The demand for love of enemy was expanded already in the Q tradition through a supplementary rationale. The original wording of the two negative examples is better maintained in Matthew than in Luke. In particular, Luke 6:34-35*a* is ascribed to the third Evangelist. Doubtless Luke provided secondary expansion of the Q tradition, reworking it in a hellenizing fashion[71] and universalizing it in adaptation to the situation of the church in all times.[72] Yet even in the Third Gospel the original sense is clearly recognizable. A rational argument supports the commandment to love one's enemy: love that is devoted only to those by whom one is loved in return is different from the love of the Father. It is only natural; it is oriented toward humanity and remains trapped on the human level. The rhetorical question, "What reward have you?" presupposes a negative answer: "None."[73] Such action is not unusual: even the tax collectors behave this way. They, however, are simply "sinners," as Luke says in a factually correct interpretation of the underlying tradition.[74] Here as elsewhere, Matthew follows the conceptual system of his model, which was common to his community. In distinction to the parable tradition in the special material of the Third Gospel,[75] the tax collectors are pictured as a negative example.

They are the representatives of mutual love and cannot satisfy the demand of God.

5:47. The second, similarly constructed example speaks of the "salute," which, of course, not only represents a polite conventional form but also, in accord with the oriental custom of the peace greeting, is a blessing. Such a greeting carries the force of a benediction (cf. 10:12-13; Luke 10:5-6). The greeting of the "brethren" is not peculiar to Jesus' followers; it does not raise the Jesus' disciples above the level of the Gentiles. It does not overcome the primitive give-and-get principle, which says that one gives in order to receive. This rule is valid for human relations in general; thus it characterizes the ἐθνικοί. Matthew employs here (as also in 6:7; 18:17) a term that implies the Jewish depreciation of the Gentile world. This original opposition of Jews and Gentiles is no longer valid for the Evangelist, since he affirms the Gentile mission and the Gentile church. Similar to the tax collectors, the Gentiles in the First Gospel are also types for non-Christian, sinful people. Thus, the intended meaning is "unconverted people."

In contrast to this, it behooves one to do "more."[76] The parallel 5:20 reveals a central idea of the Matthean ethic. There righteousness is demanded as the quantitative "more" in relation to the scribes and Pharisees as the representatives of Jewish theology; here the same thought characterizes Christian behavior in comparison with religious outsiders. The commandment of love requires more than the usual and normal. It is radical without its radical nature canceling its meaningfulness and intentionality—both are expressed in the idea of reward.

5:48. The closing verse bears genuine Matthean traits. The content, of course, goes back to Q (cf. Luke 6:36), but the concluding οὖν ('therefore') is redactional,[77] as are the adjective οὐράνιος ('heavenly')[78] and, above all, the double τέλειοι/ τέλειος ('perfect'), which is also identified as Matthean in 19:21.[79]

Rudolf Bultmann recorded the interpretation of the word τέλειος widely accepted until today.[80] It is derived from the Semitic תמים (*tamim*) with the meaning 'whole,' 'complete.'

Thus, the Matthean Jesus demanded the wholeness, undividedness of a person. Not a "both-and" but an "either-or" marks
this understanding. Human beings face a radical decision
before God. No other alternatives are left open: there is only
the choice between obedience and disobedience. Consequently, the ethic of Jesus may not be understood "in the sense of an
idealistic teaching on duty or virtue, or an ethic of goods or
worth." Instead, "all concrete moral decisions are turned over
completely to individual responsibility"; a person's decision
has a definitive character; "in it he becomes a righteous person
or a sinner."[81]

Naturally the question is whether Matthew wants to hold to
these alternatives, or whether more correctly he understands
the call to perfection as an instruction that is, of course, radical
and yet also concrete. It is illuminating that the Qumran
literature offers a wealth of documents in which תמים does not
have an exclusive, absolute meaning, but refers to a conversion
that encompasses all of the precepts and is especially aimed at
cultic correctness. There the term circumscribes a human
behavior that accords with the demands of God.[82] The
Matthean exhortation to be perfect refers expressly back to the
nature of God (v. 48b). The latter, however, is not mentioned
for its own sake; it comes to expression so that it may be
portrayed as binding for human behavior. God's benevolent
nature is valued as a model for the act of love (v. 45).

Nevertheless, the word *perfect* does not designate the highest
level of an ideal, corresponding, say, to the Greek ideal
combination of the beautiful and the good, to which the
Christian must aspire. Nor can we distinguish a Matthean ethic
of perfection that is valid only for the elite from a general
Christian ethic that is required of the remaining community
members and is limited to keeping the most important
commandments. Matthew did not present a two-stage ethic,[83]
and did not differentiate between the *praecepta* that were
necessarily followed and the *consilia* beyond what was
obligatory. The meaning of the demand for perfection is
clarified by the example of the young man in the dialogue on
the danger of wealth (19:16-30). He claims to have kept all the
commandments of the Decalogue and, according to Jesus,
lacks only one thing: "If you would be perfect, go, sell what you
possess and give to the poor" (19:21). The rich man balks at

this duty, because the one thing he lacks is the whole thing that is demanded, namely, himself. Jesus' call to perfection means the complete and concrete person. Such ethical perfection is also demanded in Jas 1:4, according to which the perfect, complete person brings forth the perfect work of steadfastness.[84]

In spite of the absolute divine claim, perfection does not stand in opposition to the concrete demand. It is also not a human superachievement that stands at the top of an ethical scale of values; it is rather the human realization of the totality of Jesus' instructions and hence identical with the demanded righteousness (5:20). The Matthean "therefore," which introduces the demand of perfection, points not to the commandment of unreserved agape (v. 44) but to the beginning of the series of antitheses (v. 20). It asserts that Jesus' teaching, as it is presented in the main part of the Sermon on the Mount, requires both: agape and righteousness! In both, attitude and action, inward and outward behavior are to become one. Through both, human hypocrisy is overcome, and the eschatological demand of the Son of God is realized. Matthew does not understand such action by the followers of Jesus as the response to a gift of divine righteousness.[85] The unconditionality of the demand leaves no room for the distinction and definition of relationship between gift and duty. Jesus' listeners are summoned to an unlimited responsibility that they cannot escape.

The standard by which the followers can measure themselves is given by Jesus' teachings and behavior. Jesus' teachings, as they are proclaimed in the Sermon on the Mount, are presented as sovereign interpretation of the Old Testament. They reveal the enduring ethical obligation of the Old Testament Torah, but also the newness of the directives spoken with authority by the Preacher on the mount. As this is assumed for the proclamation of the historical Jesus, so also the antitheses of the Preacher on the mount are defined both by Torah critique, in that Old Testament demands are replaced by new ones (5:31-32, 33-37, 38-42), and by Torah radicalization, in that Old Testament directives are intensified (5:21-26, 27-30, 43-48). At the same time, the tradition-historical development of an absolute Torah-critical prohibition of Jesus can lead to a new Matthean community rule (e.g.,

5:31-32, 33-37). In the Matthean understanding, there is no contradiction between Torah intensification or suspension and Jesus' intention not to abolish the law and the prophets but to fulfill them (5:17). In regard to the Old Testament and the tradition of the scribes and Pharisees, the Preacher on the mount does not want to teach a new law but rather to bring to expression the sovereign will of God in and in contrast to the Old Testament Torah.

Moreover, Jesus' behavior, as it is described in Matthew's Gospel, shows that Jesus accepted as binding for himself the demand of righteousness (3:15). He shuns anger (8:3; 12:12; 19:14 versus Mark 1:43; 3:5; 10:14), practices nonviolence (26:52), gentleness, and humility (11:28-30; 21:5) and submits himself in obedience to the will of his Father (26:46 versus Mark 14:39). Matthew wants to say thereby that Jesus realizes in himself the directives that he gives. From this the Christian community can learn how it is supposed to deal with the demands of the Preacher on the mount. They must endeavor to comply with the commandment of righteousness and to do what is right, without respect to persons and only in accordance with the will of God. Although the anti-Pharisee definition of righteousness (5:20; 6:1ff.) cannot exclude a nomistic understanding, the danger of legalism is, nonetheless, counteracted in that the demand of righteousness is interpreted by the commandment of love. Agape supersedes the legal question of what is just, not by repaying like with like, but by asking the blessing of God even for one's enemy. Without such agape, Jesus' demand of righteousness would become a new legal norm. In consonance with the commandment of love the demand of righteousness expresses the appeal that the community of followers do whatever is necessary in the freedom of the children of God. They are bound not only by the teaching and behavior of Jesus as criteria for proper activity; one must also point to the image of the benevolent, perfect activity of the Creator (vv. 45, 48). As little as the demanded perfection is to be exhibited in its entirety in people's concrete, everyday life, so much more is it the goal that sets an unconditional standard for human life. The community of Jesus Christ, on its way through the ages, is summoned anew everyday to direct itself toward that goal.

2.4   6:1-18   On Almsgiving, Praying, and Fasting

Betz, H. D. "Eine judencristliche Kult-Didache in Matthäus 6,1-18." In *Jesus Christus in Historie und Theologie*, FS H. Conzelmann, edited by G. Strecker, 445-57. 1975.

George, A. "La justice à faire dans le secret (Matthieu 6,1-6 et 16-18." *Bib* 40 (1959): 590-98.

Gerhardsson, B. "Geistiger Opferdienst nach Matth 6,1-6.16-21." In *Neues Testament und Geschichte*, FS O. Cullmann, edited by H. Baltensweiler and B. Reicke, 69-77. 1972.

Klostermann, E. "Zum Verständnis von Mt 6,2." *ZNW* 47 (1956): 280-81.

Maartens, J. P. "The Cola Structure of Mt 6." *Neot* 11 (1977): 48-76.

Nagel, W. "Gerechtigkeit—oder Almosen? (Mt 6,1)" *VC* 15 (1961): 141-45.

Schweizer, E. " 'Der Jude im Verborgenen . . . , dessen Lob nicht von Menschen, sondern von Gott kommt.' Zu Röm 2,28f und Mt 6,1-18." In idem, *Matthäus und seine Gemeinde*, SBS 71, 86-98. 1974.

Three catechetical pieces[1] form the core of this section. Each introduced by a ὅταν ('when') clause, they are identically constructed; they deal with almsgiving (vv. 2-4), praying (vv. 5-6), and fasting (vv. 16-18). Each is divided into two parts according to content.

1. First the forbidding example of the ὑποκριταί ('hypocrites') is presented. The ὅταν clause (2d pers. plur. except 2d pers. sing. in v. 2a) names the pious practice. Then follows a caricatured description of the actions of the hypocrites and the presentation of their inappropriate aim (linked with ὅπως 'so that'). This part concludes with the ἀμήν ('truly') message: "They have their reward!"

2. Then a positive instruction is formulated. It is constructed in the second person singular, then names the proper purpose (ὅπως in vv. 4a, 18a; infinitive in v. 6c), and concludes with a promise: "Your Father, who sees in secret will reward you!")

A comparison of structure produces the following overview of Matthew 6:2-18:

I.	"When . . . "	2a	5a	16a
	hypocrites' action	2b-c	5b-c	16b-c
	"so that"	2d	5d	16d
	"Truly . . . "	2e	5e	16e
II.	positive instruction	3	6a-b	17
	"so that"/infinitive	4a	6c	18a
	promise	4b	6d	18b

Worked into these three literary units are the heading (v. 1), the saying against the prattling prayers of the Gentiles (vv. 7-8), and the Lord's Prayer as the exemplary prayer (vv. 9-13), explained by a double saying on the obligation to forgive (vv. 14-15). In the following discussion, we will have to ask what significance these additions give to the Matthean interpretation.

2.4.1 6:1-4 On Almsgiving

[1]Beware of practicing your piety before men in order to be seen by them; for then you will have no reward from your Father who is in heaven.

[2]Thus, when you give alms, sound no trumpet before you, as the hypocrites do in the synagogues and in the streets, that they may be praised by men. Truly, I say to you they have their reward. [3]But when you give alms, do not let your left hand know what your right hand is doing, [4]so that your alms may be in secret; and your Father who sees in secret will reward you.

6:1. The introductory verse was conceived by Matthew as a heading for the entire section. Redactional composition can be demonstrated linguistically.[2] In particular, the designation of God as the "Father who is in heaven" (also in 5:16, 45; 6:9; 7:11; 18:14) and the concept of righteousness, or "piety,"[3] are typically Matthean, so that there can be no doubt: the first Evangelist consciously placed the following examples of godly Christian living under the topic of "righteousness."

With verse 1 Matthew leaves Luke and their common Q tradition, whose material he draws on in this section only in the text of the Lord's Prayer (Luke 11:2-4) and again starting with verse 19. On the other hand, the continuing line of the Q tradition that was abandoned after 5:48 is not picked up again until 7:1ff (cf. Luke 6:37ff.). On this basis it is conceivable that our section goes back to an isolated special tradition, but it is also possible that it belongs to Matthew's expanded copy of the sayings collection (Q^Matt). In comparison with the remainder of the Q tradition, the form and content are relatively independent. As a reason for its creation one may presume the catechism of the Jewish-Christian community, whose relations with the Jewish synagogue were still rather close (similarly, 5:18-19), for the criticism of the "hypocrites" begins with Jewish premises and in its outcome also accords with the presupposed Jewish conceptual scheme. On this basis one could classify the Jewish-Christian bearers of this tradition as a "reform Judaism."[4] Of course, we cannot determine the extent to which they were actually molded in a Jewish-Christian, legalistic fashion and observed the commandments of purity, circumcision, and the sabbath. In what follows it will become probable that verses 7-8 already had been added to the unit of tradition before Matthew. Here there is a pre-Matthean change of linguistic direction: instead of the Jewish "hypocrites," the reference now is to "Gentiles." Accordingly, the Evangelist Matthew got to know the tradition before him in an environment in which encounters with the Gentiles were necessary, and the church understood itself as made up of Jews and Gentiles as the "third race,"[5] as an independent entity. Apart from the heading (v. 1), only the insertion of verses 9-15 is ascribed to Matthew.

As early as 5:20 the concept of righteousness has a thematic function; thus, here it is picked up when the integrity of Jesus' disciples is expressly characterized as the result of human doing ($\pi o\iota\epsilon\hat{\iota}\nu$) and not as divine gift.[6] In Judaism the good works to be mentioned, almsgiving, praying, and fasting, belong to the recognized practices of piety.[7] They could be perceived in the diaspora independent of the Jerusalem temple cult and in Judaism after the destruction of the temple, and in the view of the first Evangelist, they must also be practiced in the Christian community. The warning not to practice them "before men in order to be seen by them" anticipates the reproach in the following verses aimed stereotypically against the "hypocrites" and waves a warning flag before the eyes of the community; as the consequence of placing oneself on exhibit before others, one must forfeit the heavenly reward, which the followers of Jesus are also promised.[8]

T. Zahn (*Evangelium*, 260) makes the following distinction: 5:21-48 speaks against the scribes and their interpretation of Scripture, 6:1-18 against the Pharisees and the piety they practice. Yet such a division is not obvious, especially since 6:19, despite a change in themes, does not name a new dialogue partner. Matthew found the phrase

"Pharisees and scribes" in the tradition before him (15:1; cf. Mark 7:1, 5) and naturally used it (5:20; 23:2ff.) without expressly differentiating; it refers to the theological representatives of Judaism at the time of Jesus, whose manner is polemically noted in order to emphasize through negative example the true attitude befitting the Christian (see also above under 5:20).

6:2. In the Jewish literature the word ἐλεημοσύνη can have the general meaning of 'charity' (cf. Dan 4:24 = 4.27 LXX), but in the New Testament it means charity that one shows to the poor and thus 'alms.'[9] The idea that the synagogue attendant blew into his trumpet when an especially large sum was given, as A. Schlatter suggests,[10] and that such a custom is presupposed here, is probably no more than an exciting speculation. The word σαλπίζειν ('to sound a trumpet') can be used in a completely symbolic sense:[11] 'do not proclaim it loudly,' that is, 'do not boast about it.'

For this reason, of course, Jesus reproaches the "hypocrites" who appear in the synagogues and streets so that they may reap fame from the people. Here as elsewhere the reproach of hypocrisy against Jesus' Jewish opponents is a part of the pre-Matthean tradition (cf. 15:7 par. Mark 7:9), and in the speech against the Pharisees becomes a focus of the Christian polemic (23:2ff.). The Pharisees and scribes live in a contradiction; their proper outward appearance does not jibe with the egoist direction of their will; they are like whitewashed tombs that on the outside are beautiful to look at but on the inside are full of dead bones (23:27-28). They adorn themselves with broad phylacteries and long fringes, they claim the most prominent seats in the synagogues, and such behavior is aimed entirely toward outward effect (23:5-6; also 23:25-26). Their hyprocrisy is an attempt to appear to be, rather than to be, to establish an image that hides their real intentions. Thus, they are prototypes of the self-alienated, divided, and thus imperfect person. The surmise that in this description Matthew is drawing a picture of an "objective self-contradiction" in which the Pharisees and scribes find themselves through no fault of their own[12] does not do justice to the intention of the first Evangelist. He is not trying to describe the unconscious sinful existence of humanity as such; for him, rather, hypocrisy is a conscious dissembling, just as its antithesis, righteousness, is a conscious human attitude. It is not coincidental that the original meaning of the Greek word ὑποκριτής is 'actor.' E. Haenchen has correctly pointed out that the cutting edge of the anti-Pharisaical polemic in Matthew's Gospel is blunted if hypocrisy is understood in an objective sense.[13] That the hypocrites are presented as conscious of their attitude and responsible for it, is also clear in the definition of its purpose: the hypocritical behavior is realized in concrete deeds that are aimed at the approval of the spectators. But, says Matthew, the meaning of good works is thereby distorted, for they are done with an audience in mind for the sake of earthly advantage.

The solemn concluding formulation, reinforced by *truly*, pronounces the judgment. The μισθός ('reward') promised for the heavenly world has been paid out. Ἀπέχειν comes from the language of business and effectively means 'to receipt a bill,' that is, 'to have received an amount.'[14] Matthew presupposes the profit motive and takes for granted its validity. The hypocrites are not denied the reward that is due them for their good works. Nevertheless, through the approbation that they seek from the spectators, they have already received their reward; there is nothing left for them to expect.

6:3. The instruction on the right way to give alms is different. The decisive difference between the right and the wrong behavior is the aim, which should be directed not toward people but toward God. Only on this premise are these two verses to be interpreted. This means that outward appearance must correspond to the inner direction of the will, which is intent on God. Obedience vis-à-vis God's demand and the outward behavior of a person may not stand in contradiction with each other. The proper benefactor is the undivided, perfect person, who can get along without outward appearance and the approval of an audience.

This provides the basis for understanding the controversial command, "Do not let your left hand know what your right hand is doing." According to a widespread interpretation it means that proper doers of good deeds are not conscious of them.[15] This would lead to the conclusion that the divinely willed work of human beings can be done by God alone (cf. Phil 2:13). Yet the Preacher on the mount aims his demand of righteousness at the doings of people who are conscious of their own selves. What is required is not a renunciation of the knowledge of one's own actions;[16] rather, the proverbial expression[17] makes clear the required action, which—because it occurs in secret—is set against the externally focused behavior of the hypocrites. The doing of good is supposed to remain hidden, not from the doer, but from the people, in order to escape public honor as the substitute for heavenly reward. This means that the doer does not want to honor himself with his work or give himself credit for his actions. It is also the sense of the following directives, according to which godly work is supposed to happen in secret. Naturally, the prayer in one's room (v. 6) can remain as little hidden from the one who prays as the secret fasting that is concealed from the public (vv. 17-18) can remain hidden from the one who fasts. In each case Matthew wants to emphasize the necessity of doing good deeds with a view toward God and not in the view of people.

6:4. The statements on secrecy are also to be seen in this light. In form this verse recalls Paul's praise for the one who is a Jew in secret and practices a spiritual circumcision of the heart, in contrast to one who is outwardly a Jew and observes external circumcision of the flesh (Rom 2:28-29). Parallels with Jewish piety can be drawn.[18] Also the First Letter of Peter contrasts the appearance of women set on outward adornment with the "hidden person of the heart," who is "of a gentle and quiet spirit" (1 Pet 3:3-4). In truth, Matthew is not concerned about an inner ethic as opposed to an outer one, or a secret versus a public ethic.[19] Crucial, rather, is the antithesis of earthly reward, which the hypocrites have received, and the heavenly compensation that may be expected from the heavenly Father alone and which is promised for human action in secret.

In distinction to the Jewish wisdom teaching, which primarily offers the prospect of earthly compensation for the good deeds of people,[20] Matthew is thinking here, as also in other places (cf. 5:12), of the future, eschatological reward. Even if the giver of this eternal reward is the heavenly Father, who demonstrates his goodness daily (5:45), Matthew is, nonetheless, not familiar with the concept of unearned compensation. Rather, in 20:8 $\dot{\alpha}\pi o\delta i\delta\omega\mu\iota$ can even have the technical meaning 'to pay out (wages)' (cf. 2 Clem. 20:4; Bar. 11:8). Even from the parable of the laborers in the vineyard (20:1-16) one cannot conclude that heavenly recompense and human achievement are mutually exclusive, but rather that the heavenly Landlord grants to the latecomers the same wage as that promised to the workers hired first. Matthew, to be sure, is not calculating future payment, but he and his community are indeed counting on a heavenly compensation, and that is eternal life.[21]

The view of Matthew as well as his tradition is that there is an unbridgeable distance between, on the one hand, the Jewish-Pharisaical standpoint and, on the other, the demand for the totality of human life and the overcoming of the contradiction between outward appearance and true inner attitude. The realm of ethical thinking, of course, has not been thereby abandoned. The calling into question of the way of the law, as it is taught by Paul, is unknown to the first Evangelist and his tradition. The idea of reward is passed down relatively without reflection. The danger that Matthew's ethic will devolve into legalism is especially clear at this point.

This leads to the question whether the pre-Matthean rules of piety could have been spoken by Jesus himself. Here it can be established that the idea of reward was presumably contained in the proclamation of Jesus, even if detailed proof remains uncertain. Yet "the naive expectation of reward was de facto overcome by the core of Jesus' message."[22] This compels the conclusion that the inferred pre-Matthean form of the three catechetical pieces presumably does not go back to Jesus. Its wisdom-like structure is quite different from the call to repentance based on the nearness of the kingdom of God and from the radical ethical demand of Jesus. One can hardly succeed in lifting out of the pre-Matthean tradition three sayings of the historical Jesus that would make the primitive calculation of godly achievement impossible.[23] The instruction on fasting (vv. 16-18) is illuminating: the affirmation of a Christian practice of fasting adapted to the expansion of time is considerably different from the situation-bound word of Jesus, according to which the presence of the bridegroom makes it unnecessary to keep the commandment to fast (9:15 par. Mark 2:19).

2.4.2　6:5-8　On Praying

⁵And when you pray, you must not be like the hypocrites; for they love to stand and pray in the synagogues and at the street corners, that they

*may be seen by men. Truly, I say to you, they have their reward. ⁶But
when you pray, go into your room and shut the door and pray to your
Father who is in secret; and your Father who sees in secret will reward
you.*

*⁷And in praying do not heap up empty phrases as the Gentiles do; for
they think that they will be heard for their many words. ⁸Do not be like
them, for your Father knows what you need before you ask him.*

6:5. Along with giving alms, prayer is named as another
important religious exercise in Judaism (cf. Tob 12:8; b. Šabb.
127a). In ancient Judaism certain times of prayer were
established. The recitation of the Eighteen Benedictions was
made obligatory three times a day (morning, noon, and
evening). The direction of the prayer points to the holy of
holies of the temple in Jerusalem. The Old Testament psalms
represent old prayer formulas of the Israelite community. The
construction of this verse—in contrast to verse 2a—with an
introductory ὅταν ('when') clause in the second person plural
leads us to think that communal prayer is understood, even if
the second singular reappears in the following verse 6. Verses
7-9, 14-16a, however, also have the plural—possibly based on
the introduction of the Lord's Prayer.

The caricaturing example shows the "hypocrites" standing
and praying in the synagogues and on the street corners. In the
Jewish world it is conceivable for prayer to be said in public if,
say, the prescribed hour of prayer required it. And praying
while standing was widespread.³⁴ The polemical reproach suggests the purpose ascribed to the hypocrites: their prayer is an
exhibition. They are displaying themselves before the people
instead of addressing God while alone. Since they satisfy their
egoistic desires under the pretext of prayer, they have received
their reward; the accounts are settled, as ἀπέχουσιν τὸν μισθὸν
αὐτῶν ('they have their reward') again asserts.

6:6. The following directive advises one—if there is to be
genuine prayer—to withdraw into a ταμεῖον and close the
door. The sentence comes from Isa 26:20, where the people of
Israel are asked to withdraw into their chamber (חדר = *cheder*)
and shut the door until the wrath of God is past. The term
ταμεῖον refers to a dark, windowless room. Whether the
author is thinking concretely of a storehouse (thus Luke 12:24)

or a shed built onto a house cannot be determined with sufficient certainty. In the New Testament the word generally has the meaning of 'inner room' (Matt 24:26; Luke 12:3; also 1 Clem. 50:4). Naturally, it does not mean that one's room is the only possible place for prayer. The object, rather, is to illustrate proper prayer. It must not satisfy a passion for public recognition but should be an act of obedience. It must concentrate exclusively on the God who is addressed in prayer. The focus of Christian prayer is on the "Father who is in secret." A number of manuscripts do not attest the article τῷ,[25] so that it is secondarily underlined that the prayer must take place in secret. To such proper prayer is granted eschatological fulfillment. No doubt the godly Jew can also understand his praying in this way.[26] Matthew is riding the wake of this tradition, since he passes on this directive on prayer without comment. He himself speaks in a different way about Christian prayer in 18:19-20. It is directed toward the Father of Jesus Christ. The presence of the exalted One is promised to the praying fellowship that gathers in the name of Jesus. On the other hand, the practice of prayer in the early Christian church shows the early influence of Jewish elements; as early as the beginning of the second century the Lord's Prayer was prayed three times a day in accordance with the Jewish times of prayer (Did. 8:3).

6:7-8. Verses 7 and 8 did not originally belong to the two foregoing catechetical units; they were presumably added to the prayer directive before Matthew. Such is suggested by the hapax legomena in verse 7.[27] By contrast, the language in verse 8 contains pre-Matthean traits, but was already partially present in Q.[28] If in their present location these verses also serve the function of a transition to the following quotation of the Lord's Prayer, they were not conceived for that purpose; for the expression of trust in the providence of God, which is recognized as effective before any praying (v. 8*b*; cf. Isa 65:24), is not a convincing prelude. As the original introduction to the Lord's Prayer, it would be more probable to contrast the garrulous praying of the Gentiles with the concise prayer of the Christian community.

Even if polemical, verse 7 incorporates current practice, good and bad, even in relation to the Gentiles. Whether

βατταλογεῖν is to be derived from the Aramaic אמר בטלתא
'empty talking' or from the Greek βατταρίζειν 'stammer,'
'stutter' remains an open question: in both cases it is a matter of
stimulating, but ultimately unprovable surmises.[29] In the
present context, the verb is characterized by πολυλογία, so that
the NEB translation "go babbling on" is appropriate. The
point is that the Gentile practice of prayer is characterized by
garrulous speech. Exactly what is covered thereby can only be
guessed: perhaps the recitation of countless names of the
ancient pantheon or incantation formulas that turn prayer
into a magical art with which one seeks to control the deity.
Seneca objected to praying with many words, because it tired
the gods.[30] In any case, our example presupposes that the
many petitionary words of the Gentiles are brought forth out
of uncertainty as to whether one's prayer will be heard at all.
Contrasted with this is the confidence of the believing
community: anyone who places his trust in the power and
goodness of God knows that the heavenly Father cares for his
children beyond all asking and understanding. Such trust is
the right presupposition for praying the Lord's Prayer.

2.4.3   6:9-15   The Lord's Prayer

Brocke, M., et al., ed. *Das Vaterunser. Gemeinsames im Beten von Juden und Christen*. 1974.
Brown, R. E. "The Pater Noster as an Eschatological Prayer" (1961). In idem, *New Testament Essays*, 2d ed., 275-320. New York, 1968.
Carmignac, J. *Recherches sur le "Notre Père"* (bibl.). Paris, 1969.
Feldkämper, L. *Der betende Jesus als Heilsmittler nach Lukas*, 179-205. 1978.
Fiebig, P. *Das Vaterunser*. BFCT 30/3. 1927.
Finkel, A. "The Prayer of Jesus of Matthew." In *Standing Before God*, FS J. M. Oesterreicher, edited by A. Finkel and L. Frizzell, 131-70. New York, 1981.
Goulder, M. D. "The Composition of the Lord's Prayer." *JTS* 14 (1963): 32-45.
Harner, P. B. *Understanding the Lord's Prayer*. Philadelphia, 1975.
Hesler, J. "Das Vaterunser" (bibl.). *NTA* 4/5. 1914.
Herrmann, J. "Der alttestamentliche Urgrund des Vaterunsers." In FS O. Procksch, 71-98. 1934.
Jeremias, J. "Das Vater-Unser im Lichte der neueren Forschung" (1962). In idem, *Abba*, 152-71.
————. *Neutestamentliche Theologie* 1:188-96.
Kuhn, J. G. *Achtzehngebet und Vaterunser und der Reim*. WUNT 1. 1950.
Kuss, O. "Das Vaterunser." In idem, *Auslegung und Verkündigung* 2:275-333. 1967.
Lohmeyer, E. "Das Vater-Unser als Ganzheit." *TBl* 17 (1938): 217-27.
————. *Das Vater-Unser*, 5th ed. 1962.
Moule, C. F. D. ". . . As We Forgive . . ." In *Donum Gentilicium*, FS D. Daube, edited by E. Bammel et al., 68-77. Oxford, 1978.

Mussner, F. "Das Vaterunser als Gebet des Juden Jesus." In idem, *Traktat über die Juden*, 198-208. 1979.

Ott, W. *Gebet und Heil. Die Bedeutung der Gebetsparänese in der lukanischen Theologie*, 92-123. SANT 12. 1965.

Schürmann, H. *Das Gebet des Herrn als Schlüssel zum Verstehen Jesu*, 6th ed. 1981.

Schulz. *Q*, 84-89.

Schwarz, G. "Matthäus VI.9-13/Lukas XI.2-4. Emendation und Rückübersetzung." *NTS* 15 (1968-69): 233-47.

Tilborg, S. van. "A Form-criticism of the Lord's Prayer." *NovT* 14 (1972): 94-105.

Vögtle, A. "Der 'eschatologische' Bezug der Wir-Bitten des Vaterunser." In *Jesus und Paulus*, FS W. G. Kümmel, edited by E. E. Ellis and E. Grässer, 344-62. 1975.

———. "Das Vaterunser—ein Gebet Für Juden und Christen?" In *Das Vaterunser*, edited by M. Brocke et al., 165-95 (nn. 272-78).

On the history of interpretation of the Lord's Prayer:

Dibelius, O. *Das Vaterunser. Umrisse zu einer Geschichte des Gebetes in der alten und mittleren Kirche*. 1903.

Dorneich, M., ed. *Vaterunser-Bibliographie*. 1982.

Walther, G. *Untersuchungen zur Geschichte der griechischen Vaterunser-Exegese.* TU 40/3. 1914.

Matthew 6	Luke 11
	²And he said to them,
⁹Pray then like this:	*"When you pray, say:*
Our Father who art in heaven,	*"Father,*
Hallowed be thy name.	*hallowed be thy name.*
¹⁰Thy kingdom come,	*Thy kingdom come.*
Thy will be done,	
On earth as it is in heaven.	
¹¹Give us this day our daily bread;	*³Give us each day our daily bread;*
¹²And forgive us our debts,	*⁴and forgive us our sins,*
As we also have forgiven our debtors;	*for we ourselves forgive every one who is indebted to us;*
¹³And lead us not into temptation,	*and lead us not into temptation."*
But deliver us from evil.	
¹⁴For if you forgive men their trespasses, your heavenly Father also will forgive you;	
¹⁵but if you do not forgive men their trespasses, neither will your Father forgive your trespasses.	

The Our Father, [31] also called the Lord's Prayer because of its origin,[32] occurs twice in the New Testament. Matthew cites it in the Sermon on the Mount as an example of prayer in connection with his instruction on prayer. In Luke's Gospel it occurs as one of three directives on prayer.[33] The Lukan version is considerably shorter. If in Matthew one normally counts seven petitions after the salutation,[34] then in Luke there are, according to the evidence of the more reliable manuscripts, five petitions. Even the salutation is reported differently, since Luke has merely the short appeal, "Father!" Luke's Gospel lacks the petition for God's will to be done and for deliverance from evil. The closing doxology, "For thine is the kingdom and the power and the glory, forever," is unknown to Luke; it is attested only in some of the manuscripts of the Gospel of Matthew[35] and is attached secondarily to the text.[36]

In all probability, the Lukan version of the Lord's Prayer is generally closer to the oldest layer of tradition, for it is revealing that the whole of the Lukan text of the Lord's Prayer fits into the Matthean version. This is also true of the five petitions; the expansions in Matthew belong to a later stage of tradition.[37] Concerning the substance of the individual petitions, preference must sometimes be given to the Matthean tradition. There were, to be sure, narrow limits on the opportunities for intrusion by the Evangelists. Presumably, they passed on in each case the version that was in use in their community. The essential expansions of the original text had already taken place before the time of Matthew. On the other hand, the interpretations by the Evangelists Matthew and Luke can be read from the different placement of the Lord's Prayer into context.

Although the original wording was composed in the Aramaic or Hebrew language,[38] even before Matthew and Luke the Lord's Prayer was prayed in different Greek versions. Perhaps during this period of tradition the substantiation for the petition for forgiveness (v. 12b) was also added.[39] Nevertheless, the occasionally expressed conjecture that the Lord's Prayer originated first in the Jewish-Christian community or even in the Hellenistic-Christian community of the early period of primitive Christianity is untenable.[40] The earliest version—derivable through synoptic comparison—belongs to the proclamation of the historical Jesus. The petition for the coming of the kingdom agrees with the conception of the kingdom of God as it decisively shaped the message of Jesus. The Father-salutation goes back to the Aramaic *abba*, which is to be ascribed to the language of Jesus. The conception and practice of the "forgiveness of sins" have an original place in the oldest Jesus tradition. The mixture of apocalyptic and wisdom elements is characteristic of both the Lord's Prayer and Jesus' proclamation. Finally, it is instructive that the Lord's Prayer text was not influenced by elements of the post-Easter profession of Christ. All of this means that the content of the Lord's Prayer not only belongs to the Jewish tradition but also is to be included in the proclamation of Jesus.

The earliest form begins with the simple Father-salutation, as it is found in Luke. Following the salutation is the first table of petitions, which speaks "theologically" of God and asks for the hallowing of his name (the *thou* petitions). Then comes the second table with the "churchly" (*we*) petitions, which concern human affairs. The two tables are also distinguished formally, for the first and second petitions of the first table are placed unconnected beside each other, while the second and third *we* petitions are linked together with *and*. The second table is more detailed and also richer in structure. Thus, the petition for forgiveness of debt is expanded through a substantiation (Luke) and a comparison (Matthew). Conspicuously, the petition not to be led into temptation is the only one to be defined by a negation; for this reason perhaps it was expanded later antithetically with the petition for deliverance from evil.

Since Jesus was of Jewish origin, it is not surprising that the literature of ancient Judaism contains prayers that exhibit far-reaching agreements with the prayer of Jesus. An example is the ancient Kaddish prayer from the temple period:[41]

> Glorified and hallowed be his great name in the world,
> which he created according to his will.
> May he let his dominion reign
> during your lives and in your days and in the lifetimes of
> the whole house of Israel
> in haste and in imminent time.
> Praised is his great name forever and ever.

Striking here is the similarity to the first two petitions of the Lord's Prayer ("Hallowed be thy name"; "Thy kingdom come"), as well as the fact that the petitions are placed side by side asyndetically.

A great influence on the Jewish practice of prayer was exerted by the שמנה עשרה *sh'moneh esre* (Eighteen Benedictions), which originated in the first half of the first century A.D. and into which the cursing of the Nazarenes and heretics (Birkath ha-minim) was later inserted.[42] It is available in Palestinian and Babylonian recensions. It comprises eighteen praise sayings *(Berakoth)* and in terms of content is divided into two parts: (1) the present situation: praise of God's deeds as Creator and Sustainer of the world, hallowing of his name, petition for knowledge of the Torah, forgiveness of sins, support in distress and sickness, petition for the fruitfulness of the earth; (2) the eschatological perfection: gathering the exiles, annihilating foreign domination, acceptance of converted Gentiles, eschatological salvation of Israel, reestablishment of Jerusalem and the temple, petition for Yahweh's reign of peace.

This distinction corresponds to the two tables of the Lord's Prayer, which, however, appear in reverse order here. Furthermore, in the Lord's Prayer the petition for bread comes first in the second table, while in the Eighteen Benedictions it is named last in the first table. Also on the individual level there are illuminating parallels: the petition for forgiveness of sins (Ber. 6) corresponds to the fifth and the petition for God's support (Ber. 7) to the sixth and seventh petitions of the Lord's Prayer.[43]

An old Jewish morning and evening prayer is recorded in the Babylonian Talmud (b. Ber. 60b, twice):

Bring me not into the power of sin,
bring me not into the power of debt,
bring me not into the power of temptation,
bring me not into the power of what is shameful.

Independently of how one may define more closely the relationship of this and other Jewish prayer texts[44] to the oldest form of the Lord's Prayer, there is no doubt that they attest the close attachment of Jesus and his prayer to Judaism and can provide reasons for interpreting the Lord's Prayer in connection with the Jewish prayer tradition.

6:9. The transition οὕτως οὖν ("then like this") points back not only to verse 7, so that the Lord's Prayer is presented as a counterexample to the garrulous prayers of the Gentiles, but also to verse 5: in connection with the admonition on prayer, the Lord's Prayer is cited as an example to which the followers of Jesus can hold when they appeal to God. Naturally, it presupposes the proper understanding of prayer, as it was explained in the preceding counterexample of the hypocrites and Gentiles.

The more detailed salutation was probably in liturgical use in Matthew's community. It clarifies the shorter Father-salutation in the Lukan version. In essence it agrees with the original wording reported by Luke, for in the *we* petitions of the second table, "Our Father!" is constantly presupposed. The typically Matthean way of speaking of the Father who is "in heaven"[45]—which is attested as rabbinical—is not only a paraphrase for the name of God; it also gives the direction of the prayer. It is directed upward. Salvation is expected from the Most High. This calls to mind the ancient multistory schema, according to which God is imagined as enthroned in heaven or above the heavens. Doubtless, behind this conception stands the patriarchal social structure as it was generally recognized in the ancient world. This also means, however, that the New Testament community, which addresses God as Father with this prayer, uses the highest predicate that it has available in its language. It can give no better and no different expression to its faith than to say that the God to whom it appeals in prayer possesses the highest authority and the greatest perfection of power.

Addressing God as a father was common in the East long before the time of the Old and New Testaments. The Greeks were also familiar with the divine father figure. Thus, in the Zeus hymn of Cleanthes, the supreme god Zeus is called "father."[46] In the Old Testament, God is represented rather seldom, but still in central assertions, as the Father of Israel, who has chosen his people to be his son and heir.[47] The theological conception of father occurs frequently in the rabbinical literature; it is the most familiar of the terms for God found there.[48] Jesus probably used the Aramaic form *abba*, which is an intimate expression (cf. Mark 14:36). It is the way a weaned child addresses his procreator. This form of address in prayer makes known that a deep trust defines the relationship between the one praying and God. It is foreign to the rabbinical literature on prayer.[49]

Jesus' Father-salutation, as attested by the New Testament Evangelists, documents a high religious self-consciousness. If Jesus addresses God as Father,[50] then he understands himself as Son. The unity of the Son of God with his Father is asserted in a way that seems to anticipate the later christological conception of the Evangelist John (cf. John 17:6-8). Also, the Evangelists' stories of the baptism, miracles, transfiguration, and crucifixion of Jesus bear witness to the Father-Son relationship with the messianic title "Son of God." In this tradition the Old Testament-Jewish belief in God as Father experienced an incisive change. The addressed Father-God is not primarily the God of the chosen people Israel but the Father of Jesus Christ. Access to him is not linked with the national expectation of a messiah but with believing devotion to the proclamation and person of Jesus. The New Testament community attests in the prayer salutation that through the message of Jesus—which after Easter is also the message about Jesus Christ—God approached them as the Father of Jesus Christ. This is reflected in the call to prayer of the Pauline communities, who used the word *abba* as a liturgical acclamation in worship (Gal 4:6; Rom 8:15).

The first petition for the hallowing of God's name recalls the third benediction of the (Palestinian) Eighteen Benedictions: "Holy art thou and fearful [is] thy name and there is no God beside thee." The petition for the hallowing of the name recognizes God's sovereign dominion. This is attested by the passive verb form. It is also found in the Kaddish prayer and presupposes God as subject. The petition is thus directed at the possibility that through his intervention God himself will effect the hallowing of his name. In the background is the Old Testament-Jewish conception that the name of God circumscribes his personal being. Reverent awe before the reality of God caused the name of God in the Old Testament to become an almost independent, personal entity (Prov 18:10; Mal 1:11). Yet the name of God is not called without an understanding of the reality of the divine revelation. If the name of God is holy, then this means that God himself is holy and his holiness is visibly revealed. Thus, along with the holiness of God's name,

Mary's Magnificat also professes the powerful reality of God (Luke 1:49; cf. Pss 30:4-5; 111:9).

If God is holy (Isa 40:25; 43:14-15), then this means that his being is withdrawn from the world and not accessible to humankind. Israelite worship was based on the conception of God's holiness and unapproachability. Only the cultically knowledgeable, the priests and the pious, have access to Yahweh, if they have been previously consecrated (cf. 1 Sam 7:1; Lev 21:1ff.). The holiness of God requires, however, not only cultic, but also ethical purity and holiness: "You shall therefore be holy, for I am holy" (Lev 11:45). Hence, to hallow the name of God means nothing other than to do the will of God and acknowledge his commandments (cf. Josh 24:19; Isa 29:23). Conversely, God's name is profaned and defiled by the sins of those who profess it (Isa 48:11; cf. 2 Cor 7:1). Therefore, the hallowing of God's name cannot occur in the first instance through people, but through God himself, through the judgment that God carries out against sinners and against his enemies. Therein is his righteousness revealed and the profanation of his name expiated (Isa 5:16). Thus, Ezekiel expects that in the promised future of his people God will assert his name as magnificent and holy (20:9 ff.; 36:20 ff.).

The Christian community that prays the first petition of the Lord's Prayer also lives in the expectation that at the end of time, God's holiness and righteousness will have the victory. Such was the anticipation of the community of the pre-Pauline christological hymn: that at the name of Jesus every knee will bow and every tongue confess that "Jesus Christ is Lord, to the glory of God the Father" (Phil 2:10-11). Yet this expectation is not directed exclusively toward the eschatological future. In praying now for the hallowing of God's name, one can experience in the present a growing number of signs that God is the righteous Judge and that his righteousness and holiness will triumph, even if such a hope is dimmed by the suffering of believers.

The glowing expectation that God himself will take care of the hallowing of his name cannot leave the people untouched in their efforts. In their thinking and acting they themselves must endeavor to be in accord with the holy will of God. Therefore, this petition contains a secondary emphasis. By teaching his disciples this prayer, he is expressing an indirect

admonition that they—as far as it lies within them—realize
holiness so that human deeds may stand before the judicial
verdict of the holy God. Such an imperative is also to be kept in
mind in regard to the remaining petitions of the first table. If
Matthew's community lives under the demand to be perfect
(5:48), then it knows that God's perfection will be demonstrated in his judgment as well as in his devotion to sinners. This is a
decisive impulse for Christian behavior in the world. The
community of followers is challenged by praying the Lord's
Prayer to take seriously the instructions that Jesus proclaims
with authority as the Preacher on the mount.

This raises the question whether the demand made by Jesus
is really fulfilled by the people. What is at stake here is not so
much the academic problem of "fulfillability"—whether,
namely, people can actually realize the perfection of God in
their lives—but, rather, the admission that such perfection and
holiness in the life of the individual Christian as well as in the
totality of Christendom cannot be determined. As far as
human behavior is concerned, the hallowing of the name of
God, the realization of the holy will of God, can be known only
in a fragmentary way. From this point there is a direct
connecting line to the fifth petition, for the forgiveness of debt
(cf. also Luke 17:10).

6:10. Like the first, the second petition refers especially to the
future kingdom of God. The word βασιλεία can designate
both the place ('kingdom') and the execution ('reign') of the
basileia. In general the two meanings are not really distinguished. Thus, the image of the feast (Matt 22:1ff.) means not
only the kingdom as a spatial entity but, at the same time, the
reality of its sovereign power.

As in the Kaddish, which asks for the establishment of God's
royal dominion in the near future,[51] the concept "kingdom" or
"dominion" refers primarily to the future. The proclamation
of the imminent divine dominion is the central assertion in the
message of Jesus in the synoptic Gospels (cf. Mark 1:15 par.;
4:26; 9:1 par.). Orientation toward the eschatological future is
characteristic of all occurrences in the Sermon on the Mount
(5:3, 10, 19-20; 6:33) and also of the majority of the remaining
instances in Matthew's Gospel. Furthermore, a few texts lead
one to think of the present or historical reality of God's

dominion (11:12; 12:28; 21:43). It is evident from them that
the Christian community professes a kingdom that has already
come in the person of Jesus Christ and expects the signs of the
self-realizing dominion of God not only at the end time but also
in the community's history.[52]

In agreement with this is the assertion of the "coming" of
God's kingdom. While in the Jewish prayer tradition one prays
not for the "coming" but for the "appearance" or "revelation"
of the coming royal dominion of God in a strictly future-
eschatological sense and thereby hopes for a definite time for
the future divine revelation,[53] the Greek term ἐλθέτω ('may it
come')[54] is not to be restricted to the eschatological time. The
coming of God's kingdom, to be sure, is not to be read as an
innerhistorical development; but, according to the report in
Mark's Gospel, the "kingdom of our father David" begins with
the entry of Jesus into Jerusalem (Mark 11:10). The parabolic
proclamation of Jesus attests the presence of God's dominion
in small beginnings (Mark 4:30-33 par.), and Matthew knows
of the reality of God's kingdom in the questionable, fragile
form of the church (13:24-30, 36-50).

On the basis of the text tradition of the Codex Bezae
Cantabrigiensis (= Cod. D), Luke 11:2 is to be translated:
"May your kingdom come to us (ἐφ᾽ ἡμᾶς)."[55] This reading
is doubtless secondary. It lifts up the anthropological-
soteriological aspect of God's kingdom, as it is taken up in the
interpretation of Martin Luther.[56] Here the legitimate concern
is expressed that the petition for the coming of God's kingdom
must include the person of the petitioner and cannot be
spoken without holding oneself to be ready for the kingdom.
Thus, it is appropriate to the monitory intention of the Sermon
on the Mount (also 24:42-44; 25:13). According to the original
understanding, however, the petition for the coming of the
kingdom does not have primarily an anthropological or ethical
sense but means, rather, the kingdom as a cosmic entity that
transcends humanity and whose eschatological realization will
encompass heaven and earth (cf. Rev. 11:15). Thus was it also
understood by the Matthean community when it expected the
coming of God's kingdom, the Parousia of the world Judge
Christ, and the end of the world all in one (Matt 13:41-43;
24:29-31).

The third petition for the happening of God's will is only transmitted in Matthew's Gospel and does not belong to the original content of the Lord's Prayer, as is made apparent by the negative attestation in the Lukan parallel. It is closely related to the theology of Matthew.[57] It is not coincidental that it lacks a parallel in the rabbinical literature.[58]

The imperative γενηθήτω ('it shall happen'), similar to the form γένηται (5:18), refers to the 'realization' or 'doing,' with the passive again designating God as the active subject. It means, may God himself realize his will and carry through his power on earth as in heaven. Without doubt this petition also stands on the horizon of eschatological expectation. When at the end of the world God visibly establishes his kingdom, then will his will have universal validity; and his cosmic authority, which encompasses heaven and earth, will find recognition. The opposition of heaven and earth is to be understood as a comparison. Does it mean that in heaven God rules over the angels, and Satan is deprived of his power (cf. Luke 10:18), and that God's will is likewise supposed to be realized on earth? Speaking for this interpretation, we may note that the comparative particle ὡς ('as') can be oriented toward a previous event.[59] Yet the conception of an already established heavenly kingdom of peace, toward which human willing and doing are directed, is unknown in Matthew's Gospel. Hence this may also express, as did the two foregoing, older petitions, the eschatological hope that at the end of the world God's will is going to be accomplished in a universal, exemplary way in heaven and also on earth. For this interpretation, the comparison would have to be made subordinate to the imperative γενηθήτω. The idea that the end time will be introduced as the age of the completion of salvation and of eternal peace through God's victory over the powers of chaos is also expressed by the apocalyptic order of events in 1 Cor 15:23-28 (cf. Heb 1:6). This eschatological happening has its effect on the present. The emphasis lies on the last two words ἐπὶ γῆς ('on earth'), without the sovereignty of God's action being restricted. The petition is directed toward the idea that God himself might accomplish his will on earth.

The believers also have their place in this heaven and earth encompassing struggle. They know themselves to be addressed by this petition and called to humble readiness to have

God's will happen in them. They do not understand the workings of God as blind fate or as Stoic natural law to which they are handed over; they are oriented instead toward Jesus, who, according to Matthew's representation, fulfills in model fashion the behavior intended here. When Jesus spoke these words in his Gethsemane prayer, he declared himself willing to accept the cup of suffering as the cup of the Father. With the words "if it be possible" (26:39), he acknowledged the free decision of God, and with the statement "thy will be done" (26:42), he subjected himself to the gracious saving will of God.[60]

The Matthean community does not speak these prayerful words without knowing that it is under an obligation. It must strive for the realization of God's will as long as that possibility is given on earth (cf. John 9:4), for entrance into the kingdom of God is open, not to the "Lord, Lord" sayers or to the miracle workers, but to the doers of God's will (7:21). To Jesus belong only those who do the will of his Father (12:50 par. Mark 3:36). In the context of the theology of the first Evangelist, the third petition has without doubt an eminently ethical orientation.

The petitions of the first table for the hallowing of God's name, the coming of God's kingdom, and the realization of God's will are not arranged in the form of a thought progression,[61] but express in different ways one petition for the accomplishment of the eschatological power of God. Thus, according to their real concern, they are eschatological petitions. We have seen, to be sure, that the praying community of Jesus Christ attests in the present the signs of the dawning *eschaton*, and that such hope must lead to ethical consequences in the Christian shaping of life. Accordingly, the first table of the Lord's Prayer presents a three-note chord. The keynote is the petition that God himself bring about his holiness, his kingdom, and the realization of his will. Next comes the admission that the believing community must allow in itself such action of God to happen and subject itself to God's judgment. Finally, linked with this is the indirect ethical demand that the community of Christ endeavor, insofar as in it lies, to realize God's claim in its fellowship and in the world in general. This point is emphasized in the third petition with the closing words καὶ ἐπὶ γῆς ('and on earth'), which at the same time have a transitional task. Here we see the anthropological dimension of the Lord's Prayer, which defines the petitions of the second table.

6:11. The fourth petition is reported in variant form in Luke's text. Instead of the imperative in the aorist δός (with ingressive meaning: 'begin to give'), Luke has the present imperative δίδου ('give') and indicates thereby that he is thinking of a continuing gift. The words τὸ καθ᾽ ἡμέραν ('daily') also have this meaning. Different from Matthew, according to whom the gift is requested for "this day" (σήμερον), the aim of the petition in Luke is that the gift of bread will happen day by day. From many passages in Luke's Gospel and in Acts, we may conclude that Luke's community has set in for the duration of human history.[62] The text of the Lukan parallel is stamped with this consciousness of the "extension of time." Thus, the version in Matthew's Gospel comes closer to the original wording.

The word ἐπιούσιος represents a *crux interpretum*; it is attested neither in Greek literature nor in the Greek vernacular, and thus Origen held that it was coined by the Evangelists (*De Orat.* 27:7). In recent time, however, an instance has been found in an upper Egyptian papyrus, which, admittedly, belongs to the fifth century A.D. and is not interpretable with certainty according to the grammatical evidence.[63] Hence, it is not surprising that this word in Matt 6:11 and Luke 11:3 (also in Did. 8:2) is interpreted in quite different ways. Of the numerous interpretations,[64] we will name three that are relevant to the issue.

1. According to a derivation from ἐπιέναι, "future," the requested bread is identified with the heavenly bread of life, the heavenly manna, which is expected at the end time. This is appropriate to a purely eschatological interpretation of the Lord's Prayer.[65] The aim of this petition would be the bread of the coming kingdom. But can the gifts of the eschatological bread and the coming of the kingdom be requested for "this day" in such a direct way? This would be in contradiction to the sovereignty of God, who through his omnipotence sets the time of arrival of his kingdom in a way that is inaccessible to humanity (cf. Mark 13:32 par.). Since allegorization is also foreign to the other petitions of the Lord's Prayer, this interpretation should be rejected as the least probable.

2. Similarly, the translation 'for tomorrow' is derived from ἐπιέναι.[66] It does not have to contradict the first one and can also be proclaimed with an eschatological interpretation.[67] The church father Hieronymus reports that in the Jewish-Christian Gospel of the Hebrews, written in Aramaic, he found at this point the word *mahar* and translated it with *crastinum* ('for tomorrow').[68] But since the Gospel of the Hebrews presupposes the Gospel of Matthew, its message can only mean that Aramaic-speaking Jewish Christians understood the Lord's Prayer in this way. On this basis nothing can be concluded about the original understanding. Even if nothing is to be brought against the translation 'for tomorrow' with philological arguments,[69] there are still considerations of content. The petition for bread for tomorrow stands in tension with Jesus' admonition not to be anxious for tomorrow,[70] and to the sending out of Jesus' disciples with "no bread, no bag" (Mark 6:8 par.). It would announce a planning intention, for it shows itself concerned about God's help when it is not immediately needed. Hence preference must be given to a third possible translation.

3. Through division into ἐπί and οὐσία, we derive the translation 'needed for existence,' that is, 'necessary'; so that one can also translate, "Give us this day the bread we need." Even if for this, as for every other translation, there is no exact parallel to be found in Greek or Old Testament-Jewish literature, the idea that vital human needs may be entrusted in prayer to the providence of God is widespread in the religious-historical environment. Thus, in the old Israelite wisdom tradition a prayer reads, "Give me neither proverty nor riches; feed me with the food that is needful for me" (Prov 30:8; cf. LXX translation: "Grant me what is needful and sufficient"). And the ninth of the Eighteen Benedictions reads, "Bless us, Yahweh our God, this year . . . and satisfy the world from the treasures of your good things."

The word *bread* here designates a primary means of nourishment. It represents everything else that can satisfy the material and spiritual needs of humankind.[71] When this petition is spoken, the one praying is giving expression to his will to be contented with the most necessary things that God apportions to him. Like the Christian community as a whole, he is convinced that everything that is encountered in human life is part of the generous creative power of God. If no sparrow falls to the ground without the will of the heavenly Father, then the community, which is of more value than many sparrows (10:29-30), can have certainty in such trust. The psalmist also knew this confidence: "The eyes of all look to thee, and thou givest them their food in due season. Thou openest thy hand, thou satisfiest the desire of every living thing" (Ps 145:15-16).

In the fourth petition, reference is made for the first time in the Lord's Prayer to humanity in its creaturely existence. The following petitions of the second table will put other human and interpersonal problems into words. In comparison to the first table, it brings a new viewpoint. Nevertheless, the anthropological dimension of the *we* petitions does not stand unrelated beside the foregoing *thou* petitions. Rather, the person who includes here in the prayer his everyday life and his profane problems is the same one who considers God's powerful reality to be the decisive perspective of his life. His standing before God affects every detail of his life. This is true not only for the Matthean and Lukan communities, which, affected by the delay of the Parousia, prepare for everyday life for the long term, but also for Jesus and the disciples. Vis-à-vis the currently dawning dominion of God, Jesus does not entrust discipleship in the interim to himself but turns it over to the generous goodness of his Father.[79]

6:12. In the fifth petition, also, Matthew has the original wording. When Luke speaks of the "sins" (ἁμαρτίας) whose forgiveness is prayed for, this is a secondary generalization.[74] Without doubt the Matthean reading ὀφειλήματα ('debts') is closer to the original text, because in the following clause in Matthew and Luke the same root appears.[75] In a further important variation, the second clause is constructed with the aorist (ἀφήκαμεν) in Matthew versus the present (ἀφίομεν) in Luke. The Lukan tradition is clearly secondary; it stresses the duration of the forgiving behavior: forgiveness on the part of people is always a repeated and a to-be-repeated activity.

The petition for forgiveness of debts uses expressions from the language of business. The word ὀφειλήματα in Greek designates owed sums of money.[76] This agrees with the original meaning of ἀφιέναι, 'to forgo repayment (of a loan)' (cf. Matt

18:27). Thus, we have a symbolic use of language: in the figurative sense the "forgoing of repayment" is a "forgiveness of shortcomings" or, as Luke correctly interprets, of "sins."[77] After what has been said, the inclusion of this petition in the proclamation of the historical Jesus does not need special substantiation. The radical nature of Jesus' ethical demands as they are proclaimed exemplarily in the antitheses of the Sermon on the Mount require discernment and acknowledgment of human guilt. In particular Jesus' critique of Pharisaism exposes human failure. That human beings fall short of the demands of God and are dependent on forgiveness of their guilt is already presupposed in John's "baptism of repentance for the forgiveness of sins" (Mark 1:4 par.). The Q tradition preserves the image of Jesus as a "friend of tax collectors and sinners" (Matt 11:19). He forgives and overcomes sins through his words and his deeds (Mark 2:5, 10; Luke 7:47ff.).

The eschatological orientation of Jesus' proclamation suggests that the aim of this petition is divine forgiveness at the final judgment. This was doubtless the way Matthew understood it when he sharpened the admonition to be reconciled before the day of judgment (5:25-26), and when he closed the parable of the Unmerciful Servant with the warning that everyone who is not ready to forgive his brother will have to reckon with the unrelenting judicial punishment of the heavenly Father (18:35). On the other hand, the Matthean community knows that through the Christ event God's forgiveness has come to them and that in the sacraments, for example, in the Lord's Supper, the individual Christian is concretely addressed (26:28). Moreover, the discipline of Matthew's church presupposes that the power of forgiveness of sins is turned over to her and is perceived in the community assembly (18:18-19). Hence, on the level of the First Gospel, the petition for God's forgiveness refers not only to the final judgment but also to the experiences of the community in its present life and history.

The second clause (Matt 6:12b; Luke 11:4b) may not have belonged to the original version of the Lord's Prayer, since it goes beyond the series of individual petitions. The form attested in Matthew expresses with ὡς καί ('as also') a comparison that at the same time has a substantiating significance.[78] The aorist ἀφήκαμεν is translated into the English perfect: 'as we also have forgiven.' Recourse to a hypothetical Aramaic model[79] contributes nothing to the understanding of the Matthean version, since Matthew's community prayed the Lord's Prayer in the Greek language. In contrast to the first line, the second clause marks a gradation. The petitioners declare that they are also ready to forgive their debtors, indeed, that they have already actualized such readiness to forgive. Accordingly, the presupposition of the proper petition for forgiveness is that one has forgiven in turn. If Matthew interprets the parable of the Unmerciful Servant in the same sense (18:35), then he also teaches in other places the Christian's duty to forgive (5:25-26; 18:21-22). It precedes every other religious obligation (5:23-24). This also accords with the Matthean idea of reward, according to which only the doer of right deeds may be certain of the eschatological gift of God (cf. 5:12, 46; 6:1ff.). This asserts not only a correspondence between divine and human forgiveness: God's forgiveness is linked to the priority of the deed of human forgiveness. Thus is it expressly repeated by the Evangelist in what follows (vv. 14-15).

The idea that human forgiveness is made the very condition for God's forgiveness differentiates Matthew's theology from Paul's message of justification, according to which the deeds of the believer are understood as the consequence, not as the precondition, of God's redeeming and forgiving activity (Gal 5:25; Rom 6:1ff.). Here Matthew—as also the pre-Matthean version of the Lord's Prayer that was expanded in this way—stands in the tradition of Jewish thinking, according to which human readiness to forgive is demanded as the prerequisite of divine forgiveness of sins. Thus, Sir 28:2 reads, "Forgive your neighbor of the wrong, and then(!) your sins will be forgiven when you ask it." In the Matthean understanding, the fifth petition is not only the expression of the Christian certainty of forgiveness but also the demand of Jesus that the Christian community must be ready to forgive.

6:13. Deviating from the remaining petitions, the sixth contains a negative assertion. The construction μή with the subjunctive has the meaning of an imperative: "Lead us not into temptation!" In content there is a connection with the foregoing petitions. If forgiveness is requested there for past offenses, then here the prayer is directed toward the future, in which the existence of the believers will be threatened. The purely eschatological interpretation relates the petition to the tribulations of the end of the world, from which one would like to be spared.[80] Actually, according to the early Christian apocalyptic view, the woes of the end time place in great danger the existençe of the community as well as that of the individual Christian (Mark 13:4 ff. par.; Rev 3:10). And the possibility should not be dismissed that Jesus' proclamation of the coming dominion of God also contained the instruction to his disciples to pray that they be spared the dangers of the final catastrophe and be taken up directly into the kingdom of God. Nonetheless, it is hardly an accident that the prayer speaks only of temptation and not *the* (eschatological) temptation. As with the other petitions of the second table, a purely eschatological understanding is not suggested here. Rather, the one praying has in mind all the dangers that threaten the followers of Jesus on their way and call their faith into question. Even Luke is familiar with a group of community members who only "believe for a while and in time of temptation fall away" (Luke 8:13).

There is no corresponding petition in the Old Testament, where prayers are directed, rather, toward God putting the godly man to the test, for the latter is conscious of God's right way (Ps 139:23-24). Similarly, the prologue of the Book of Job makes clear the certainty that the believer will not let himself be diverted from the way once shown, and the temptation of Satan will not achieve its goal (Job 1:6-12).[81] The Epistle of James also has a positive attitude about the testing of the godly: the testing of faith is joyfully greeted, for from it come patience and pious work (1:2). Therefore, the man is called blessed "who endures trial, for when he has stood the test he will receive the crown of life" (1:12).

By contrast, in this petition Jesus is not speaking of a petty testing whose fortunate outcome is prescribed; the trial intended here makes faith radically subject to disposal. It is an existential threat, and it does not even leave room for the prayer for preservation in temptation, but necessitates asking that God not allow such a test to come up. The seemingly obvious question whether God himself causes the temptation is not raised. A reflection on the relationship of God's gracious to his wrathful being or on the theodicy problem seems as obvious as the thesis that the evil aspirations of a person from youth on produce that person's temptation and fall (cf. Gen 8:21). In truth, it is a question of the sober recognition that a person faced with the radical eschatological claim must confess his frailty, as the preceding petition implies. Here, there is no choice but to flee from *deus absconditus* to *deus revelatus*,[82] the Father of Jesus Christ. The idea that in the eschatological perspective human existence is always comprehended as threatened existence is also expressed in the Talmudic prayer text: "Lead me not into the power of temptation!"[83]

In the time of persecution, the Matthean community experiences many threats. The possibility of falling away is one of the dangers it has to anticipate (cf. 10:17ff.; 24:4 ff.). In this situation it can look toward the image of God's Son, who in his temptations withstood people and the devil (16:1ff.; 4:1ff.; cf. Luke 22:28). If it needs the warning of the suffering One, "Watch and pray that you may not enter into temptation" (Mark 14:38 par.), then this indicates that its way will often be marked by human failure. This gives reason to comprehend and speak ever anew the sixth petition.

The closing seventh petition interprets the immediately preceding one and takes up its positive side. Since it remained unknown to Luke and his community, this expansion does not belong to the original content of the Lord's Prayer. Yet one cannot demonstrate, even with linguistic arguments, that Matthew formed this petition himself;[84] instead, like the third petition, it may have already been a part of the Lord's Prayer of the first Evangelist's community and have been added to fill out the group of seven. For this is also seen elsewhere as a structuring principle of the pre-Matthean tradition.[85]

If the Christian community expects from the Parousia of Jesus that he, as the Son of God, will "deliver" them from the coming wrathful judgment (1 Thess 1:10), then such deliverance can already be experienced in an anticipatory way in the conversion of individual Christians (Col 1:13; cf. Rom 3:24). Faced with the concrete perils of his service, Paul can also speak of deliverance (2 Cor 1:10; cf. Rom 15:31; 2 Thess 3:2). The question what is meant in our text by "deliverance" or "liberation" is answered by an understanding of the expression ἀπὸ τοῦ πονηροῦ ('from evil').

We must distinguish between evil in general and evil in the personified sense (= "devil"). Both possibilities are demonstrable in Matthew's Gospel. Evil in general is the topic of 5:11 (πᾶν πονηρόν); possibly also in 5:37 (ἐκ τοῦ πονηροῦ); the latter instance is assuredly redactional, while the former depends on Q (Luke 6:22). The "evil one" ('devil') is named in 13:19 (ὁ πονηρός), perhaps also in 13:38 (υἱοὶ τοῦ πονηροῦ 'sons of the evil one'); by contrast, in 5:39 it is indeed masculine, but refers to an ἀνθρώπῳ ('person') that is to be supplied. The first named instance is assuredly redactional, the second probably pre-Matthean. Thus, we can make out no tradition-historical tendency that could suggest a solution. The history of interpretation also gives no indication, but attests both possible understandings (neuter: Did. 10:5; masculine: Ps. Clem., Hom III 55:1-2).

Since neither the Matthean nor the pre-Matthean use of language offers an unambiguous answer, the safest interpretation of verse 13*b* comes from its antithetical attachment to the sixth petition. If there the talk was also of the eschatological temptation and the request to be removed from such a peril, then here the request is expressed that God's eschatological victory may bring the final deliverance for all who follow Jesus. Conversely, if at the same time the object of the sixth petition is that the faith not collapse in time, then here the petition is expressed for deliverance from all dangers that block humanity's way to God in history. In concrete encounters with evil, the Christian faith has always seen the effectiveness of the power of evil—so teach the New Testament writers and a two-thousand-year history of theology, so that it did not require a "theology after Auschwitz" to comprehend the existence of evil as a historical reality and theological problem. Therefore, with the petition for deliverance from the dangers threatening them, Matthew's community probably also prayed for liberation from the deadly power of Satan.[86] Here, as in the Lord's Prayer in general, it expresses its trust in the power of God, who as Judge is unapproachable, but as the Father of Jesus Christ has come near.

6:14-15. A typically Matthean interpretation of the Lord's
Prayer comes from the two attached verses 14 and 15. These
have an apparent parallel in the Gospel of Mark (11:25-26).
Yet there it is presumably a matter of post-Markan glosses that
presuppose our text.[87] Matthew is following an independent
tradition. Proclaimed here is a legal statement that passes
judgment according to the principle of retribution. The ἐάν
('if') and ἐὰν μή ('if not') each introduce a judicial "case." It is a
matter of an antithetical parallelism. A positive assertion is
followed by a negative one. The two parts of each verse are
related as condition and result. The monitory aim is essential.
Verse 14 takes up the petition for forgiving debts (v. 12). If
there the topic is the ὀφειλήματα ('debts'), then here it is the
παραπτώματα, the ethical "trespasses." It was shown that in
verse 12, human readiness to forgive was presented plainly as
the precondition for the forgiving action of God. This idea is
repeated here in more pointed form. The forgiveness of the
heavenly Father presupposes human forgiveness, as conversely the nonforgiving person also does not experience God's
forgiveness. Human action is thus the preparation for gracious
action of the heavenly Judge.

Matthew added these two verses to the quotation of the
Lord's Prayer because for him the admonition to the
community to be ready to forgive carried great weight. As
elsewhere in the Gospel of Matthew, at stake here also is the
practical action of the believers. Christian life is supposed to be
shaped concretely in accordance with the demand of the
Kyrios, which is obligatory for the church in all times. And it is
characteristic that this closing admonition is not limited to the
relationship of Christians to each other. The practice of the
readiness to forgive is valid for all "men"—not for just the
brothers alone. Forgiving love is supposed to be bestowed on
the whole of humanity, as Christ demands (cf. 5:13-16 and
5:43-48).

The original meaning of the Lord's Prayer cannot be
grasped unless one becomes aware of the central thought of
Jesus' proclamation, the message of the approaching dominion of God (cf. Mark 1:14-15 par.). The eschatological
dimension of this proclamation is impressed on the Lord's
Prayer. Jesus expected everything from the mighty coming of
the kingdom of God, with which God will change the course

of an unholy history. This expectation determined Jesus' behavior vis-à-vis the people, his fellowship with tax collectors and sinners. That it is of prime importance for the understanding of the Lord's Prayer is shown in the second petition, which is expressly aimed toward the coming of God's kingdom (v. 10a). This hope has significance for each individual petition. Only in the confident expectation of God's kingdom—more clearly stated: of God's dominion—can one pray for the hallowing of God's name, or is it possible to speak the petition for the bread needed for today. This expectation defines the petitions for the forgiveness of human debt and deliverance from temptation and evil. The petition for the realization of God's dominion is the *cantus firmus*; everything else is interpretive accompaniment. Thus says even the salutation, for the God who is addressed by Jesus as Father is the same one who will visibly bring in his dominion.

This expectation is common to Jews and Christians. Hence, the Lord's Prayer was also named an "ecumenical prayer"; it can be prayed by Jews as well as Christians.[88] Of course, we have already seen that the orientation of the messianic kingdom in Judaism was different from that of the Christian hope of the kingdom of God. The former is a national expectation that remains tied to the history and self-understanding of the Jewish people. For the early Christian community, on the other hand, the hope for the realization of the reign of God is linked with the coming of God's Son Jesus Christ. It looks back to the Easter event; it bears witness to the conviction that Jesus of Nazareth is the crucified and resurrected One, who was raised to the right hand of God and now has already appeared in his dominion. The Christ event is the foundation for the prayer of the community. When it closes the prayer of its Lord with the word "amen," then it knows about this seal—one almost wants to say: about this guarantee—for "amen" means that I have the certainty that God will accept my prayer.[89] This confidence is based on the event of Golgatha, on the cross and resurrection of Jesus Christ.

The church cannot go back behind this fact in its history. This was already true for the New Testament writers and, not least of all, for the Evangelists who transmit the Lord's Prayer.

Luke presents the Lord's Prayer in the first of three sections that deal with prayer: the Lord's Prayer (11:2-4), the parable of the Importunate Friend (11:5-8), and the saying on the answering of prayer (11:9-13). This instruction on prayer is introduced by the request of one of the disciples for Jesus to teach them to pray as John the Baptist had done for his disciples (11:1). The Lord's Prayer is thus a prayer for the followers of Jesus, a prayer of the community that knows that it is established by the Christ event and—as the durative element reveals, especially in Luke 11:3-4—has settled in for a not inconsiderable duration of history.

Luke appends to the directive on the Lord's Prayer two further sections, in order to demonstrate the certainty of the answering of prayer.[90] This series of pericopes is brought to an end with the statement: "If you . . . know how to give good gifts to your children, how much more will the heavenly Father give the Holy Spirit to those who ask him?" (11:13). Luke reads "Holy Spirit" in distinction to Matthew's "good things" (7:11). Did Luke want to "spiritualize" the text attested as original by Matthew? It is clear, in any case, that according to the Lukan understanding the standard of the Holy Spirit is to be applied to prayer. The gift of the Spirit represents the fulfillment of every prayer. From this gift is derived the assurance of the answering of prayer. The one praying does not ask primarily for the fulfillment of his wishes; rather, proper praying opens itself to the gift and subjects itself to the decision of God. This right attitude of the one praying is what is meant by the promise of the Holy Spirit.

As we have seen, Matthew places the Lord's Prayer likewise in the context of a catechetical section. In the middle of directives on almsgiving and fasting is a discourse on proper prayer, into which the Lord's Prayer is inserted as an example of prayer. The "hypocrites," the Pharisees and scribes, serve as the representatives of incorrect praying. For their prayer they seek the public in order to be acknowledged by people. By contrast, proper prayer should happen in the absence of the public. It should be directed only to the heavenly Father, who sees in secret and grants fulfillment to the prayer devoted exclusively to him (6:5-6). A further counterexample is the prayer of the "Gentiles," for whom garrulous talk is typical. Proper prayer, on the other hand, should be satisfied with few words—so says Jesus to his disciples and the listening crowd

(6:7-8). The Lord's Prayer is taught as such a concise prayer. A final typically Matthean interpretation of the Lord's Prayer follows from the appended verses 14-15, in which a finer point is put on the duty to forgive as a presupposition to the proper petition for forgiveness on the part of the heavenly Father. This confirms the ethical line of interpretation that is generally characteristic of the First Gospel and is apparent in the individuality of the Matthean version of the Lord's Prayer, especially in the third, fifth, and sixth petitions. Matthew is trying to say that the instruction of the Son of God is the radical and at the same time practical law that sets the only binding standard for life in the Christian communion as well as in the relationship of the community to the world.

2.4.4   6:16-18   On Fasting

For bibliography see 2.4 above on 6:1-18.

16When you fast, do not look dismal, like the hypocrites, for they disfigure their faces that their fasting may be seen by men. Truly, I say to you, they have their reward. 17But when you fast, anoint your head and wash your face, 18that your fasting may not be seen by men but by your Father who is in secret; and your Father who sees in secret will reward you.

6:16. As the last of the catechetical sections Matthew adds a teaching on fasting. Like the foregoing directives on almsgiving (vv. 2-4) and on praying (vv. 5-8), it is of pre-Matthean origin and like them symmetrically structured. The ὅταν ('when') clause is followed by a warning against a wrong attitude, as demonstrated by the sharply drawn counterexample of the "hypocrites." They look "dismal" or "sad" (KJV).[91] They make their faces "unseemly," so that they will "seem" to men to be fasting.[92] In demonstrative fashion they put their pious action on display. Their object is to achieve recognition from the people, which was also the motivation of their previously named pious works (vv. 2d and 5d). Such an attitude is subjected to the solemn pronouncement of judgment: "They have their reward." The heavenly μισθός ('reward') has been paid out and the "account settled."

6:17-18. The instructions for a Christian practice of fasting, on the other hand, say that when fasting one is to take care of one's body as usual.[93] Thus, the Jewish custom of fasting is indisputably presupposed yet defined in a new way. According to the Mishna tractate Yoma, it is forbidden at the feast of the atonement to eat, to drink, to bathe, or to anoint oneself.[94] Naturally, the Jewish practice of fasting was not restricted to official days of fasting or mourning. The godly Jewish person had the opportunity for private, individual fasting (cf. Luke 18:12). This should be observed especially on the days of the week designated for that purpose, Monday and Thursday. Thus, apparently in dependence on the Matthew text but in disagreement with the Jewish fasting custom, the Didache, the "Teaching of the Twelve Apostles," which originated at the beginning of the second century, determined that, "Your fasting shall not happen with the hypocrites, for they fast on the second and fifth days of the week. You, however, shall fast on the fourth day (Wednesday) and on the day of preparation (Friday)" (8:1).

Our text says nothing of a temporal difference between Christian and Jewish fasting. This makes even clearer the conditions under which Christian fasting is supposed to take place. It is not required that the one who fasts forgo anointing his head with oil or washing his face. This would, indeed, be nothing but putting on a display, which contradicts the true character of fasting. For fasting is not supposed to count on the people's approbation but to happen for God's sake. Hence, the summons to fast in such a way that the orientation toward God is ensured. In a time when the Christian community is feeling the absence of the "bridegroom," it can be meaningful through moderation to hold oneself ready in regard to the will of God (cf. 9:15). This does not need to stand in contradiction to the fact that they already live now in eschatological joy. Rather, the transference of the early Christian custom of fasting into the present leaves open many possibilities. The crucial point, says Matthew, is that a person's inner attitude should agree with the image of his outer appearance. The totality of human life and conduct is demanded, which, to be sure, will not be fully realized in this world but turns its eschatological fulfillment and final judgment over to the Father of Jesus Christ.

2.5   6:19-7:12   Individual Directives

2.5.1   6:19-24   On Wealth

Mees, M. "Das Sprichwort Mt 6,21/Lk 12,34 und seine ausserkanonischen Parallelen." Aug. 14, 1974, 67-89.
Pesch, W. "Zur Exegese von Mt 6,19-21 und Lk 12,33-34." *Bib* 41 (1960): 356-78.
Steinhauser. *Doppelbildworte*, 236-49.

Betz, H. D. "Matthew VI.22f and ancient Greek theories of vision." In *Text and Interpretation*, FS M. Black, edited by E. Best and R. McL. Wilson, 43-56. Cambridge, 1979.
Brandt, W. "Der Spruch vom lumen internum." *ZNW* 14 (1913): 97-116, 177-201.
Edlund, C. *Das Auge der Einfalt*. ASNU 19. 1952.
Fensham, F. C. "The Good and Evil Eye in the Sermon on the Mount." *Neot* 1 (1967): 51-58.
Fiebig, P. "Das Wort Jesu vom Auge." *TSK* 89 (1916): 499-507.
Hahn, F. "Die Worte vom Licht Lk 11,33-36." In *Orientierung an Jesus*, FS J. Schmid, edited by P. Hoffmann et al., 107-38. 1973.
Schwencke, F. "Das Auge des Leibes Licht." *ZWT* 55 (1914): 251-60.
Sjöberg, E. "Das Licht in dir: Zur Deutung von Matth. 6,22f Par." *ST* 5 (1952): 89-105.

Groenewald, E. P. "God and Mammon." *Neot* 1 (1967): 59-66.
Rüger, H. P. Μαμωνᾶς." *ZNW* 64 (1973): 127-31.
Safrai, S. and D. Flusser. "The Slave of Two Masters." *Imm.* 6 (1976): 30-33.

[19]*Do not lay up for yourselves treasures on earth, where moth and rust consume and where thieves break in and steal,* [20]*but lay up for yourselves treasures in heaven, where neither moth nor rust consumes and where thieves do not break in and steal.* [21]*For where your treasure is, there will your heart be also.*

[22]*The eye is the lamp of the body. So, if your eye is sound, your whole body will be full of light;* [23]*but if your eye is not sound, your whole body will be full of darkness. If then the light in you is darkness, how great is the darkness!*

[24]*No one can serve two masters; for either he will hate the one and love the other, or he will be devoted to the one and despise the other. You cannot serve God and mammon.*

In the following section, Matthew joins sayings of various content from the Q tradition. The first group of sayings concerns the problem of wealth. It begins with the opposition of treasures on earth with treasures in heaven (vv. 19-21), and closes with the saying on the question of God or mammon (v. 24). These brackets suggest that the saying of the eye as the light of the body (vv. 22-23) is to be understood in the Matthean sense as a statement on the attitude of the individual regarding wealth.

6:19-21. In the Matthean version, the saying on laying up treasures is skillfully constructed. Each of the first two verses contains three lines. First, the prohibition is expressed (v. 19); then follows the commandment (v. 20). This antithetical double saying is summarized with a closing substantiation (v. 21). Its structure clearly exhibits echoes of the Jewish wisdom tradition.[1]

The parallel tradition Luke 12:33-34a is not found in the Sermon on the Plain, but in an independent composition that begins with the parable of the Rich Fool (12:13-21), continues with the sayings on anxiety and gathering treasures (12:22-34 par. Matt 6:25-33, 19-21), and ends with an apocalyptic parable of watchfulness (12:35-46; cf. Matt 24:43-51). This allows the surmise that the sayings on anxiety and on laying up treasures were already bound together in the pre-Matthean Q tradition.

Comparison of Matt 6:19-21 with the Lukan parallel shows that Luke transmits only the positive commandment to gather "treasure in the heavens that does not fail" (12:33), and the following substantiation (v. 34). The introductory admonition, "Sell your possessions and give alms" (v. 33a) exhibits Lukan linguistic material,[2] and its content agrees with Lukan theology (cf. 14:33; 11:41; Acts 9:36; 10:2, 4; and elsewhere). Although in Matthew's Gospel we can demonstrate an antithetical shaping of the sayings units by the redactor (cf. 5:31-32, 38ff., 44ff.), the group of sayings in verses 19-21 is probably of pre-Matthean origin.

The admonition to lay up treasures, not on earth, but in heaven is substantiated with two statements from experience. Earthly possessions are exposed to deterioration through σής ('moth') or subject to βρῶσις ('rust'—lit., 'eating').[3] An additional danger is posed by thieves, who dig through[4] the wall of the house. Thus, it is rationally argued that the collecting of earthly possessions is not sensible, because they are subject to loss. It behooves one, rather, to lay up treasures in heaven, for these are not threatened with destruction.

The opposition of earthly and heavenly treasures is also known in apocalyptic and rabbinical Judaism. The underlying idea is that good works result in a heavenly accumulation of credit that is paid out on the day of final judgment.[5] Thus, it corresponds to the Matthean concept of reward, according to which the heavenly compensation is not calculated, to be sure, but still—on the basis of good works in discipleship to Jesus—is a firm component of the eschatological expectation (cf. above on 5:12; 6:1).

The closing substantiation (v. 21) may have originally been passed down independently.[6] In the present connection, it means that the θησαυρός ('treasure') determines an individual's existential orientation. If the treasure is an earthly one, the person becomes lost in earthly things; if it is a heavenly one, the person lives with an orientation toward heaven; his will[7] is not egoistically aimed toward himself, but toward God (cf. 6:1ff.). In spite of the eschatological perspective, such reasonable, wisdom-like argumentation is nothing like a prophetic cry of alarm and could have had an original context in early Christian instruction. Nonetheless, we cannot exclude the possibility that this admonition goes back to the proclamation of the historical Jesus, for traditional wisdom elements are also found in his message; they have the task of instructing the hearers of Jesus and convincing them on rational grounds. At this point Matthew, in harmony with tradition, does not demand a radical renunciation of possessions, although in an exceptional situation, the Matthean demand for perfection can also be realized in giving up possessions (19:21). Basically similar to Luke,[8] who with the word ἐλεημοσύνη is thinking about liberality vis-à-vis the poor (12:33), Matthew expects the proper attitude regarding possessions to be made concrete in social deeds (cf. 6:2-4).

6:22-23. The sayings unit on the lamp of the body is not a parable but an elaborated image saying, whose application is not expressed and thus can only be inferred. Comparison with the Lukan parallel (11:34-36) shows that the content was present in Q. The basic statement proclaims a general truth: "The lamp of the body is the eye." Σῶμα designates not only the human body but the human person (cf. Matt 5:29-30; versus 6:25; 10:28 par.). Lifted up is the overarching significance of the eye for a person. Thus, it is clarified through antithetical twin sayings of two lines each (vv. 22*b*-

23*a*). If the eye is ἀπλοῦς ('pure'), then the whole person is φωτεινόν ('full of light'); if the eye is πονηρός ('evil'), then the whole person is σκοτεινόν ('dark'). This generally insightful statement is closed with a consequence that concerns the "light in you"; this was available to both Matthew and Luke, but it goes beyond the assumed image and may not have belonged to the earliest tradition.

The original assertion in the sayings source (Q) may have related to the Greek distinction between the whole body and its individual members,[9] say, in the sense that the insignificant organ of the eye has an extraordinarily important function for the whole person ("little causes, big effects"). Yet in keeping with the overall character of the sayings source, it is a matter not only of a factual description of the relationship of the eye to the human person but also of an ethical state of affairs. This could be related to the perception of a person; that is, in the eye a person's inner makeup can be read (cf. *T. Benj.* 4:2: "The good man has no dark eye, for he has pity on all . . . "). It is more likely that the overall behavior of the person is indicated: just as the whole person lives in the dark when the eye is not sound, where the proper understanding or the proper ethical attitude is lacking, the whole person is possessed by darkness and falls prey to godlessness. Conversely, as a result of the proper understanding and the proper ethical attitude, the person stands completely in the light and is near God. So also in the Testament of the Twelve Patriarchs, human purity is understood in an ethical, monitory fashion. The good person "walks in purity and sees everything in rectitude. He does not accept the evil eyes of the enticement of the world, so that he does not have a twisted view of the commandments of the Lord."[10]

The continuation in verse 23*b*, which was already present in Q, speaks no longer of the person's body possessed by darkness but of the φῶς ('light'). Outward blindness is set over against inner blindness: if the inner light (of faith?) is extinguished, then the darkness is total. Thus, the passage can be understood even in Q as an admonition not only to faith but also to obedience to the law.[11]

Luke, who presents the saying in a version expanded by verse 36, places it in the context of a judgment speech of Jesus. The image of the pure eye is supposed to make the proper understanding clear to Jesus' followers. It is precisely to this that Jesus' listeners are summoned, as underlined by the Lukan imperative σκόπει (v. 35: 'be careful').[12]

Matthew, on the other hand, presents our sayings unit in a tighter form,[13] in order to clarify one's proper relationship to possessions. At this point, it is illuminating that the Greek ἁπλούς can mean not only 'pure' but also 'generous' (Prov 22:9; Jas 1:5); also, πονηρός can be rendered not only as 'evil' but also with the word 'greedy' (cf. Deut 15:9; Pro 23:6; 28:22). It means that whenever someone looks greedily at earthly possessions, the whole person goes bad; and conversely, whoever is generous with his wealth, to him belongs the light. In the Matthean understanding, the closing statement of verse 23b means the same thing. In the rabbinical way of speaking, the human soul is designated "light" or "lamp of God."[14] When the soul is darkened by subjection to earthly possessions, the person is ruled totally by darkness. This anticipates already the demand for decision in the following verses.

6:24. The saying on double service is attested word for word for Q through Luke 16:13.[15] It begins with a proverbial expression (v. 24a). This is substantiated through a symmetrical parallelism (v. 24b-c: ἤ . . . ἤ 'either . . . or') and ends with a final conclusion (v. 24d).

P. Billerbeck points out that cases are well known to Jewish legal practice in which a slave is the property of more than one master.[16] Such a legal possibility, however, is at best the exception that proves the rule set up here. It is a question of a proverbial assertion that comes from a generally recognized experience: unrestricted service can be given only to one master!

The substantiation employs the Semitic opposition of ἀγαπᾶν ('to love') and μισεῖν; in this text the latter does not have the usual, emotionally loaded meaning of 'to hate' but of 'not to love' (cf. Luke 14:26). In like manner, the verb used in the following sentence, καταφρονεῖν (lit., 'despise'), is to be understood from its opposite as 'not to hold to.'[17]

Thus, the presented issue itself forces a decision. In the closing sentence, it is expressed in the second person plural as direct address: "You cannot serve God and mammon" (at the same time). The Greek word μαμωνᾶς is also found in Aramaic; its etymological derivation is obscure, yet the meaning in our text (as also in Luke 16:9, 11, 13) is unambiguous. The personified locution refers to earthly possessions.[18] The either-or before which the Preacher on the mount places his followers does not mean that one should fundamentally renounce possessions. Even if according to the report in Matthew's Gospel the disciples left everything in order to follow Jesus (4:18-22; 19-27), the Evangelist does not hold to an ideal of poverty.[19] A complete separation from money and means is not demanded; rather, the call to decision is defined by the verb δουλεύειν ('serve'). Recognition of the dominion of God excludes service under the law of wealth. Enslavement to earthly possessions cannot be brought into harmony with service to the community of Jesus Christ.

Thus, in verse 24 Matthew means basically the same thing that he said in verses 19-21. He admonishes the community to turn their vision away from earthly possessions and direct it toward God. Similarly, like greed and avarice, this also calls into question an economic order that claims for itself an absolute position, and thus becomes the representation of humanity-enslaving mammon. On the other hand, the saying does not demand freedom from any economic order or absolute separation from possessions. The either-or aims rather at the realization of a freedom that has its origin in commitment to God and is realized every day as service to God in that it "deals with the world as if it had no dealings with it" (1 Cor 7:31).

2.5.2   6:25-34   On Anxiety

Fuchs, E. "Die Verkündigung Jesu. Der Spruch von den Raben." In *Der historische Jesus und der kerygmatische Christus,* edited by H. Ristow and K. Matthiae, 385-88. 1960.

Jacquemin, E. "Les options du chrétien (Mt 6,24-33)." *AsSeign* 68 (1964): 31-44.

Riesenfeld, H. "Vom Schätzesammeln und Sorgen—ein Thema urchristlicher Paränese." In *Neotestamentica et Patristica,* FS O. Cullmann, edited by W. C. van Unnik, 47-58. NovTSup 6. 1962.

Steinhauser. *Doppelbildworte,* 215-35.

Zeller. *Mahnsprüche,* 82-94.

[25]Therefore I tell you, do not be anxious about your life, what you shall eat or what you shall drink, nor about your body, what you shall put on. Is not life more than food, and the body more than clothing?

²⁶Look at the birds of the air: they neither sow nor reap nor gather into barns, and yet your heavenly Father feeds them. Are you not of more value than they? ²⁷And which of you by being anxious can add one cubit to his span of life? ²⁸And why are you anxious about clothing? Consider the lilies of the field, how they grow; they neither toil nor spin; ²⁹yet I tell you, even Solomon in all his glory was not arrayed like one of these. ³⁰But if God so clothes the grass of the field, which today is alive and tomorrow is thrown into the oven, will he not much more clothe you, O men of little faith? ³¹Therefore do not be anxious, saying, "What shall we eat?" or "What shall we drink?" or "What shall we wear?" ³²For the Gentiles seek all these things; and your heavenly Father knows that you need them all. ³³But seek first his kingdom and his righteousness, and all these things shall be yours as well.

³⁴Therefore do not be anxious about tomorrow, for tomorrow will be anxious for itself. Let the day's own trouble be sufficient for the day.

Matthew found the following sayings unit before him in the written Q tradition, as its far-reaching agreement with Luke 12:22-31 guarantees. Only in a few cases are the Matthean intrusions of real importance—especially in the introduction of the concept of righteousness in verse 33. Luke, on the other hand, more definitely shaped the form of the inherited text.[20] Since the attachment to the parable of the Rich Fool (Luke 12:13-21) is certainly Luke's work, the question remains open as to the location of this unit of tradition in the Q source.[21]

Here we have a collection of wisdom sayings, at the beginning of which stands the fundamental warning against anxiety (v. 25a). It is aimed directly at Jesus' listeners and is substantiated in various ways in the following text: by the placing of life above nourishment and the body above clothing (v. 25b), by the example of the birds of the air (v. 26), by the indication of the inability of a person to lengthen his life (v. 27), and by the example of the lilies of the field (vv. 28-30). The first summary, with its repeated warning about anxiety and the admonition to orient oneself toward the kingdom of God and his righteousness, represents a provisional closing (vv. 31-33). The second summarizing conclusion is not attested in Luke and is a secondary addition (v. 34).[22]

6:25. The beginning with διὰ τοῦτο ("therefore"), which was already present in Q, links this section with the preceding one.

The required service to God (v. 24) means not only distance
from possessions but also renunciation of anxiety. A distinction between an address to the rich (vv. 19-24) and to the poor
(vv. 25-34) is not intended, since even the poor are, of course,
threatened with the danger of losing themselves in striving for
possessions, just as, conversely, the rich fall prey to anxiety—
not least of all through their possessions.[23] Nor is Matthew
thinking especially of the disciples of Jesus, who through Jesus'
word are to be freed from the drudgery of work;[24] instead, he
continues the admonition to the community: one who is
committed to the reign of God may not let himself be attacked
by anxiety (cf. 1 Pet 5:7).

The authoritative instruction[25] of the Preacher on the mount
that one should not be anxious is made concrete first in the
example of the ψυχή (lit., 'soul'). This is not, in the Platonic
sense, the immortal part of a human being; rather, analogous
to the Hebrew נפש (nefesh), it is the life, or life force, that is
maintained through nourishment.[26] The σῶμα, as the ani-
mated human "body," is the object of anxiety about clothing.[27]
The appended rabbinical deductive procedure draws the
conclusion in interrogative form[28] a maiori ad minus (v. 25b): if
the greater is present, then the lesser will also follow. The logic
of this argumentation is borne by the conviction that the
creative power of God, which brought life and body, will also
provide food and clothing.

6:26. Different, however, is the deductive procedure in verse
26 (and vv. 28-30), which goes from the lesser to the greater. If
God takes care of the birds of the air,[29] even though they make
no provision for their own existence, how much more must this
also apply to Jesus' hearers! Expressed here is an optimistic
view of nature, which has parallels in Stoic[30] and rabbinical
texts.[31] As for the struggle to preserve the species of nature
against the natural catastrophes to which animals and plants
fall victim, our text says nothing. At the same time there is no
doubt that Matthew knows not only about suffering and death
in his community but also about distress in the animal world
(cf. 10:29-31). Nevertheless, wherever there may be well-
founded reason for fear and anxiety, this is overcome through
faith in the providence of God, whom the community
addresses as its Father (cf. 5:45; 6:9).

6:27. Another motif in not being anxious is named with the example of the ἡλικία ('age'). In graphic language it demonstrates that no one is in a position to lengthen his alloted span of life.[32] This thought goes beyond the immediate context; it does not refer to the providence of the Creator but presents anxiety in general as meaningless. However much one may endeavor to lengthen life—and even with prominent success in recent times through modern medical means—the measure granted by God cannot be exceeded nor death avoided through such anxiety. Hence, over such endeavor stands ultimately the verdict: in vain!

6:28-29. The example of the life of nature is taken up again by pointing to the κρίνα ('lilies'). In combination with the genitive τοῦ ἀγροῦ ('of the field'), particular wildflowers are probably not intended, and thus attempts to identify them (for example, as iris or wild roses) promise no success. The flowers growing wild perform no man's work in the field (οὐ κοπιῶσιν) nor woman's work in the house (οὐδὲ νήθουσιν).[33] Yet one can look at them and tell that God himself cares for the smallest one, for the proverbial splendor of King Solomon (cf. 2 Chron 9) cannot be compared with them.

6:30. This example also is given full value in a conclusion *a minori ad maius* (cf. v. 26). If the goodness of God adorns the grass of the field[34] in this manner, then how much more does the community of Jesus Christ have reason to rely on God's providence. The word ὀλιγόπιστοι[35] makes clear that what is demanded is not a blind trust, which, in illusionary fashion, passes over natural and human catastrophes and fails to acknowledge situations of persecution and distress. The demand, rather, is for the risk of that trust—the *nevertheless* of faith—which relies on the creative power of God, who calls into existence the things that do not exist (Rom 4:17).

6:31-32. With the Matthean concluding οὖν ('therefore'; cf. 5:48; 6:9), the Evangelist introduces the logical conclusion by repeating the prohibition of being anxious and makes it concrete by taking up the questions of verse 25. The ἔθνη ('Gentiles'—cf. ἐθνικοί in 5:47; 6:7) are named as counterexamples.[36] They represent the mass of unconverted, godless people, who have reason, to be sure, to be anxious about food, drink, and clothing, since they are oriented to this world and know nothing of the alternative of trust in God. All the more urgently this passage (as earlier in 6:8) points to the providential knowledge of the heavenly Father. His work is not a collection of facts that follow natural laws and can be determined objectively, however much God's goodness may become visible in the context of creation (cf. 5:45). His providence occurs, rather, in the liberating claim of Jesus' word, which sets for humankind the goal and norm of life and opens the way into the kingdom of God (cf. 5:17-20).

6:33. The kingdom of God and his righteousness are explicitly brought to expression in this closing section. They are a goal worth striving for, which—when it becomes the aim of human life—makes all anxiety superfluous.

The text is variously attested. The following is based on the underlying reading τὴν βασιλείαν καὶ τὴν δικαιοσύνην αὐτοῦ. The injection of the genitive τοῦ θεοῦ (after βασιλείαν), which quantitatively is not poorly attested, is secondary polishing; it is apparently supposed to avoid the difficult construction in which two "status constructi" are dependent on the genitive αὐτοῦ. The original Q text is passed on in the Lukan parallel (Luke 12:31). From this we learn that Matthew inserted the words καὶ τὴν δικαιοσύνην before αὐτοῦ. This is all the more probably, since all instances of δικαιοσύνη are of redactional origin in the First Gospel. The striving of the Evangelist to treat the Q model as protectively as possible led to the linguistic unevenness of the text.

The personal pronoun αὐτοῦ ('his') refers back to the preceding ὁ πατὴρ ὑμῶν ὁ οὐράνιος (v. 32: 'your heavenly Father'). Both the "kingdom" and the "righteousness" are accordingly marked by their relationship to God and designated as the aim of human striving. What does this mean? Clearly, the thinking and doing of the individual is to be oriented toward the kingdom of God as a reality that transcends human existence and is promised to the followers of Jesus in the future (cf. 5:3, 10, 20; 6:10). How is righteousness related to the content of this hope? Does Matthew distinguish between "your righteousness" (5:20; 6:1), absolute "righteousness" (5:6, 10), and "his (God's) righteousness" (6:33)?[37] The Evangelist makes no distinction between the righteousness demanded of the disciplies and the concept of righteousness used absolutely, which designates an attitude for the sake of which Jesus' followers are persecuted. Hence, there is no differentiation between divine righteousness as a gift and human righteousness as a duty, such as might be presumed from the perspective of Pauline theology. Rather, God's righteous being is revealed in the goodness with which God sustains his creation (5:45). He is the ideal and model of what Jesus' eschatological demand requires, the righteousness of humanity. Therefore, God's righteousness comes to expression as it is demanded of human beings. Through such "righteousness" alone is entrance to the "kingdom" to be gained, as already stated in 5:20. In a presumably secondary reading, the Codex Vaticanus (Cod B) interpreted the text correctly when it exchanged the two terms and placed "righteousness" before "his kingdom."[38] "Righteousness" and thereby the "kingdom" are supposed to be the primary goal of human endeavor. The Matthean πρῶτον ('first') stresses the point: in view of the eschatological demand and its promise, everyday cares seem small and can be left to God's providence. Anyone who hears this instruction of the Son of God has reason enough to place trust in the providence of the heavenly Father.

6:34. The closing verse returns to the beginning (v. 25); it is presumably a secondary, pre-Matthean addition that was not known to Luke. The admonition not to be anxious is given a new basis and closed with a proverbial expression: "Let the day's own trouble be sufficient for the day." Tomorrow will bring new conditions and therewith the possibility and necessity of dealing with tomorrow's problems—a rational argument that is equal to the foregoing flow of wisdom. Thus is it also stated in the rabbinical literature: "Worry not about the worries of tomorrow, for you do not know what the day will bring forth; perhaps tomorrow you will be no more, and then you would have worried about a world that will belong to you no more" (b. Sanh. 100*b*). Greek and Latin writers also recommend concentrating on today.[39] Of course, the motivation for such advice varies. The present text is not intended to express a general ethical recommendation, but rather is a component of the concrete summons of the Preacher on the mount. It is understood by the Evangelist as community admonition, and it is addressed to the Christians who hear the demand of the Son of God and shape their lives with an upward glance toward God. Hence, the warning against anxiety implies a positive commandment. If anxiety about the self goes along with a lack of faith (v. 30), then πίστις ('faith') in Matthew's Gospel has almost a general meaning of 'trust' (8:10; 9:2, 22, 29; 15:28; and elsewhere). Anxiety is opposed to trust. Demanded is the act of trust, an attitude that holds itself ready for service (v. 24) today[40] and assigns the worries about tomorrow to the One who sends the good as well as "the day's own trouble" and will lead his kingdom upward.

The synoptic Evangelists, of course, are also familiar with justified, responsibly executed planning for the future (cf. Luke 14:28-32). Our present text, however, speaks of anxiety as the wrong approach to the future. Anyone who is anxious proves thereby that he is trying to take his life into his own hands. By anticipating the future in a scheming way, he attempts to protect himself (v. 34). Such an attitude is marked by fear and anxiety (Luke 12:32). The Preacher of the Sermon on the Mount admonishes his followers to overcome anxiety. It is in vain, for worry never leads to the desired goal (v. 27). It is unreasonable because every day has its own trouble, and the new day will bring new problems (v. 34). Above all, it is needless, since it denies God the necessary trust in him as Creator and Sustainer of life (v. 26, 28-30). Even if the details of the wisdom-like argumentation are to be questioned, the call to overcome anxiety points beyond itself. It contains the warning not to throw trust away (Heb 10:35) but to place oneself without reservation at the disposal of the promised "kingdom" and the demanded "righteousness" (v. 33).

2.5.3   7:1-6   On Judging

Couroyer, B. "De la mesure dont vous mesurez il vous sera mesuré." *RB* 77 (1970): 366-70.
Neuhäusler, E. "Mit welchem Masstab misst Gott die Menschen?" *BibLeb* 11 (1970): 104-13.
Rüger, H. P. "Mit welchem Mass ihr messt, wird euch gemessen werden." *ZNW* 60 (1969): 174-82.

Jeremias, J. "Matthäus 7,6a" (1963). In idem, *Abba*, 83-87.
Maxwell-Stuart, P. G. " 'Do not give what is holy to the dogs' (Mt 7:6)." *ExpTim* 90 (1979): 341.

Perles, F. "Zur Erklärung von Mt 7,6." *ZNW* 25 (1926): 163-64.
Schwarz, G. "Matthäus VII 6a. Emendation und Rückübersetzung." *NovT* 14 (1972): 18-25.
Steinhauser. *Doppelbildworte*, 259-80.

Matthew 7

¹Judge not, that you be not judged.

²For with the judgment you pronounce you will be judged,

and the measure you give will be the measure you get.

³Why do you see the speck that is in your brother's eye, but do not notice the log that is in your own eye? ⁴Or how can you say to your brother, *"Let me take the speck out of your eye," when there is the log in your own eye? ⁵You hypocrite, first take the log out of your own eye, and then you will see clearly to take the speck out of your brother's eye.*

⁶Do not give dogs what is holy; and do not throw your pearls before swine, lest they trample them underfoot and turn to attack you.

Luke 6

³⁷"Judge not, and you will not be judged; condemn not, and you will not be condemned; forgive, and you will be forgiven; *³⁸give, and it will be given to you; good measure, pressed down, shaken together, running over, will be put into your lap.* *For the measure you give will be the measure you get back."* *³⁹He also told them a parable: "Can a blind man lead a blind man? Will they not both fall into a pit? ⁴⁰A disciple is not above his teacher, but every one when he is fully taught will be like his teacher.*

⁴¹Why do you see the speck that is in your brother's eye, but do not notice the log that is in your own eye? ⁴²Or how can you say to your brother, 'Brother, let me take out the speck that is in your eye,' when you yourself do not see the log that is in your own eye? You hypocrite, first take the log out of your own eye and then you will see clearly to take out the speck that is in your brother's eye."

With verse 1, Matthew picks up the thread of the Q tradition, which he had dropped in 5:48. The parallel from the Sermon on the Plain (Luke 6:37-42) attests our pericope for Q. The present version of the Matthew text may come very close to the original Q tradition.

Synoptic comparison identifies a Lukan surplus in verses 37b-38; vis-à-vis Matt 7:2 this is presumably secondary.[41] Verses 39-40 were available to Luke from another Q connection (cf. Matt 15:14; 10:24-25) and were redactionally inserted. The following shows far-reaching agreement; yet especially in verse 42 Lukan linguistic intrusions can be established. In the context of Luke's Gospel, verses 37-42 clarify the commandment to be merciful (v. 36). The text is elaborately constructed in that two prohibitions (v. 37a-b) and two commandments (vv. 37c-38a) are opposed to each other, and two sayings on "measure" are added (v. 38b-c). Bultmann sees that in terms of tradition history, the sayings group passed on by Matthew does not represent a single unit, and he makes a separation between verses 1-2 and verses 3-5 (*Synoptische Tradition*, 90); it is more correct, however, to distinguish tradition-historically between verse 1, verse 2, verses 3-5, and verse 6.

7:1. The absolute prohibition of judging (κρίνειν) leaves no room for harmonization attempts. It represents another ethical radicalism of Jesus, corresponding to the absolute demands in the antitheses of the Sermon on the Mount. If the second clause ("that you be not judged") seems close to understanding judging as condemnation, the Greek concept does not distinguish between judging and condemning. It is presupposed that every human judgment contains the beginnings of an element of condemnation. The eschatological demand is made without restriction. The followers of Jesus, who are sworn to the commandment of love (cf. 5:38-48; 22:34-40), are forbidden any kind of judgment-passing that reduces one's neighbor to an object of one's own interests. For them, judging is precluded as an attitude that is identical with lovelessness.

The prohibition is based on a purpose (ἵνα 'so that'). Thus, the last judgment is not just threatened as an unavoidable consequence;[42] instead, the behavior of Jesus' followers is to be intentionally oriented toward the end. From there God's judgment is expected, as the passive "be judged" indicates.[43] This apocalyptic perspective motivates the right behavior vis-à-vis one's neighbor. Thus, it is in tune with Jesus' proclamation of the kingdom of God. The call to repentance occasioned by the nearness of the kingdom becomes concrete in the prohibition of judging. It allows no possibility of distinguishing between judgment and condemnation. Even if the administration of justice by the state lies beyond the proclamation of Jesus, he does not distinguish between private judgment and the activity of a judge.[44] There is nothing left for the individual to use to justify himself in regard to Jesus' demand. All of Jesus' hearers are included in the *massa perditionis*. All are summoned to repentance, to turning away from an egocentric life-style and toward devotion to the pardoning and judging God, who will pass the final judgment.

7:2. In contrast to Jesus' initial prophetic cry of alarm, the continuation brings a wisdom-like admonition. It contains first a two-line substantiation (v. 2), then a graphic example that ends with a final admonition (vv. 3-5). This directive is likewise substantiated with a view toward the future final judgment; it advises, however, not the renunciation but the proper use of judging. Thus, it is in keeping with the situation of a community that is prepared for the duration of history. The establishment of order and discipline requires it to answer the question, how does one judge correctly (cf. 18:15-20). In the process it is in danger of overestimating the criteria at its disposal. Paul also knows of a human self-overestimation that goes with judging and observes that the judging of one's neighbor ultimately turns against the one who judges (Rom 2:1-6, 17-24). This principle, practiced in the Q tradition and also in Matthew's community, has a foundation in the Old Testament conviction that God repays a person according to his actions (Prov 24:12; Ps 62:13; cf. Rom 2:6). From this it follows that judging in the community must be validated by God's judgment.

The same is asserted with the saying on accurate measure. It has literal parallels in rabbinical writing.[45] The maxim "measure for measure"[46] leaves open the possibility of choosing different units of measure. Whether one uses a narrow or a broad dry measure, whether one is generous or stingy, God's judgment will fall in like measure. Such casuistry comes from wisdom thinking, which likewise orients ethical instruction toward the concept of repayment (cf. Wis 11:16). The following saying about the speck and the log explains that in judging and measuring the Christian community is supposed to let itself be led by the commandment of love (cf. 5:7: the merciful have the promise that they will receive mercy).

7:3-4. From the form-historical viewpoint, the two rhetorical questions about the speck in the brother's eye and the log in one's own eye are to be designated metaphors. The intended subject goes beyond the image. As exaggerated as the statement may be, as inconceivable as a log in one's own eye is, the meaning needs no further explanation: insight into one's own imperfection should lead to a careful, loving interaction with one's neighbor. In applying the admonition of verse 2, the use of the standard of love and mercy is demanded.

Whether the rabbinical literature knows a similar tradition and this is presupposed by Rabbi Tarphon (c. A.D. 100), or whether the rabbis took a polemical stand in regard to our text, it is impossible to say here.[47] As other parallel texts make clear, this rule is, in any case, not foreign to Jewish thinking. More important is the fact that it is handed down in this location as an utterance of Jesus and addressed to the community and the world.

In the synoptic tradition the word ἀδελφός generally refers to one's Christian brother. Yet the Sermon on the Mount is addressed not only to the disciples but also to the listening people. Also, the universalistic ethic of Matthew forbids that the demand of Jesus be restricted to the relationship of Christians to each other (cf. above on 5:24, 47). Speaking here is the exalted one, who is given power over heaven and earth. His word lays claim to recognition beyond the bounds of the church (cf. 28:16-20). It demands that brotherly love rule relations between people without any limitation.

7:5. The "hypocrite" closes himself off from such a demand. He lives in a contradition (cf. on 6:2ff.), since he undertakes putting his brother on the right path, but does not eliminate his own imperfection. His behavior is that of the blind guide who wants to lead another blind person, so that both come to a fall (Luke 6:39 par. Matt 15:14; cf. Rom 2:19). By contrast, Jesus

demands that one first eliminate one's own fault, then
undertake the attempt to correct that of the brother. The
statement is introduced by the future διαβλέψεις ('you will
see'), which takes up the imperative in verse 5*a* and clearly
represents a retarding element. It means that the application
of the measure of love requires sober consideration and
restraint. It presupposes that one not only confess one's fault
but also remove it. It is thus appropriate to the monitory theme
of this pericope.

7:6. The sayings unit ends with a dramatic, three-line image
saying of the dogs and the swine which is handed down only in
Matthew's Gospel. Matthew found it either in his copy of the
sayings collection (Q^{Matt}) or in an isolated special tradition. The
structure shows a clear division. The first two lines are related
in parallel fashion (μή . . . μηδέ 'not . . . and not'). The last
line brings the final substantiation (μήποτε 'lest'); it is
chiastically constructed in that the first part refers to the swine
and the second to the dogs. The original meaning is puzzling.[48]
In any case, something especially valuable and holy is set over
against unclean animals. In Old Testament-Jewish writing the
"holy" is often identified with sacrificial flesh (e.g., Exod
29:33-34; Lev 2:3 LXX). In this way, the image becomes more
graphic without developing a genuinely religious statement.
Presumably, it is a question of a profane, proverbial expression
with the meaning: you should not turn over something
precious to someone who does not know how to appreciate it;
otherwise you yourself will suffer.

The profane meaning is attested by numerous texts for the New
Testament environment which contain near parallels to the first two
lines. To verse 6*a*: "One does not remove something holy in order to
have it eaten by the dogs" (b. Ber. 15*a* on Deut 12:15). To verse 6*b*:
"Words of the wise man to the fool are like pearls to a sow" (Ginza R
VII 218:30). The uncleanness of dogs and swine is not exclusively a
Jewish concept; for example, it was also known to Horace: "Canis
immundus vel amica luto sus" (ep. I 2:26).

Since the life situation and the context in the oral or written
pre-Matthean tradition are unknown, the presynoptic interpretation will always remain in dispute. Present interpretations exhibit a broad spectrum. According to predisposed

position, the "holy" is identified with gnostic secret knowledge, ecclesiastical teaching, or a Jewish-Christian scribal position.

(a) Logion 93 of the Gospel of Thomas reveals a gnostic-esoteric conception: "Do not give what is holy to the dogs, lest it be thrown on the manure pile. Do not throw pearls to the sows, lest they. . . ." Since even the context (log. 92: Matt 7:7b; log. 94: Matt 7:8c) presupposes the connection with Matthew's Gospel, this tradition is relevant for the history of influence, but not for the original meaning of Matt 7:6. The logion contains a warning against profaning gnostic secrets.[49]

(b) An interpretation from ecclesiastical politics is represented by Hilarius of Poitiers (d. 367), who identified the "dogs" with Gentiles and the "swine" with heretics (in Mt VI 1). In another interpretation, the "dogs" are equated with apostates, the "swine" with the unconverted,[50] without producing any clues that suggest such an interpretation for the pre-Matthean tradition.

(c) Scarcely less improbable is the exegesis that is to be deduced from the first Christian novel, the Pseudo-Clementines (second-fourth centuries), in which a Jewish-Christian tradition is treated. Here, Matt 7:6 is connected with the theory of falsified scriptural pericopes.[51] Over against the Gentile-Christian church at large, the Jewish-Christian scribal interpretation appeals to our text and thereby differentiates itself from its opponents.

If Matthew inserted this saying in the present context, then there is also, in terms of content, a great distance from the tradition-historical starting point, that is, the absolute prohibition of Jesus (v. 1). On the problem of judging, the Evangelist transmits a supplementary instruction: even if one is to exercise restraint in criticizing one's brother (vv. 2-5), this does not mean, however, that the Christian should refrain from any kind of judgment. On the contrary, there are situations in which, for the sake of the issue, a clear judgment is necessary. There is thus a limit to not judging. When the truth of the faith stands in the balance, it may be necessary to make an unambiguous profession and draw a clear line of demarcation. The application of church discipline raises the question of *status confessionis*. The disciplinary power granted to the community can also be expressed in treating the unrepentant sinner as "a Gentile and a tax collector" (18:17). For the sake of Christ's commission, the lifting of ecclesiastical fellowship may become necessary in light of the common obligation to the law of the Lord. Naturally, the commanded separation also applies to relations with outsiders. Such decisions are not to be avoided when the faith is endangered and the identity of the community threatened (v. 6c). But they cannot be made in the Christian community without being mindful of Jesus' absolute demand (v. 1) and being aware of one's own failure.

2.5.4   7:7-11   On the Answering of Prayer

Greeven, H. "Wer unter euch . . . ?" *Wort und Dienst* 3 (1952): 86-101.
Piper, R. "Matthew 7:7-11 par. Luke 11:9-13: Evidence of Design and Argument in the Collection of Jesus' Sayings." In *Logia—Les Paroles de Jésus*, Mem. J. Coppens, edited by J. Delobel, 411-18. Leuven, 1982.
Steinhauser. *Doppelbildworte*, 69-79.

[7]Ask, and it will be given you; seek and you will find; knock, and it will be opened to you. [8]For every one who asks receives, and he who seeks finds, and to him who knocks it will be opened. [9]Or what man of you, if his son asks him for a loaf, will give him a stone? [10]Or if he asks for a fish, will give him a serpent? [11]If you then, who are evil, know how to give good gifts to your children, how much more will your Father who is in heaven give good things to those who ask him?

Prayer has already been considered in the passage 6:5-15. When here again a position is taken on this theme, it is clear that even though Matthew is following systematic viewpoints in the outline of the Sermon on the Mount, he feels closely bound to his sources and preserves the independence of verses 7:7-11, which were already connected in Q (cf. Luke 11:9-13).[52] This theme appears, to be sure, in a new perspective. In place of a prayer directive that teaches the right way to pray and demonstrates with counterexamples, here we find a repeated summons to prayer and detailed reasons why prayer will be answered.

From this standpoint, the often posed question of how our text is related to the foregoing section on judging loses its importance. Is it presupposed that a false kind of self-criticism, self-destructive insight into one's own shortcomings, leads to distrustful thoughts that make confident prayer impossible?[53] Should one pray for instruction from God in order to be prepared to judge one's brother, as Jas 1:5 seems to suggest?[54] Or since this text concludes the main part of the Sermon on the Mount immediately before verse 12, does it affirm the central position of the Lord's Prayer?[55] The following will show that verse 12 reaches back to 5:17-20, and summarizes the preceding monitory sections, in each of which the demand for righteousness is concretized with regard to the disciples. Hence, our text is also to be understood as a piece of monitory teaching that is placed alongside the foregoing directives. The righteousness of Jesus' followers includes, for example, not only the right relationship to possessions (6:19-24), the overcoming of anxiety (6:25-34), and the right kind of judging (7:1-6), but also the confidence that prayer will be answered.

This sayings unit breaks down into two parts. Verses 7-8 contain twin sayings of three lines each, which are symmetrically related to each other. Of course, the fact that the verbs in the first and second lines in verse 8 are constructed in the present active (instead of the future passive) detracts from the symmetrical structure, but makes no difference in content.[56] The unit of verses 9-11 includes first two rhetorical questions of two lines each, which are arranged in parallel. Then in verse 11 comes a final conclusion, which at the same time has the function of substantiating the whole section.

7:7-8. In the form of a wisdom speech,[57] the listeners are summoned to pray confidently. The piling up of imperatives underlines the urgency of the admonition. Just as the Son of God is presented praying (11:25; 14:23; 19:13; 26:36ff.), so also his disciples stand as petitioners before God (cf. 24:20; 26:41). The future passive, appended each time with a consecutive καί ('and'), expresses the certainty that God will grant fulfillment of the petition. These statements about the petition as well as the favorable response remain closely bound to the wisdom tradition. In contrast to the preceding text, the aim of prayer is not the future-eschatological kingdom (6:10a, 33) or the apocalyptic final judgment (7:1-2). The gift of God occurs, rather, in everyday human life (cf. 6:25ff.). As urgently as the admonition is expressed, no compulsion can be exercised through human prayer. Proper prayer is in harmony with the third petition of the Lord's Prayer; it subjects itself to the will of the Father, who is entrusted not only with the answering but also with the fulfillment according to his will (6:10b).

7:9-10. The comparison with the requests that are usual in an earthly father-son relationship makes clear that being a child of God is fundamental to prayer and to the relationship of humanity to God. The parallel in Luke 11:11-12 offers the examples of fish/snake and egg/scorpion and emphasizes the sharp contrast between the request and the gift, since both the snake and the scorpion are harmful animals for people. Matthew, on the other hand, has the idea—probably closer to the original—that the form of the gift corresponds to what was requested, so that the bread could be confused with a stone or an eel-like fish with a snake. Both examples describe a response of the giver that is normally unthinkable in earthly father-son relationships, for it is part of the recognized image of a human father that the son submits to the father a request with warranted trust. Hence, the two rhetorical questions can expect the answer, "No one!"

7:11. The conclusion, introduced with οὖν ('then'), applies the deductive process *a minori ad maius*. If even human parents grant the requests of their children, how much more will the heavenly Father grant fulfillment. Like the Pharisees in 12:34, the people are called πονηροί ('evil')—not, of course, in regard to inherited sin as a sinful, original condition of humanity. Matthew probably knows that the unconverted person does not reach salvation apart from the word of the Son of God and lives accordingly in a salvationless condition, and also that Christians do not exist in the state of perfection, however much they are summoned to perfect action. These ideas, however, do not lead to the development of a theological system. The statement that people are evil is supposed to stress their distance from God. For God is good (19:17 par.) and proves daily his goodness in relation to good and evil people (5:45 par.). Therefore good things can be requested of him and confidently expected.[58]

2.5.5 7:12 The Golden Rule

Dihle, A. *Die Goldene Regel.* Studienhefte zur Altertumswissenschaft 7. 1962.
———. "Goldene Regel." *RAC* 11 (1981), 930-40.
Strecker, G. "Compliance—Love of One's Enemy—The Golden Rule." *AusBR* 29 (1981): 38-46.

Matthew 7   Luke 6

¹²So whatever you wish that men   *³¹And as you wish that men would*
would do to you, do so to them; for   *do to you, do so to them.*
this is the law and the prophets.

In central position, as the closing of the main body of the Sermon on the Mount, Matthew placed the so-called Golden Rule. In Luke's Gospel, it is found after the commandment to love one's enemies and to forgo retaliation (6:27-30), and before the explanation of the commandment to love one's enemy, which is brought to a close with the demand to be merciful (6:32-36). Presumably, in Q it followed the prohibition of retaliation (Luke 6:29-30 par. Matt 5:39b-42).[59]

If the Golden Rule is formulated positively in both the sayings source and in Matthew and Luke, in the world around the New Testament it was generally known in a negative version (that is, what you do not want anyone to do to you, do not do that to anyone else). This is attested in Confucianism, where it is interpreted with the principle of reciprocity.[60] Moreover, it can be demonstrated in Asiatic and Near-Eastern cultures. It is attested in Greek literature as early as Herodotus.[61] It is cited in almost all literary genres in both the Greek and the Roman cultural areas. Yet it is not found in the philosophical ethics of early Hellenism. Since it seems to be directed toward one's fellow human being and to promote the principle of retaliation as the criterion of human behavior, it was not appropriate for an individual ethic or ethic of attitude oriented toward a moral ideal. This means, on the other hand, that it "has belonged since the fourth century to the integrating component of a common ethic formulated in maxims."[62] Greek-speaking Judaism adopted it from the Greeks and used it primarily in its negative version.[63] It was also common in Hebrew-speaking Judaism.[64] It was granted an important significance in rabbinical teaching. It is cited by Rabbi Hillel (c. 20 B.C.) as a summary of the Torah:

> One time a Gentile came to Shammai; he said to him, "Accept me as a proselyte, with the condition that you teach me the whole Torah while I stand on one leg." He pushed him away with a stick that he had in his hand. He went to Hillel; this one accepted him as a proselyte. He said to him, "What is

displeasing to you, do to no one else; that is the whole Torah, and the rest is explanation. Go and learn!" (*Šabb.* 31*a*)

There is no doubt that the summarizing function creates a parallel between Hillel's understanding and the summary formula of Matt. 7:12. Matthew, of course, cites the positive version. At this point the conclusion seems obvious that in contrast to the rabbinical negative Golden Rule, Christian tradition consciously used the positive form. And in terms of substance, it seems that the intention of the negative formula is merely to protect one's fellow human being from injury, while the positive version is to be understood as a summons to the active giving of help to one's neighbor.[65] Nonetheless, even with Hillel the negative version aims at the active doing of good, for the Golden Rule, as the sum of the Torah, is a summary of not only the prohibitions but also the commandments of the Old Testament, especially since the intention of Hillel's statement is to lead beyond the Golden Rule to the Torah as its "explanation."[66] It is significant that in the post-New Testament period there was no distinction between the positive and negative forms; instead, both versions were cited as Christian ethical maxims.[67] Even in Confucianism the negative Golden Rule was interpreted in the sense, "to want the best for someone" or "to exercise benevolence toward another."[68] In the Epistle of Aristeas, written around 100 B.C., the negative is linked with the positive form,[69] just as also in rabbinism, the negative version is advanced as an interpretation of the commandment to love one's neighbor (Lev 19:18).[70] The formal difference between the two versions does not result in different ethical conceptions; they refer to one and the same ethical content.

At first glance, the Golden Rule seems to express the idea that one's own actions in regard to one's fellow human being must be oriented toward the behavior of the other person. On this basis the verdict seems justified that this ethical maxim reflects the "morality of a naive egoism."[71] Yet this is valid only when one considers the saying in isolation, interprets it *in malam partem*, and overlooks the fact that the standard for one's own actions toward one's neighbor is based, not on actual current modes of behavior or on return favors, but on desired (good) deeds on the part of the other person.[72] The ideal requirement of the other person becomes the standard of one's own actual behavior. Thus, the ethical norm of the Golden Rule exceeds both the reciprocity and the reality of human behavior. For characteristic of its realization is the idea that one does not let oneself be governed by the will or deed of another, but knows that one is placed under the unrestricted demand to do the good that one wishes for oneself and not to do the evil that one would not like to suffer oneself.

The standard of value that is established with the Golden Rule is, accordingly, distinct from a *do ut des* principle. It is comparable rather to the categorical imperative of Immanuel Kant, according to which a person should act "so that the maxim of your will could at any time also be valid as a principle of general legislation."[73] Of course, Kant begins with a philosophically based idealism of the subjective will and draws consequences of universal moral claim. The Golden Rule, on the other hand, in keeping with its roots in common ethics, presupposes a conceptual world, not of theoretical, but of practical ethics. Although a formal principle of action, it is aimed at the concrete situation. The material context that is determinative for it decides on which level and with what content it will be put into action.

Did Jesus use the Golden Rule in his proclamation? Since wisdom elements are a part of his message and the prophetic, eschatologically motivated call to repentance can also be expressed in the form of a wisdom saying or in connection with a wisdom-like admonition, it is conceivable—if not strictly demonstrable—that Jesus taught this ethical principle.[74] At this point, it is clear that Jesus' ethic does not simply oppose human autonomy with the heteronomous principle of action of God's sovereignty, but—and this applies generally to early Christian ethics—adopts the ethical content and standards of the Jewish and Hellenistic surroundings and in view of the approaching kingdom of God makes room for the freedom of the individual for ethical values and brotherly action.

The legacy of the Q source lies not so far back in the darkness of tradition history. Here for the first time the Golden Rule is linked to the demands of compliance and love of enemy. The commandment of unconditional love defines its application. It is thus a component of the community admonition that is explained through examples[75] and proclaimed with eschatological authority as the word of the earthly and exalted Son of God. In this connection, the Golden Rule is expressly removed from a concept of retaliation that promotes the achievement of reciprocity to an ethical principle (Matt 5:46-47 par. Luke 6:32-33). It marks the "more" that the Christian community must do in discipleship to Jesus if it wants to be certain of the promise.

Basically, the understanding is not different in Luke, who stresses even more the relationship between the Golden Rule and the renunciation of retaliation as well as the commandment to love one's enemies (6:27-36). The monitory context makes it probable that ποιεῖτε (v. 31*b*: 'do') is to be understood not as indicative but as imperative.[76] The Lukan ὁμοίως ('in the same way') is not to be viewed as substantially different from the original οὕτως ('likewise').

Matthew interprets the Golden Rule in an especially penetrating manner by freeing it from its original literary context and placing it at the close of the main section of the Sermon on the Mount. With such a central position, it points back to the theme of the Sermon on the Mount, the demand of righteousness (5:17-20), which is taken up here again in a summarizing and concluding fashion, since in the following verses only final warnings and parables appear.

The redactional πάντα οὖν ὅσα ἐάν (lit., 'all things therefore whatsoever')[77] makes clear the summarizing function. The Golden Rule summarizes "all things" that were proclaimed in the foregoing individual directives. Thus, it matches the Matthean tendency toward fundamental principles, which in the Sermon on the Mount is recognizable in the compositional caesuras (apart from 5:20 esp. 5:48; 6:1) and is often attested in the First Gospel. Above all, the closing formula οὗτος γάρ ἐστιν ὁ νόμος καὶ οἱ προφῆται ('for this is the law and the prophets'), which on linguistic and material grounds goes back to the Evangelist (cf. 22:40 red.), has the task of characterizing the Golden Rule as an overarching principle of behavior. Similar to the manner in which it is possible in the rabbinical tradition, this maxim, according to the Matthean understanding, renders the sum of the Old Testament, which Jesus interprets with eschatological claim in the Sermon on the Mount, since he came not to abolish the law or the prophets but to fulfill them (5:17). As a rendering of the Old Testament will of God, it is at the same time the summary representation of the ethical instructions of Jesus. This standard for the right behavior of the followers expresses what the Lord demands: a better righteousness (5:20), perfection (5:48), mercy (5:7; 9:13; 12:7; cf. Hos 6:6), and love of enemy as an expression of the unrestricted love of God and neighbor (5:44; cf. 19:19; 22:34-40).

Even if from the tradition-historical and religious-historical point of view such instructions are of various kinds—since Jesus' demand for love of enemy represents a radicalization of the commandment of love of neighbor, and the Golden Rule was originally an ancient, common sense maxim—for Matthew there is still a fundamental unity in all of this. For him the Golden Rule is identical in terms of content with the commandment of agape. It gives the principled demand of agape a practical orientation toward the neighbor in his actual existence. On the other hand, its connection with the command of love excludes the misunderstanding that Christian interpersonal relations are formed on the basis of reciprocity. The harmony of the Golden Rule with the demand of compliance, the commandment of love of enemy, and, more broadly, with the commandment of love in general means that the agape practiced toward one's neighbor is the meaning and goal of the ethical law of the Preacher on the mount. This, however, is nothing other than the demand for righteousness, which lays the foundation for the new communion of followers of Jesus Christ.

2.6   7:13-27   Closing Admonitions and Parables

2.6.1   7:13-14   The Gate and the Way

Denaux, A. "Der Spruch von den zwei Wegen im Rahmen des Epilogs der Bergpredigt (Mt 7,13-14 par. Lk 13,23-24). Tradition und Redaktion." In *Logia—Les Paroles de Jésus*, Mem. J. Coppens, edited by J. Delobel, 305-35. Leuven, 1982.

Hoffman, P. "πάντες ἐργάται ἀδικίας. Redaktion und Tradition in Lk 13,22-30." *ZNW* 58 (1967): 188-214.

Mattill, A. J. "The Way of Tribulation." *JBL* 98 (1979): 531-46.

Schwarz, G. "Matthäus VII 13a. Ein Alarmruf angesichts höchster Gefahr." *NovT* 12 (1970): 229-32.

Steinhauser. *Doppelbildworte*, 148-57.

¹³*Enter by the narrow gate, for the gate is wide and the way is easy*
that leads to destruction, and those who enter by it are many. ¹⁴*For the*
gate is narrow and the way is hard that leads to life, and those who find
it are few.

With this image saying, Matthew begins the closing section of
the Sermon on the Mount. Thus, as much as the image relates
to Jesus' demands as a whole, which are also summarized in the
Golden Rule, it is not only to be understood as a continuation
of verse 12.¹ Instead, verses 13-14 anticipate the parables of
verses 24-27 and form with them the framework of the final
part of the Sermon on the Mount. Like the latter, they
articulate the call to decision that is defined in terms of content
by the following individual parts.

The presence of this image saying in Q can be presumed
from the parallel Luke 13:23-24, even if the Lukan text is in
the form of a school dialogue and exhibits many Lukan traits.²
The admonition in Luke to enter by the narrow door (θύρα)
reflects the substance of the saying, but for the most part it is
found in its original form in Matthew.

The structure of the prophetic, wisdom-like call to decision is
transparent. The introductory exhortation (v. 13) is followed by two
ὅτι ('for') clauses with parallel constructions; that is, each contains two
lines joined by καί ('and'). The oldest form of the text is in dispute.
According to the majority of the manuscripts, the phrase ἡ πύλη ('the
gate') is to be read in verse 13b following πλατεῖα ('wide'). That lets
the parallelism between verse 13 and verse 14 seem flawless, but for
that very reason it could be secondary polishing. The omission of ἡ
πύλη is supported by ℵ, it, and by some church fathers and has in its
favor the argument of *lectio difficilior*. A further variant is found in
verse 14a, where a few manuscripts (Min 5:44, lat, church fathers) do
not report the phrase ἡ πύλη; because of weak attestation this can be
judged a secondary reading. Also, the manuscript tradition in verse
14a varies between the reading τί ('as'), which is also favored by
Nestle²⁶, and ὅτι, which is supported by ℵ, B, as well as a broad
manuscript foundation and, because of the parallelism (cf. v. 13b), will
be presupposed in the following discussion. The variant τί can be
explained as scribal error.

At this point in the New Testament, we have the Old
Testament-Jewish teaching of the two ways.³ Its roots reach
back to the Old Testament blessing-curse concept. Blessed by

God is the one who walks in the way of God's commandments, but cursed is the one who strays from those commandments (Deut 11:26; cf. 30:15). The ways are related to each other as life and death (Jer 21:8). Although the wisdom tradition was familiar with a teaching of two ways (cf. Sir 2:12), it was especially the Jewish apocaplyptic that prepared for the Christian understanding, since it linked monitory aims with apocalyptic motivation.[4] As a monitory cliché, it is widespread in the post-New Testament period[5] and in the rabbinical tradition.[6]

Thus, the presynoptic tradition reached back to a known view when it linked the two-ways teaching with the image of the wide and narrow gates. The combination of prophetic call to decision, wisdom teaching, and apocalyptic motivation had already left its stamp on the proclamation of the historical Jesus.[7] In the Q source the image saying has a monitory function. The relationship here between the gate and the way need not concern us. Perhaps there is an underlying conception of a fortified municipal design in which the city is protected first by outer gates, then by a street restricted by protective walls. It is also possible that gate and way represent parallel concepts and two different images for the one assertion that finding the entrance into life is difficult, but the way to destruction is easy to locate. In any case, the two sayings are not to be interpreted allegorically (for example, gate = systematic doctrine; way = ethical conduct of life), and in the Q tradition they were already a component of ethical admonition to the eschatological community. The aim is the summons to keep in mind the risk of the way and to recognize as binding the instruction of the Son of man/Judge of the world. The saying also has an eschatological-monitory direction in Luke's Gospel. There it occurs in the redactional context of a judgment speech of Jesus, which—placed in the Lukan travel report with the focal point of Jerusalem (13:22)—holds out the prospect to the "first" that they will knock on the door in vain and be counted among the "last" and the left out (13:25-30). The hearers of Jesus, on the other hand, are invited to strive, so that they can enter through the door (13:24).

When Luke adopts from the Q saying, not the word "gate,"

but the conception of the "door," it refers to the image of an entrance to a banquet room in which the meal of the kingdom of God will be celebrated. By contrast, Matthew follows the original Q tradition, since, through the parallelism of the image saying, he offers a choice between two possibilities of comprehending human life. This call to decision invites the community and the world to recognize the claim of the *Kyrios*. If his instruction is not recognized by the πολλοί ('many'), then they are pronouncing judgment on themselves; they are on the way to destruction.[8] For the ὀλίγοι ('few'), however, the eschatological-ethical demand of Jesus is the prerequisite to salvation, for it opens the entrance to life (cf. 18:8; 19:16, 29; 25:26). This means nothing other than that they will be granted entrance into the kingdom of God (5:20; 19:23-24; cf. 22:12; 23:13) and participation in the eschatological joy (25:21, 23). The assertion that only a few will find this way (cf. also 11:25; 22:14) does not cause Matthew to comprehend the providence of God rationally,[9] nor to understand salvation as a gift,[10] but rather establishes the urgency of the admonition.

2.6.2   7:15-20   The False Prophets

Barth, G. "Das Gesetzesverständnis des Evangelisten Matthäus." In G. Bornkamm et al., *Überlieferung* (54-154), 68-69, 149-54.

Böcher, O. "Wölfe in Schafspelzen. Zum religionsgeschichtlichen Hintergrund von Matth. 7,15." *TZ* 24 (1968): 405-26.

Cothenet, É. "Les prophètes chrétien dans l'Évangile selon saint Matthieu." In *L'Évangile selon Matthieu*, edited by M. Didier, 281-308. BETL 29. 1972.

Daniel, C. "'Faux Prophètes': surnom des Esséniens dans le Sermon sur la Montagne." *RevQ* 7 (1969): 45-79.

Hill, D. "False Prophets and Charismatics: Structure and Interpretation in Matthew 7,15-23." *Bib* 57 (1976): 327-48.

Krämer, M. "Hütet euch vor den falschen Phopheten." *Bib* 57 (1976): 349-77.

Marguerat. *Jugement*, 168-211.

Minear, P. S. "False Prophecy and Hypocrisy in the Gospel of Matthew." In *Neues Testament und Kirche*, FS R. Schnackenburg, edited by J. Gnilka, 76-93. 1974.

Schürmann, H. "Die Warnung des Lukas vor der Falschlehre in der 'Predigt am Berge' Lk 6, 20-49" (1966). In idem, *Traditionsgeschichtliche Untersuchungen zu den synoptischen Evangelien*, 290-309. 1968.

Schweizer, E. "Matthäus 7,14-23" (1973). In idem, *Matthäus und seine Gemeinde*, 126-31. SBS 71. 1974.

Zumstein, J. "La condition du croyant dans l'évangile selon Matthieu." *Orbis Biblicus et Orientalis* 16 (1977): 178-87.

Matthew 7   Luke 6

*15Beware of false prophets, who
come to you in sheep's clothing but
inwardly are ravenous wolves.
16You will know them by their
fruits. Are grapes gathered from
thorns, or figs from thistles?
17So, every sound tree bears
good fruit, but the bad tree bears
evil fruit.
18A sound tree cannot bear evil
fruit, nor can a bad tree bear good
fruit.*

*43For no good tree bears bad
fruit, nor again does a bad tree
bear good fruit;
44for each tree is known by its
own fruit. For figs are not
gathered from thorns, nor are
grapes picked from a bramble
bush.
45The good man out of the good
treasure of his heart produces
good, and the evil man out of his
evil treasure produces evil; for
out of the abundance of the heart
his mouth speaks.*

*19Every tree that does not bear
good fruit is cut down and thrown
into the fire.
20Thus you will know them by
their fruits.*

A person who decides on the narrow and hard way and
accepts the word of God's Son as the sole binding instruction is
still not secure. He must be on his guard, since many dangers
press in on him and on the community as a whole. Such a threat
are the ψευδοπροφῆται ('false prophets'). Their appearance
can divert not only individual Christians but also the total community from the right way. They are named in this section as
an example of the possible dangers in the history of the church,
and at the same time the criterion is made known which will
help unmask false prophecy, in order to escape its threat.

The literary criticism of this text is especially complicated. Even a first comparison with the parallel Luke 6:43-45, however, will show that Matthew took the theme of the false prophets from an older Q pericope, whose tradition he also used in 12:33-35, bound it with partially disparate material, and placed it independently in the middle of this section.

The Q parallel Luke 6:43-45 contains a parable that divides into symbolic and objective parts. Verses 43-44 present three images (of the good and bad trees and their fruit, of the thorns that bear no figs, and of the bramble bush that bears no grapes); verse 45 expresses the application (of the treasure of the good and evil men and their words). Although the details differ,[11] there is no doubt that Matthew had before him, in the Q tradition available to him, not only the essential part of the images but also the application. For Matt 12:33-35 attests the image of the good and bad trees and their fruit, as well as the relationship to people's words (v. 34) and the application of the treasure of good and evil people (v. 35). Even the problem of the standard of recognition (Luke 6:44a) is reported in Matt 12:33c and belongs to the Q tradition.

On this basis, the following statements can be perceived as pre-Matthean: corresponding to Luke 6:44, the substance of verse 16a (the standard of recognition) and verse 16b (the image of the thorns and thistles); parallel to Matt 12:33, the positive image of the good and bad trees in verse 17, even if in the present context it appears as a "secondary doubling of verse 18."[12] The negative image of the good and bad trees in verse 18 is also reported in Luke 6:43. Finally, the connection of the tree and judgment motifs in verse 19 (cf. 3:10 par. Luke 3:9) is pre-Matthean.

From this we may conclude that the redactor Matthew is essentially responsible for the framing of the tradition. The warning against false prophets (v. 15) and the closing admonition ("You will know them by their fruits"—v. 20) give the piece its redactional orientation. Beyond that, the Matthean insertion of the judgment motif (v. 19) is of special significance for the interpretation.

7:15. Matthew found before him the conception of the false prophets, which was known from the Old Testament,[13] in connection with the Markan apocalypse. There false prophets are named along with false Christs; both want to lead astray even the elect through wonders (Mark 13:21) and are counted among the apocalyptic signs of the present (Mark 13:5). Matthew distinguishes more clearly than Mark between the appearance of the future false prophecy of the end time (Matt 24:5, 11, 24) and the present situation of his community. Thus, the foretelling of apocalyptic persecution (Mark 13:9-12) is anticipated in the mission speech, for the church of Matthew's time was threatened with acute persecution (Matt 10:17-21; cf. 5:11-12). The fact that the Preacher on the mount expresses in our text the warning against false prophets makes clear the tension in which Matthew's community lives: on its way it is threatened by false prophecy, not later in the eschatological future that is still to come, but now, in the present.

The attempt to identify the false prophets with specific contemporary groups has led to numerous suggestions. A. Schlatter thinks of "the zealot movement within Jewry" at the time of the Jewish war. This thesis is based on the idea that "the separation between the two religions" had not been completed[14]—an improbable assertion when one considers that the prophets belong to the community and (according to 24:5) appear in the name of Christ. Moreover, this suggestion implicitly presupposes the priority of Matthew and the composition of this tradition during the Jewish war.[15]

There is a greater probability for the supposition that Matthew is polemicizing against a group of opponents who taught the abolition of the law and also practiced it as libertines and antinomians.[16] The texts giving apparent support to this suggestion are 5:17, the connection of 7:15-20 with 7:21-23, and 24:11-12. In particular, 24:11-12 seems to suggest a close link between seduction by false prophets and the rise of lawlessness and "cooling of love," and to reveal the adversaries as an antinomian movement. Yet 24:11-12 attests no direct connection between false prophecy (v. 11) and the increase in lawlessness (v. 12: $\dot{\alpha}\nu o\mu\dot{\iota}\alpha$), but only the assertion that in the end time various oppressions and threats to the Christian community are expected, which are listed in this context without any material connection. As much as immorality and lack of love, along with persecution and the appearance of false prophets, are counted among the apocalyptic events, it does not say directly that false prophets will appear as teachers of lawlessness, and to do so would unjustly restrict the Matthean conception of the overdue event of the end time. In 5:17, likewise, the Evangelist does not have an antinomian group in mind. He mentions only a theoretical possibility, namely, that Jesus came to abolish the law.[17] In regard to our present text, the following section (vv. 21-23) only appears to illustrate the Matthean image of false prophecy. In truth the generalizing beginning (v. 21: $o\dot{\upsilon} \pi\hat{\alpha}\varsigma$ 'not every one') means a new declarative direction in terms of content; it is repeated in the likewise generalizing introduction of the closing parables (verses 24, 26: $\pi\hat{\alpha}\varsigma$ 'every one'). Both times Jesus addresses the behavior of his hearers, that is, the Christian community as a whole; there is no special reference to a certain intrachurch party.

When the Preacher on the mount warns of false prophets, and thereby takes up Old Testament traditions, he is not confronted with a particular group of opponents but is indicating, rather, a danger that threatens the church in all times.[18] Similarly, in his farewell address at Miletus, the Apostle Paul warned the elders that from the ranks of the community "fierce wolves" would appear, and he summons them to watchfulness in face of such a threat. The historian Luke is not thinking here of a particular heresy, but is consciously putting in Paul's mouth a warning that can be applied to the heresies of all ages (Acts 20:29-30). The same is true for Matthew: at the close of the Sermon on the Mount, the view is broadened to the future of the church. As the Lord of the universe, the Son of God gives obligatory instruction "to the close of the age" (28:20). The Christian community is threatened not only by persecution from without but also by seduction from within. The danger of false teaching and prophecy will accompany the community on its way through history, without the concrete utterances of the pseudoprophets being predictable, and without the element of unpredictability and unrecognizability being taken from them in advance (cf. 13:24-30).

When the false prophets present themselves as wolves in sheep's clothing, this idea presupposes that the Christian community understands itself as a "flock."[19] Hardly likely is the idea that the false prophets will actually be clothed in garments of sheepskin, as is often presumed on the basis of Mark 1:6. The sense of the image is rather that the seducers cannot be distinguished outwardly from ordinary members of the community. All the more dangerous is their appearance. As "ravenous wolves" they devastate and destroy the Christian fellowship.[20]

7:16. The image of the thorns that bring forth no grapes and of the thistles that produce no figs[21] also has, according to widespread interpretation, the task of illustrating the possibility of confusion. Thus ἄκανθα ('thorns') would be equivalent to wild grapevines that bear no genuine grapes, while τρίβολι ('thistles') are identical to wild fig trees.[22] Hence, the idea seems to offer itself that the fruits of these plants can be confused with genuine grapes and genuine figs, and that community members, faced with the attractive external appearance of the false prophets, can be easily deceived about their true intentions. Yet the twin concepts of "thorns and thistles" is attested in the religious-historical environment frequently and unambiguously for the weeds in a field,[23] so that such an idea has little probability. Rather, this image points to an assertion about the nature of false prophets and their works: if their nature is comparable to that of weeds and rapacious wolves, then nothing good can be expected from their works either.[24]

7:17-18. Thus is it explained in the double antithetical parallelism of the good and evil trees, which follows immediately. Although οὕτως ('so') seems to introduce a subsequent application, the positive assertion about the fruits of the trees (v. 17) is hardly an original continuation. Also, it is not a question of an application but of another image. The negatively constructed saying (v. 18) continues better the train of thought of verse 16. Nonetheless, Matthew may have found verse 17 already in this location (cf. 12:33). This verse, in combination with verse 18, contains an explanation of the nature of tempters and the relationship of their nature to their deeds. If—as the Q tradition has already established—it is not possible for a sound tree to produce evil fruit or a bad tree good fruit, then this also asserts the agreement of the evil nature and evil deeds of false prophets. It goes without saying that we should not ask the critical question of whether a good tree could also bring forth bad fruit and vice versa; nor is it a question here of a fundamental reflection on the abstract nature of humanity or of false teachers.[25] Rather, the image may have been used polemically even in the Q tradition, in disagreement with Jesus' opponents (cf. Matt 12:34). The sense of the argumentation is that out of the asserted identity of nature and deed can be derived the criterion for recognition: the evil person can be known by his evil works (verse 16a, 20).

7:19. The almost literal incorporation of the threatening words of the baptismal sermon (3:10) underlines the seriousness of the situation and of the warning. As an unfruitful tree falls prey to annihilation, thus also is the fate of false prophecy. The word πῦρ ('fire') points beyond the image of the tree and contains the idea of apocalyptic punishment, which threatens those who take offense and turn from the way of Jesus (cf. 13:42, 50; 25:41). It is identical to the loss of eternal life

(18:8-9; 25:40). Naturally, the community is also addressed with this warning and indirectly admonished to bring forth "good fruit." This prepares the way for the assertion in the following section (vv. 21-23).

7:20. With the concluding particle ἄρα γε ('thus'), the application is attached, and—as already indicated in verse 16*a*—it represents the actual theme of the section. The warning against false prophecy is a summons to the community vis-à-vis the threat of heresy to apply the offered criterion of recognition and watch the "fruits." The future ἐπιγνώσεσθε has imperative meaning ('you shall know!'). This admonition anticipates the later heresiological identification of false doctrine and immorality.[26] The Didache affirms that such a trait of recognition was practiced in the early Christian communities of Syria and explains how it was used.[27] Even if it seems to have little application in the individual case, it implies the timeless demand of the Christian community not to put itself on the same level as the false prophets but to meet the ethical demand of Jesus with proper action.[28]

2.6.3 7:21-23 The Necessity of Deeds

Betz, H. D. "Eine Episode im Jüngsten Gericht (Mt 7,21-23)". *ZTK* 78 (1981): 1-30.
Schneider, G. "Christusbekenntnis und christliches Handeln. Lk 6,46 und Mt 7,21 im Kontext der Evangelien." In *Die Kirche des Anfangs*, FS H. Schürmann, edited by R. Schnackenburg et al., 9-24. 1978.
Otherwise cf. Marguerat, *Jugement*, 192, and above on 7:15-20.

Matthew 7	Luke 6
[21]*Not every one who says to me, "Lord, Lord," shall enter the kingdom of heaven, but he who does the will of my Father who is in heaven. [22]On that day many will say to me, "Lord, Lord, did we not prophesy in your name, and cast out demons in your name, and do many mighty works in your name?" [23]And then will I*	[46]*"Why do you call me 'Lord, Lord,' and not do what I tell you?"*

declare to them, "I never knew
you; depart from me, you evil-
doers."

The criterion of the right deed is not to be applied only with
regard to false prophecy: it is all the more valid for the
Christian community with all its members. The fact that the
following generalized beginning with οὐ πᾶς ('not every one')
will be taken up by the likewise generally aimed final parables
(verses 24, 26: πᾶς 'every one') makes clear that after the
subtheme "false prophecy," the whole community and,
indeed, all hearers of Jesus are now addressed and are the
object of the admonition.

Again, the literary criticism of this section is not without complication.
Verse 21 has a parallel in Luke 6:46, whose location corresponds to
the Matthean composition. The fact that immediately before the
closing parables, in both the Sermon on the Plain and the Sermon on
the Mount, judgment is pronounced on the "Lord, Lord" sayers
reveals that in Q there was already a summons to action at the close of
this composed speech. Verse 21 is decisively marked by Matthew's
language;[29] even the antithetical formation (οὐ . . . ἀλλ' 'not . . . but')
is redactional. In dispute and ultimately not to be answered is the
question whether in the Q source verses 22-23 followed verse 21.[30]
Originally, they were passed down as an isolated saying, as the parallel
Luke 13:26-27 makes probable. According to form and content,
Matthew has priority over Luke. Whereas Matthew addresses the
community and has especially Christian charismatics in mind, Luke
directs the statement against the Jews. The fact that Luke thereby
adopts the intention of his context (13:22-33) speaks for secondary
status.[31] Luke also strongly influenced the text linguistically. By
contrast, Matt 7:22-23 exhibits a non-Matthean flow of language.[32]
The quotation from Ps 6:8 in the last part seems to have been
assimilated by Matthew to the LXX (τὴν ἀνομίαν: lit., 'the
unlawfulness'); the first part of the quotation in Luke 13:27, however,
is closer to the LXX. Result: verses 22-23 are for the most part
pre-Matthean. Luke eliminated their focus on the Christian
charismatics and, by applying it to Jewish contemporaries of Jesus,
softened the original meaning.

7.21. Attaching a key word with the verb ποιεῖν ('do'; vv. 21,
19) stresses again at the end of the Sermon on the Mount that
the ethical deed represents for the life of Christians a binding
necessity. The "admittance saying with definitive character"[33]

proclaimed by verse 21 takes up the theme of the Sermon on the Mount (5:20).

The conditions of the kingdom of God are not fulfilled by the one who only joins in the community cry κύριε κύριε ('Lord, Lord'). This Semitically shaped double naming reflects the *Kyrios* Christology that leads back to the Aramaic liturgical acclamation *maranatha* (1 Cor 16:22: "Our Lord, come!"), and in the Pauline communities corresponds to the cry "Jesus is Lord" (1 Cor 12:3). In numerous instances, the first Evangelist makes known that the title *Kyrios* contains a confessional assertion.[34] Thus, the apocalyptic parables speak of the coming κύριος who will certainly come, even if his arrival is delayed (24:42, 44; 25:19), and on the judgment day, his verdict will fall severely (24:46, 50). He is the "bridegroom" whom those who come too late will beg in vain for admittance with the cry κύριε κύριε (25:11 par. Luke 13:25). It is characteristic of Matthew that the *Kyrios* form of addressing the earthly Jesus comes exclusively from the disciples and the sufferers who beg for healing.[35] Jesus' adversaries, on the other hand, use the title "teacher."[36] From this it follows that, according to Matthew, the "Lord, Lord" sayers belong to the Christian community. It does not matter where they make their *Kyrios* confession—in worship vis-à-vis the exalted One, as the last generation before the Son of God/Judge of the world, or as disciples vis-à-vis the earthly Jesus as a teacher—such a confession will do them no good. The decisive foundation of Christian existence is not the word but the deed.[37]

The deed that is expected of Jesus' followers is the realization of God's will (cf. 12:50; 21:31), which is authoritatively interpreted and proclaimed by Jesus.[38] The ethical attitude demanded by him as Lord of the community is different not only from a libertine or antinomian way of life, but also from the demeanor of the Pharisees, as polemically delineated in the First Gospel (cf. 6:1ff.; 23:1ff.). The ethical conduct of life of Christians is oriented neither toward a worldly realm nor toward the human ego; it is directed toward the God who is proclaimed as the Father of Jesus Christ,[39] and who, through such proclamation, makes possible sonship of God for the followers of Jesus (5:9, 16; 6:25ff.).

7:22. The statement that before the Judge of the world at the final judgment "many" will refer in vain to their membership in the community recalls 7:13, where "many" will take the broad road to destruction (cf. Luke 13:24). "On that day,"[40] earlier verbal profession of Jesus will not suffice, nor will the fact that one has completed pneumatic deeds in the name of Jesus. It is well attested that the early Christian communities had experiences of the Spirit,[41] and thus we may also assume that Matthew's church was familiar with and practiced charismatic utterances. As "prophecy" these are related to the proclamation of the word. Thus, the persecuted community can console itself that it stands in the tradition of the Old Testament prophets (5:12). It grants prophets a hospitable reception (10:41) and counts them with wise men and scribes as Christian officeholders (23:34). Charismatic consciousness also appears in exorcisms and other mighty works. In this the Matthean community finds itself in continuity with the demeanor of Jesus. Just as Jesus drove out demons with the Spirit of God (12:28; cf. 4:23; 11:20; 12:15; and elsewhere), so also in the early Christian communities demon expulsions and miraculous deeds were effected through the Spirit (cf. of the disciples: 10:8; 12:10). For this reason, like Jesus they draw the Beelzebul reproach (10:25; cf. 9:34). Such mighty deeds occur ἐν τῷ ὀνόματι ('in the name') of the *Kyrios*. With the appeal of prayer or only with the expression of his name, the exalted, coming Lord is present in his church and powerfully active through the Spirit (18:20; 28:20).

7:23. With the word ὁμολογήσω ('I will declare'), Matthew takes up antithetically the declaration of the "many" (v. 21-22). On the day of the final judgment, no reference to a declaration for the *Kyrios* will save anyone from the verdict. In an antideclaration, the Judge of the world will distance himself from the "Lord, Lord" sayers. He will meet them with the banishment formula that he "never knew" them.[42] While the closing quotation of Ps 6:8 by the Evangelist comes close to the concept of "unlawfulness" of the LXX, here the content of verse 21 is taken up antithetically: the community is obligated to doing the will of God, which is the "law" that demands from it unconditional fulfillment.[43]

Since the call to decision forms the framework of this closing section,[44] this passage also has a monitory direction. The antithetical structure of verse 21 points to an admonition. The summons to action (vv. 22-23)—like the ethical instruction of Jesus in general—is motivated by the prospect of the *eschaton* (cf. v. 19). If the ethical demand in the Sermon on the Mount points up the necessity of obedience to the will of God, then its direction becomes clear in this text.

What is new in our text is that the object of the warning is the charismatic life of the community. No doubt a certain caution is thereby expressed: pneumatic mighty works cannot and ought not to be constitutive of the Christian life. Perhaps this was said even in the Q tradition in response to the misuse of charismatic gifts. During the Pauline period, an excess of enthusiastic phenomena is attested for Corinth. Mark 9:38-41 gives an example of how one should regard the relationship of community order to exorcists. There a more tolerant position is documented. Since "no one who does a mighty work in my name will be able soon after to speak evil of me" (verse 39), the nonfollower is allowed to carry out exorcisms in the name of Jesus. By contrast, Matthew seems less ready for concession and overlooks this Markan pericope. For him it is crucial that the name of Jesus be acknowledged through right action. A miracle is useless if it is done with an attitude of "unlawfulness." In reporting the miracles of Jesus, the redactor of the First Gospel lifts up the "word" and often transforms the synoptic miracle stories into exemplary didactic tales.[45] Accordingly, in our text charismatic works are relativized and subordinated to the ethical demand. The message of the Preacher on the mount to the community is not to trust in miraculous experiences but to do what is right!

2.6.4   7:24-27   The Closing Parables: On the Wise and Foolish Builders

Flusser, D. *Die rabbinischen Gleichnisse und der Gleichniserzähler Jesus* 1:98ff. 1981.
Jeremias. *Gleichnisse*, 193.
Ornella, A. "Les chrétiens seront jugés. Mt 7,21-27." *AsSeign* 40 (1972): 16-27.

Matthew 7	Luke 6
[24]*Every one then who hears these words of mine and does them will be like a wise man who built his house upon the rock;* [25]*and the*	[47]*Every one who comes to me and hears my words and does them, I will show you what he is like:* [48]*he is like a man building a*

rain fell, and the floods came, and the winds blew and beat upon that house, but it did not fall, because it had been founded on the rock.

²⁶And every one who hears these words of mine and does not do them will be like a foolish man who built his house upon the sand; ²⁷and the rain fell, and the floods came, and the winds blew and beat against that house, and it fell; and great was the fall of it.

house, who dug deep, and laid the foundation upon rock; and when a flood arose, the stream broke against that house, and could not shake it, because it had been well built.

⁴⁹But he who hears and does not do them is like a man who built a house on the ground without a foundation; against which the stream broke, and immediately it fell, and the ruin of that house was great.

As the parallel Luke 6:47-49 demonstrates, in the Q source the double parable of the Wise and Foolish Builders already stood at the close of the speech. Its form of faultless antithetical parallelism places an impressive capstone on the structure of the Sermon on the Mount.

Literary-critical analysis shows that the symmetrical construction in the Matthean version was largely destroyed in Luke, who links the parable to the foregoing context. With the words ὁ ἐρχόμενος πρός με ('who comes to me') verse 47 connects with the summation of Jesus' healings (6:18).[46] Moreover, Luke writes more graphically; he describes the execution of the house building, particularly the activity of the builders. According to Luke, the house is erected on a floodplain (cf. the singular ποταμός 'river,' 'stream'—v. 48-49), whereas Matthew is apparently thinking of construction on a sloping landscape, so that the house could be endangered by rain-swollen streams from the mountain.[47] Linguistic observations reveal that Luke's version is more Greek that the Matthean parallel; it may go back largely to the third Evangelist himself. By contrast, among the Matthean linguistic traits are the introduction from the context (οὖν 'then,' τούτους 'these'), the finite verb ὁμοιωθήσεται (vv. 24, 26: 'will be like'; vs. Luke 6:47: ὅμοιος 'like'), perhaps also the more concrete indication ἀνήρ ('man' vs. ἄνθρωπος 'human being'), and the identification with φρόνιμος and μωρός (vv. 24, 26: 'wise' and 'foolish').[48]

Unlike Luke, Matthew stresses not the activity of the builders but the fate of the two houses, which are threatened by the elements of nature, by the βροχή ('rain'), by the ποταμοί ('floods') streaming from the mountain, and by the ἄνεμοι ('winds'). While the house built on the rock withstood this assault, the one erected on sand fell. That its fall is "great" could indicate the parabolic nature of the image, but is probably only a proverbial way of speaking.[49] Also in other respects the parable may not be allegorized. The term οἰκία ('house') is not used symbolically for the community—this assumption is excluded by the personal pronoun αὐτοῦ ('his') in verse 24. Also, we are not to think that the powers of nature are supposed to represent the "temptations of life,"[50] or that the catastrophic flood in Genesis provides the model for the threat of inundation.[51] As A. Jülicher has explained in detail, allegorization is foreign to Jesus' proclamation in parables.[52] Matthew's intended main point is to be derived from the opposition of the two builders and their houses: the double parable is nothing but a graphically executed call to decision.

The call to decision and to repentance is an essential component of the language of the Revealer.[53] It is present in the blessing and curse sayings of the Old Testament as well as in the later Jewish-apocalyptic teaching of the two ways.[54] The rabbinical literature exhibits near parallels. Thus the following parable is ascribed to Elisha ben Abuja (c. A.D. 120):

> With whom can we compare a person who has many good works and has learned much Torah? With a person who builds underneath with stones and afterward with adobe; even if a great deal of water comes and remains beside them, it will not loosen them from their place. But with whom can we compare a person who has no good works and learns no Torah? With a person who first builds with adobe and then with stones; even if only a small amount of water comes, it will topple them at once.[55]

Also Rabbi Eleazar ben Azarja (c. A.D. 100) says:

> What is one like whose knowledge surpasses his deeds? A tree whose branches are many and whose roots are few; when the wind comes, it will uproot it and overturn it. . . . But what is one like whose deeds surpass his knowledge? A tree whose branches are few and whose roots are many; even if all the winds in the world come and blow into it, they will not move it away from its place.[56]

These rabbinical parables relate the context of decision to the relationship between the person's deeds and his knowledge of the Torah. Thus, as in our text, the relationship between hearing and doing lies at the center of the parabolic assertion: it is not enough to study the Torah and hear its teaching; its instruction must be carried out! In the placing of doing above hearing, the Q tradition and Matthew agree with the rabbinical understanding.[57] But Matthew, more clearly than the sayings source, relates the hearing and doing not to the Torah but to the words of Jesus.[58] In the Sermon on the Mount, the Son of God claims for himself the authority that Judaism accords to the Torah. His demand calls his hearers to decision and gives them the choice of behaving like the smart or the stupid builder.[59] The "wise man" is the person who grasps the eschatological situation created by Jesus and makes it his own by doing the word. The "foolish man" is anyone who shuts himself off from the eschatological situation and does not observe Jesus' demand. The forces of nature described in the parable are thus not to be identified with dangers that threaten the individual Christian on his life's way; they symbolize, rather, the verdict in the final judgment. There it will be decided whether human existence is built on sand or on rock.[60] Whoever fulfills the demand of the *Kyrios* can look forward confidently to that time. The foolish man, on the other hand, whose hearing does not lead to action, will be subjected to the πτῶσις, the great "fall." Thus, it is not just that the hearing of Jesus' words is supposed to be followed up with appropriate action; rather, only in action does proper hearing take place. This rejects an unreflective activism as much as an escapist piety. Blind involvement misses the will of God as much as fruitless theologizing. The salvation-filled meaning of the words of the Preacher on the mount is discovered only through meeting his demand.

If Matthew in his Gospel represents Jesus as the *Kyrios* who will appear in judgment at the end of the world as the Son of man, he also holds that the epiphany of the Judge of the world will be determined by his appearance on earth. The judgment verdict will be related to the fulfillment or nonfulfillment of the words of the earthly Son of God. If these words in our text are the subject of the demand for decision of the Preacher on the mount, so also is his disciples' world-encompassing mission to the nations (28:20*a*). Jesus' demand receives an eschatological and a soteriological meaning. In his Gospel Matthew attempts to explain that this demand is obligatory. No one can escape its radicality under the pretext of its unrealizability; it is rather a directive instituted to be fulfilled. It keeps before our eyes the goal that obligates both the individual Christian and the community as a whole to the unconditional service of discipleship while on their way through time.

2.7   7:28-29   Epilogue

28And when Jesus finished these sayings, the crowds were astonished at his teaching, 29for he taught them as one who had authority, and not as their scribes.

With the solemn καὶ ἐγένετο ('and it happened'), borrowed from the language of the LXX, Matthew returns to the situation described at the beginning of the Sermon on the Mount. In the Q source there was already a formula at the end of the speech, as attested in a similar way by the parallel Luke 7:1*a*. If this establishes the end of the Sermon on the Mount,[61] the Matthean demonstrative pronoun τούτους ('these') refers back expressly to the words of the Preacher on the mount.[62]

The first Evangelist combines Q and the Markan tradition. In Q the ὄχλοι ('crowds') were presupposed as hearers of the speech (cf. Luke 7:1*a*; Matt 5:1), and Mark also reports on the effect of Jesus' teachings (Mark 1:22, 27). The listeners "were astonished" (ἐξεπλήσσοντο), either out of fear (thus 19:25 par. Mark 10:26) or out of amazement (also 22:33 par. Mark 11:18). Since the crowds in the First Gospel are generally presented as the applauding accompaniment of Jesus,[63] such a statement seems at first nothing but a rhetorical device for emphasizing the significance of Jesus' teaching. Because the ἐξουσία of Jesus is named as the reason for the astonishment, however, a specifically christological assertion is involved here. This 'authority' is different from that of the scribes. The personal pronoun αὐτῶν[64] indicates a distance. Matthew carries back into Jesus' time the dissociated relationship of his community and their scribes vis-à-vis the rabbis of Judaism. In this way the independence of Jesus' authority is emphasized.

Different from the Jewish scribes, the Son of God does not formulate his instruction in connection with and as interpretations of inherited doctrinal opinions. His authority is that of the Lord of the community. It stands not only over the claim of the Jewish scribes but also over the Torah of Moses. As the *Kyrios* invested with eschatological authority, Jesus proclaims the will of his Father. His demand has a significance that excludes all other instructions.

3 Outlook

3.1. As we have seen, through probability judgments—not least of all through the "growth criterion"—the oldest material in the Sermon on the Mount can be shown to be a component of the proclamation of the historical Jesus. This historical core is more extensive than previous critical research has been ready to assume yet not as encompassing as presupposed in conservative-fundamentalist interpretation. Included above all are the three oldest beatitudes, a series of three antitheses, the Lord's Prayer, and other verbal material that in the course of tradition history has experienced manifold changes before the redactor Matthew put it into its final form.

The message of Jesus must be interpreted in connection with the disparate Judaism of his time. Indeed, Jesus lived as a Jew in Galilee and Judea, and he died in Jerusalem, the capital of Judaism. As Mark and Matthew make known, his message is the proclamation of the approaching kingdom of God, which is linked to the call to repentance: "Repent, for the kingdom of heaven is at hand" (Matt 4:17*a*). In a similar way before him, of course, the Old Testament prophets and John the Baptist had called for repentance; yet his message—as the antitheses of the Sermon on the Mount show—makes a new claim that is highly concrete in terms of content. This is seen already in the first antithesis: Jesus starts with an Old Testament commandment from the Decalogue (Exod 20:13)—which he can presume to be known and acknowledged by his hearers—so that he can oppose it with his own "but I say to you," a counterthesis that does not revoke the Old Testament demand but attempts to make clear its true content and claim. Not just the one who kills his brother will be brought to judgment but also the one who is angry with his brother (5:21-22*a*).

The interpretation that Jesus gives to the fifth commandment lies beyond the traditional Jewish possibilities of exegesis. The claim made by Jesus for himself and his teaching is that of

174

a new interpretation of the Torah that strengthens the validity of the Torah in a way that reveals the true radical nature of the Decalogue's demand. With this, not only a quantitative but also a qualitative change is achieved vis-à-vis the traditional understanding. With Jesus' radical exegesis of the fifth commandment, which consigns to judgment not only the murderer but also the angry person, a fundamental shift in the theological horizon has occurred.

This becomes clear when one asks about the judgment that is presupposed here. In Jesus' time, the court to which a murderer was consigned according to Jewish legal practice was the Sanhedrin, which in accordance with the Torah imposed either exile or the death penalty.[1] This court of justice was to some extent both secular and divine judgment in one. Jesus is not thinking of that same judicial forum when he has the angry person consigned to judgment; he has in mind the eschatological judgment of God. The validity of his Torah interpretation will be proved before the final judgment and will serve there as the criterion of justice, which he proclaims with radical seriousness. For Jesus, it is thus not a matter of an ethical refinement according to human standards, for which Jewish parallels can be indicated, but of the revelation of the true eschatological forum of justice and the nonhuman justice of God.[2]

The following two antitheses, which in terms of content belong together, also confirm this image. Although Jesus equates the lustful look with the carrying out of adultery (5:27-28), such a fundamental assertion stands in the tradition of Jewish Torah exegesis. It is already formulated with similar sharpness by Jewish wisdom teaching as well as in the rabbinical tradition.[3] But here, too, a shift in accent has occurred: in the context of Jesus' proclamation, there is no interest in a casuistic interpretation of the commandment. The legal standard for establishing guilt or innocence in the Torah community is completely turned back to the relationship between the individual and God. What Jesus reveals is the inner, secret disobedience of the heart—so aptly expressed by Matthew—with which the person seeks to hide himself before God and his commandment. Before God there are no pretexts for circumventing obedience to the commandment. The demand is for the undivided obedience of outward action and inward effort. In view of this interpretation of the law by Jesus, it is clear that here a person's brokenness before God becomes apparent and will be finally disclosed in the eschatological judgment. In the revelation of the absolute claim of the law, the proper sphere of Jesus' proclamation is found anew.

No less than his statement on adultery, Jesus' absolute prohibition of divorce, which forms the tradition-historical point of origin of the third antithesis, goes beyond the rabbinical Torah exegesis (5:31-32). Although the rabbis recognized more or less legitimate grounds for divorce according to the school to which they belonged, Jesus' commandment opposes them with unconditional, uncompromising radicality. When Jesus absolutely rejects any grounds for divorce, we can no longer speak of a strengthening of the Torah; it is a question, rather, of a fundamental critique and revision of the Torah. The Old Testament provides a regulated procedure for divorce (Deut 24:1ff.). Jesus' interpretation, however, expounds the fundamental incompatibility of the institution of divorce with the sixth commandment and proclaims a new, more radical law that forbids divorce. With the claim of the eschatological prophet, Jesus gives a hearing to the holy will of God, even against the wording of the Torah.

This is recognizable in the demand to turn the other cheek, which in the Matthean context is opposed to the Old Testament law of retribution ("an eye for an eye"—5:38-42). Even in the Old Testament, there is beside the principle of retribution an idea that goes beyond the juridical understanding of righteousness (cf. Lev. 19:18). In the proclamation of Jesus, it can be reduced to an unambiguous common denominator: in the future what will satisfy the demand for righteousness is no longer derivable from a legal claim vis-à-vis one's neighbor, but is realized, on the contrary, precisely in a fundamental renunciation of rights. At this very point, the old symbol of worldly righteousness—the scales of justice that attempt to establish a visible balance through the calculation of guilt and punishment—is turned into injustice.

Not only is the way to public judgment blocked for the hearers of the Sermon on the Mount, however, but also the humanly understandable judgment of one's brother before one's own internal court of justice. From Jesus' instruction not to retaliate for a deed that does me personal injury, a direct line leads through the admonition to renounce judgment of my neighbor (7:1) to the challenge not just to ignore or to spare my enemy but to love him (5:44). With this the last, decisive step is taken toward a radical Christian ethic. Jesus demands not only a passive indulgence, but also an active attitude of love even and precisely toward one's enemy. The commandment of love of enemy is of such unambiguous precision and radicality that it has plainly become the epitome of Christian teaching far beyond the realm of the church. By this first principle of Christian ethics, the followers of the Preacher on the mount have been repeatedly measured and—as history shows— found guilty of their failure vis-à-vis Jesus' claim. In the nature of this extreme demand of Jesus lies the reason why the history of the church—like the history of humankind in general—can be written as a history of closing oneself off from this commandment.

In Jesus' sense, love of enemy is not a principle of action that was developed from human rights or social-cultural models of behavior. It is, as the word itself says, a *paradox*, a commandment from beyond this world. It is the eschatological law of God. The obligation of this commandment is established for the Christian faith through the person of Jesus as the exalted Lord of his community.

Certainly, the commandment of love of enemy is anticipated and rooted in Judaism. The Old Testament-Jewish wisdom tradition teaches, "If your enemy is hungry, give him bread to eat; and if he is thirsty, give him water to drink" (Prov 25:21). This quotation, to which others could be added, shows that even in the Old Testament we find the demand for concrete, loving service to the enemy in need as the commanded attitude of the godly. A broad stream within Jewish thinking anticipates Jesus' commandment of love of enemy. Yet, not until Jesus did it become an ethical demand that claims universal validity beyond religious and national boundaries. The commandment to love one's enemy can be considered the highpoint of God's demands, which Jesus placed up against the Torah and its Jewish tradition. Bound up in this commandment are the essential traits of his sermon. The radical nature of this claim makes his appearance an event without analogy. In the area of the history of religion, the person and teaching of Jesus are a unique and isolated phenomenon. David Flusser has correctly pointed out that there is a considerable difference between this sermon of Jesus oriented toward Judaism and the handing down of the sermon by the Evangelists.[4] The French modernist Alfred Loisy perceived that "Jesus proclaimed the kingdom of God, and what came was the church![5] Without doubt, there is a discrepancy between what Jesus said and wanted and what has become of his teaching.

Jesus and his message stand alone, however, even in the Judaism of his time. His radical call to repentance is directed first of all toward Jewish listeners. His call for inward and outward obedience of the commandments, for renunciation of justice vis-à-vis one's neighbor, for love of enemy—all of this created astonishment and horror (7:28) and caused more misunderstanding and incredulity than faith and obedience. In a time that takes for granted the extinction of the Spirit, Jesus enters as one who defines anew the will of God with pneumatic authority. Also, his demand is always linked with *paraclēsis*, with eschatological exhortation, as the beatitudes (5:3-12) and the Lord's Prayer (6:9-13) indicate. In his claim Jesus is comparable to the Old Testament prophets, and yet he is more than these, since he understands himself, as the herald of God's will, to stand immediately before the end of the world. Today as then the ways of people separate on the question whether in this Jesus the God of the Old Testament has given a new and final, an unconditional form to the revelation of his will. The eschatological Prophet of Nazareth is a *skandalon*—for his Jewish contemporaries as well as for the church in all ages.

3.2 The Sermon on the Mount of the Evangelist Matthew is not to be equated with the message of the historical Jesus. Between the proclamation of Jesus and the writing down of the Sermon on the Mount in Matthew's Gospel lie the cross and the resurrection of Jesus Christ, the Easter event that constitutes the new faith of the Christian church. This faith says that Jesus of Nazareth is the One sent by God, the now exalted *Kyrios*, Messiah, Son of God, and Judge of the world.

The time interval between the Easter event and the composition of Matthew's Gospel amounts to more than forty years. During this time in Palestine and in the other provinces of the Roman Empire, the first Christian communities were forming and gradually leaving the sphere of influence of the synagogue. In them was developing the brisk activity of collecting and passing on the words of Jesus; above all, however, they worked on the proclamation and interpretation of the message of the crucified and resurrected one. As a result of this manifold process of growth and interpretation, Matthew's Gospel came into being as the presentation of a history of Jesus Christ.

For understanding the theological accomplishment of the unknown author, who was schooled in the Jewish Christian scribal tradition, the Sermon on the Mount is significant. In this first of a total of five composed speeches in his work, he interprets Jesus' proclamation for a community that knows the disappointment of the hope of imminent expectation and despite the delay of the Parousia holds fast to this hope—namely, that the crucified and resurrected One will appear as the Son of man/Judge of the world and visibly bring in the kingdom of God. The demands of the Sermon on the Mount are founded on this eschatological future, and yet, at the same time, they receive their authority from the past appearance of Jesus. By accommodating itself to the apocalyptic and wisdom-like teaching of Jesus, the community acknowledges that teaching as the binding claim of its Lord. It understands the Sermon on the Mount as the binding law of the *Kyrios* who is coming and has already come.

At this point, Matthew and his community make no distinction between indicative and imperative, such as we find in the theology of the Apostle Paul; also the differentiation between law and gospel, as it corresponds to the Reformation confessions, is unknown to them. More important, rather, is the fact that the Preacher on the mount, with all of his own radicalism, demands concrete ethical behavior. For Matthew, the Sermon on the Mount is first of all admonition, which is directed toward the followers of Jesus, and only in the second place—in connection with the call to repent—is it intended for the non-Christian world. With it the exalted *Kyrios* gives instruction to a church that is subject to the problems of ongoing time. His proclamation appears in Matthew's Sermon on the Mount, not as an exclusive call to repentance, but as an

offering of ethical demands that culminate in the Golden
Rule (7:12).

That these demands are supposed to be realized in the
practice of the Christian community is shown by Matthew in
exemplary fashion in Jesus' prohibition of divorce. Although it
basically forbids any divorce, and in this respect stands in
contradiction to the Old Testament Torah and Jewish legal
life, the reality of the Christian community, by contrast,
requires a regulation that is adequate for its problems. Hence
Matthew, in agreement with his community, admits an
exception by inserting the condition, "except on the ground of
unchastity" (5:32; cf. 19:9), and thus the marital unfaithfulness of the wife is declared a legitimate reason for divorce.

In similar fashion, the Evangelist changed the fourth
antithesis. If the absolute prohibition of swearing originally
read, "You shall not swear at all," and in the pre-Matthean
tradition was added to the commandment on truthfulness
("Let your yes be yes and your no be no"), then Matthew, by
contrast, reformed the truthfulness commandment into a
formula of a solemn declaration. By saying, "Let what you say
be simply 'Yes' or 'No'; anything more than this comes from
evil" (lit., "yes yes, no no"), he introduces a substitute oath,
which could be used in his community in place of a sworn oath
in the name of God (5:37).

All of these are changes and interpretations of the original
proclamation of Jesus; they make the claim of formulating the
binding will of the exalted One in a new situation and must be
questioned critically, against the background of the message of
Jesus, as to whether they do justice to their claim. Here
occurred, already in the time of the New Testament, what the
church in all ages has the task of doing: it must comprehend
and interpret anew in a changed situation the will of God as
expressed in the message of Jesus. Matthew did this by
interpreting Jesus' radical call to repentance as an ethically
binding demand, and he put this into understandable
language when, with the words *righteousness, perfection,* and
love, he summarized the ethical meaning of the Sermon on
the Mount.

Matthew's community does not maintain that its reality
matches such high demands. It does not claim for itself the
condition of perfection or of unreserved love of God and

neighbor. Rather it knows itself called into service through the word of the Preacher on the mount. From him, it receives the eschatological goal, toward which it moves ever anew through concrete deeds in the everyday world.

3.3. The current importance and attention that the Sermon on the Mount is given in public discussion has its causes least of all within the sphere of the church; rather, the dialogues about and with the Sermon on the Mount have been newly revived by political problems and controversies. There are apparently times in which Jesus' call to repentance is heard more clearly and urgently than in others, especially since the problems humankind has to overcome today have assumed a magnitude hitherto unknown. For the first time in its history, the human race sees itself not just theoretically, but actually faced with the possibility that human life on this earth could be annihilated; and indeed not—as those in the realm of religion were ever and again ready to assume—through an apocalyptic final event effected from beyond, but through a self-initiated atomic blast of annihilation. In the face of this possibility, the key word "love of enemy" acquires importance in the rational calculation of survival, even in politics, where it has been kept out—and not just since Bismarck.[6] It requires no great imagination to determine that there is a similarity of atmosphere and reality between the present-day feeling of a total threat to existence and the eschatological expectation of a world catastrophe that beset many people in the time of Jesus. These are existential questions for which answers are being sought today with the help of the Sermon on the Mount. At this point, the contribution of a New Testament scholar cannot offer any final, comprehensive help in decision-making. His contribution to the discussion, nonetheless, can help to understand the textual foundations better through exegetical analysis and, thereby, to prepare critical standards that make it possible to recognize and reject incorrect interpretative approaches and incorrectly posed exegetical alternatives.

We must start with the idea that the question of the criteria for proper exegesis and truthful obedience of the Sermon on the Mount is, in an ultimate sense, not to be answered and yet not to be abandoned. Agreement with the original literal meaning is a criterion of truth with only limited validity. In the individual case, the very deviation from what is literally commanded can mean obedience in spirit, as one sees realized, for example, in Dietrich Bonhoeffer's lonely decision to resist the Third Reich. The criterion of truth for an appropriate exegesis of the Sermon on the Mount must lie in the question whether it succeeds in transporting the original message of Jesus across the centuries and into the present without losing the spirit in which it was spoken. A review of this translation process reveals wrong paths, and there have been exegetical paths of different kinds that have led to controversies, and even today still stand side by side unreconciled.

An example of past exegetical strife is the question of the audience. In contrast to the medieval Scholastic interpretation, today it is broadly recognized that the Sermon on the Mount is directed not just at a special group of Christians who want to achieve perfect obedience: it is for all believers. It is an unconditional, general call to discipleship! The differentiation of a two-stage ethic, such as that shaped in the old (pre-Reformation) church, has now been overcome. Martin Luther understood the claim of the Sermon on the Mount as equally binding for all Christians, but at the same time warned against simplifying its application.[7] His statement of the problem still stands: how in a hostile and unredeemed world can the Christian protect and preserve, not his own life, but that of his neighbor, for whom he is responsible according to the commandment of love? Luther's answer binds the individual, insofar as his own person is concerned, to the Sermon on the Mount, that is, to love of enemy and renunciation of one's own right. In one's responsibility for third parties, however, Luther refers even the Christian to worldly and rational means of protecting and maintaining right. The criterion of this line of interpretation of double responsibility remains the irreversible priority of the purpose—namely, the fulfillment of the commandment of love—over the employment of the means. Where the priority of the love commandment is not longer in view, there Jesus' call to repentance is silenced.

Through analysis of the text layers of of the Sermon on the Mount, it has become clear that the tradition of the early

Christian community, and especially Matthew, has an elementary interest in the practicability of Jesus' ethical demands. The correction and new interpretation of the prohibition of divorce offer an emphatic example of this. One can see in this example that the practicability of the Sermon on the Mount as a whole as well as the ethical claim of its directives in particular was not in doubt in early Christianity—and the same can be demonstrated for exegesis of the Sermon on the Mount in the old church.

A fundamental doubt as to the practicability of the Sermon on the Mount, that is, its character as ethical commandment, did not arise until after the New Testament. If one understands the Sermon on the Mount exclusively as Jesus' preaching of the law (which is supposed to lay before a person his undeniable sinfulness, from which deliverance is obtained only through Jesus' absolute obedience and atoning death), this viewpoint is of critical significance because it appeals to Jesus' radical call to repentance, which comes to expression especially in the Torah-critical assertions of the Sermon on the Mount. At the same time, however, this restriction to an exegesis based purely on the theology of justification has to be rejected. In the sense of the Matthean Sermon on the Mount, there is no alternative between the dimension of the *usus elenchticus legis* and the demand for the followers of Jesus to act concretely in accordance with the commandment of love. This recognition is perhaps the most important one that the exegete can bring into today's discussion of the Sermon on the Mount. It provides the motivation for the necessity of Christian activity, according to generally prudent, rational standards in a world that is reconciled through the Christ event but not yet visibly redeemed.

We also must reject yet another alternative that, again only recently—since the nineteenth century—has widely defined the exegesis of the Sermon on the Mount. Here the individualistic perspective gained the upper hand. It was no longer the concrete deed that counted as fulfillment of the better righteousness, but the attitude in the depth of one's heart, as presented, for example, by Wilhelm Herrmann and Adolf von Harnack. By contrast, the historical significance of the countermovement of a Leo Tolstoy or a Leonhard Ragaz consisted in stressing the social ethical dimension and attempting a correction of the narrowing to an individual ethic; at the same time, however, they run the risk of sinking into a new one-sidedness: legalism.

We have seen that the spectrum of themes in the antitheses by itself excludes the choice between a purely individual and a purely social ethical interpretation. Furthermore, we maintain the following as negative conclusions: no two-stage ethic, no special ethic for a Christian elite, no opposition of *usus elenchticus legis* and the character of ethical commandment!

From this standpoint, both are concretely conceivable: the radical, eschatologically based call to repentance of Jesus and the practicable, ethically obligatory instruction as it is presented by the Sermon on the Mount in the context of the Gospel of Matthew. Appropriate action and an accurate, contemporary translation of the meaning of the Sermon on the Mount will come only when Jesus' call to repentance is understood and concretized anew in a changed situation as a call that here and now is addressed to me individually and seizes my whole person. Theological reflection must grasp mentally the dialectical contradictions that result from the confrontation of the Sermon on the Mount with the reality of the world; Christian action must dare and bear these tensions, because the message of Jesus is both: admonition to repent and exhortation to act.[8]

All discussions that are held in the spirit of the Sermon on the Mount must work toward this way of repentance and obedience vis-à-vis the commandment of love—toward the realization of agape and righteousness, even and precisely with respect to one's enemy. They should be in harmony with the seventh beatitude, the demand to make peace among people (5:9). Even if the Sermon on the Mount does not place in our hands a political, juridically derivable concept of action by which states and peoples can be governed, we may not infer from this a revocation of its claim. Thus, as Jesus himself, in his life and death, set a universally valid example, the Christian community is called to place itself under the word of its Lord, to shape the realm of the church in accordance with the Sermon on the Mount, and to realize an exemplary existence that will shine into the world like the light into the darkness (5:16). This path of signal existence will best do justice to the missionary claim of the exalted One, as emphasized by Matthew at the end of his Gospel. With these words let us remember the Christians' commission: "Go therefore and make disciples of all nations . . . teaching them to observe all that I have commanded you."

Bibliography

Albright, W. F. and C. S. Mann. *Matthew* 2d ed. AnBib 26. 1973.
Allen, W. C. *A Critical and Exegetical Commentary on the Gospel According to St. Matthew*, 3d ed. ICC. 1912.
Arnold, E. *Salz und Licht: Über die Bergpredigt.* 1982.
Aukrust, T. "Bergpredigt II: Ethisch." *TRE* 5:618-26.
Bammel, E. "Das Ende von Q." In *Verborum Veritas*, FS G. Stählin, edited by O. Böcher and K. Haacker, 39-50. 1970.
Banks, R. *Jesus and the Law in the Synoptic Tradition*. SNTSMS 28. 1975.
Barth, G. "Bergpredigt I: Im Neuen Testament." *TRE* 5:603-18 (bibl.).
Beare, F. W. *The Gospel According to Matthew*. New York: Harper and Row, 1982.
Berger, K. *Die Amen-Worte Jesu: Eine Untersuchung zum Problem der Legitimation in apokalyptischer Rede.* BZNW 39. 1970.
———. *Die Gesetzauslegung Jesu I.* WMANT 40. 1972.
Berner, U. *Die Bergpredigt: Rezeption und Auslegung im 20. Jahrhundert*, 3d ed. GTA 12. 1985. (Literature).
Betz, H. D. *Essays on the Sermon on the Mount.* Philadelphia: Fortress, 1985.
Beyschlag, K. "Zur Geschichte der Bergpredigt in der Alten Kirche." *ZTK* 74 (1977): 291-322.
Böcher, O., et al. *Die Bergpredigt im Leben der Christenheit.* Bensheimer Hefte 56. 1981.
Bonhoeffer, D. *Nachfolge*, 10th ed. 1971.
Boring, M. E. *Sayings of the Risen Jesus: Christian Prophecy in the Synoptic Tradition.* SNTSMS 46. Cambridge, 1982.
Bornhäuser, K. *Die Bergpredigt: Versuch einer zeitgenössischer Auslegung*, 2d ed. 1927.
Bornkamm, G. "Der Aufbau der Bergpredigt." *NTS* 24 (1978): 419-32.
———, G. Barth and H. J. Held. *Überlieferung und Auslegung im Matthäusevangelium*, 7th ed. WMANT 1. 1975.
Bornkamm, G., et al. "Bergpredigt I-III." *RGG* 1, 3d ed. (1957), 1047-54.
Braun, H. *Spätjüdisch-häretischer und frühchristlicher Radikalismus*, 2 vols., 2d ed. BHT 24/1, 2. 1969.
Brinkel, W., et al. *Christen im Streit um den Frieden.* Aktion Sühnezeichen Friedensdienste, 1982.
Brown, J. P. "The Form of 'Q' Known to Matthew." *NTS* 8 (1961/62): 27-42.

Bultmann, R. *Die Geschichte der synoptischen Tradition*, 9th ed. FRLANT 29. 1979.

Burchard, C. "Das doppelte Liebesgebot in der frühen christlichen Überlieferung." In *Der Ruf Jesu und die Antwort der Gemeinde*, FS J. Jeremias, edited by E. Lohse, 39-62. 1970.

————. "Versuch, das Thema der Bergpredigt zu finden." In *Jesus Christus in Historie und Theologie*, FS H. Conzelmann, edited by G. Strecker, 409-32. 1975.

Carson, D. A. *The Sermon on the Mount*. Grand Rapids, 1978.

Davies, W. D. *The Setting of the Sermon on the Mount*. Cambridge: Cambridge University Press, 1964.

Descamps, A. D. "Le Discours sur la Montagne." *RTL* 12 (1981):5-39.

Dibelius, M. "Die Bergpredigt" (1940). In *Botschaft und Geschichte I*, 80-174. 1953.

————. *Die Formgeschichte des Evangeliums*, 3d ed. 1959.

Didier, M., ed. *L'Évangile selon Matthieu*. BETL 29. 1972.

Edwards, R. A. *A Theology of Q*. Philadelphia, 1976.

Eichholz, G. *Auslegung der Bergpredigt*. BibS(F) 46. 1965.

Fenton, J. C. *The Gospel of St Matthew*, 5th ed. Harmondsworth, 1973.

Fiebig, P. "Der Sinn der Bergpredigt." *ZST* 7 (1930): 497-515.

Frankemölle, H. *Jahwebund und Kirche Christi*. NTA n.s. 10. 1974.

Friedländer, G. *The Jewish Sources of the Sermon on the Mount*. New York: KTAV Publishing House, 1969.

Fuchs, E. "Jesu Selbstzeugnis nach Matthäus 5" (1954). In idem, *Zur Frage nach dem historischen Jesus*, 100-125. GAufs. 1960.

Gaechter, P. *Das Matthäusevangelium*. 1963.

Goppelt, L. "Das Problem der Bergpredigt." In *Christologie und Ethik*, 27-43. 1968.

Grant, R. M. "The Sermon on the Mount in Early Christianity." *Semeia* 12 (1978): 215-31.

Grundmann, W. *Das Evangelium nach Matthäus*, 4th ed. THKNT 1. 1975.

Guelich, R. A. *The Sermon on the Mount*. Waco, 1982.

Gundry, Robert H. *Matthew: A Commentary on His Literature and Theological Art*. Grand Rapids: Eerdmans, 1982.

Hengel, M. "Das ende aller Politik: Die Bergpredigt in der aktuellen Diskussion." *Evangelische Kommentare* 14 (1981): 686-90; 15 (1982): 19-22.

Hochgrebe, V., ed. *Provokation Bergpredigt*. 1982.

Hoffmann, P. "Die Anfänge der Theologie in der Logienquelle." In *Gestalt und Anspruch des Neuen Testaments*, edited by J. Schreiner and G. Dautzenberg, 134-52. 1969.

————. "Die Jesusverkündigung in der Logienquelle." In *Jesus in den Evangelien*, edited by W. Pesch, 50-70. SBS 45. 1970.

————. *Studien zur Theologie der Logienquelle*. NTA n.s. 8. 1972.

————, and V. Eid. *Jesus von Nazareth und eine christliche Moral*. Quaestiones Disputatae 66. 1975.

Hübner, H. *Das Gesetz in der synoptischen Tradition*. 1973.

Hummel, R. *Die Auseinandersetzung zwischen Kirche und Judentum im Matthäusevangelium.* BEvT 33. 1963.

Jeremias, J. *Abba: Studien zur neutestamentlichen Theologie und Zeitgeschichte.* 1966.

———. *Die Gleichnisse Jesu,* 9th ed. 1977.

———. *Neutestamentliche Theologie* 1, 2d ed. 1973.

———. *Die Sprache des Lukasevangeliums.* KEK Sonderband. 1980.

Kantzenbach, F. W. *Die Bergpredigt.* 1982.

Kilpatrick, G. D. *The Origins of the Gospel According to St. Matthew,* 2d ed. Oxford, 1950.

Kingsbury, J. D. *Matthew: Structure, Christology, Kingdom.* Philadelphia, 1975.

Kissinger, W. S. *The Sermon on the Mount: A History of Interpretation and Bibliography.* Metuchen, N. J.: Scarecrow Press: 1975.

Kittel, G. "Die Bergpredigt und die Ethik des Judentums." *ZST* 2 (1925): 555-94.

Klostermann, E. *Das Matthäusevangelium,* 4th ed. HNT 4. 1971.

Künzel, G. "Studien zum Gemeindeverständnis des Matthäusevangeliums." *CTM* 10. 1978.

Lagrange, M. J. *Évangile selon Saint Matthieu.* Paris, 1941.

Lambrecht, J. *Ich aber sage euch: Die Bergpredigt als programmatische Rede Jesu (Mt 5-7; Lk 6,20-49).* 1984.

Lange, J., ed. *Das Matthäus-Evangelium.* Wege der Forschung 525. 1980.

Lapide, P. E. "Es geht um die Entfeindungsliebe: Realpolitik, wie sie die Bergpredigt eigentlich meint." *Lutherische Monatschefte* 20 (1981): 505-8.

———. *Wie liebt man seine Feinde?* 1984.

———. *The Sermon on the Mount: Utopia or Program for Action?* Mary Knoll, N. Y.: Orbis, 1986.

Lerle, E. "Realisierbare Forderungen der Bergpredigt?" *KD* 16 (1970): 32-40.

Lohff, W. "Manifest der Zuversicht: Verheissung und Forderungen der Bergpredigt." *EK* 14 (1981): 502-4.

Lohmeyer, E. *Das Evangelium des Matthäus,* 4th ed. KEK Sonderband. 1967.

Lohse, E. *Die Ethik der Bergpredigt und was sie uns heute zu sagen hat.* Vorlagen 21. 1984.

Lührmann, D. *Die Redaktion der Logienquelle.* WMANT 33. 1969.

Luz, U. *Das Evangelium nach Matthäus (Matt 1-7).* EKKNT 1/7. 1985.

Marguerat, D. *Le jugement dans l'évangile de Matthieu.* Geneva, 1981.

McArthur, H. K. *Understanding the Sermon on the Mount.* New York: Harper, 1960.

Merk, O., and E. Würthwein. *Verantwortung.* 1982.

Merklein, H. *Die Gottesherrschaft als Handlungsprinzip.* FzB 34. 1978.

———. *Jesu Botschaft von der Gottescherrschaft: Eine Skizze.* SBS 111. 1983.

Miegge, G. *Il sermone sul monte: Commentario esegetico a cura di B. Corsani.* Turin, 1970.

Moltmann, J., ed. *Nachfolge und Bergpredigt.* Kaiser-Traktate 65. 1981.

Müssle, M. *Die Humanität Jesu im Spiegel der Bergpredigt.* 1971.

Nissen, A. *Gott und der Nächste im antiken Judentum: Untersuchungen zum Doppelgebot der Liebe.* WUNT 15. 1974.

Pamment, M. "The Kingdom of Heaven according to the First Gospel." *NTS* 27 (1981): 211-32.

Pokorný P. *Der Kern der Bergpredigt: Eine Auslegung.* 1969.

Polag, A. *Die Christologie der Logienquelle.* WMANT 45. 1977.

———. *Fragmenta Q,* 2d ed. 1982.

Ragaz, L. *Die Bergpredigt Jesu.* 1945.

Räisänen, H. *Paul and the Law.* WUNT 29. 1983.

Reuter, H. R. "Die Bergpredigt als Orientierung unseres Menschseins heute." *ZEE* 23 (1979): 84-105.

Robinson, J. M. "ΛΟΓΟΙ ΣΟΦΩΝ: Zur Gattung der Spruchquelle Q." In *Zeit und Geschichte,* FS R. Bultmann, 77-96. 1964.

Rothfuchs, W. *Die Erfüllungszitate des Matthäusevangeliums.* BWANT 88. 1969.

Sand, A. *Das Gesetz und die Propheten.* Biblische Untersuchungen 11. 1974.

Schenk, W. *Synopse zur Redenquelle der Evangelien.* 1981.

Schlatter, A. *Der Evangelist Matthäus,* 4th ed. 1957.

Schmithals, W. *Einleitung in die drei ersten Evangelien.* 1985.

Schnackenburg, R. *Alles kann, wer glaubt: Bergpredigt und Vaterunser in der Absicht Jesu.* 1984.

———. "Die Bergpredigt Jesu und der heutige Mensch" (1966). In *Christliche Existenz nach dem Neuen Testament* 1, 109-30. 1967.

———, ed. *Die Bergpredigt: Utopische Vision oder Handlungsanweisung?* 2d ed. 1984.

Schneider, G. *Botschaft und Bergpredigt,* 2d ed. 1973.

Schniewind, J. *Das Evangelium nach Matthäus,* 12th ed. NTD 2. 1968.

Schrage, W. "Das Ende aller Politik? Kritische Fragen an Martin Hengel." *Evangelische Kommentare* 15 (1982): 333-37.

———. *Ethik des Neuen Testaments.* GNT 4. 1982.

Schulz, S. *Q: Die Spruchquelle der Evangelisten.* 1972.

———. *Die Stunde der Botschaft.* 1967.

Schürmann, H. *Traditionsgeschichtliche Untersuchungen zu den synoptischen Evangelien.* 1968.

Schweizer, E. *Die Bergpredigt* (based on the following work). 1982.

———. *Das Evangelium nach Matthäus,* 15th ed. NTD 2. 1981.

———. *Matthäus und seine Gemeinde.* SBS 71. 1974.

Soiron, T. *Die Bergpredigt Jesu: Formgeschichtliche, exegetische und theologische Erklärung,* 2d ed. 1944.

Steck, O. H. *Israel und das gewaltsame Geschick der Propheten.* WMANT 23. 1967.

Steinhauser, M. G. *Doppelbildworte in den synoptischen Evangelien.* FzB 44. 1981.

Stendahl, K. *The School of St. Matthew and Its Use of the Old Testament,* 2d ed. Philadelphia, 1969.

Strack, H. and P. Billerbeck. *Kommentar zum Neuen Testament aus Talmud und Midrasch,* 5th ed. 1969 (= Str-B).

Strecker, G. "Das Geschichtsverständnis des Matthäus" (1966). In idem, *Eschaton und Historie,* 90-107. 1979.

————. "Glauben und Handeln in der Theologie des Matthäus." In idem, *Handlungsorientierter Glaube,* 36-45. 1972.

————. *Der Weg der Gerechtigkeit: Untersuchung zur Theologie des Matthäus,* 3d ed. FRLANT 82. 1971.

Stuhlmacher, P. "Jesu vollkommenes Gesetz der Freiheit: Zum Verständnis der Bergpredigt." *ZTK* 79 (1982): 282-322.

Taylor, V. "The Original Order of Q." In *New Testament Essays,* FS T. W. Manson, edited by A. J. B. Higgins, 246-69. Manchester, 1959.

Tilborg, S. van. *The Jewish Leaders in Matthew.* Nijmwegen, 1972.

Trilling, W. *Das wahre Israel,* 3d ed. SANT 10. 1964.

Venetz, H.-J. *Provokation der Freiheit: Bergpredigt heute.* 1982.

Vögtle, A. *Was ist Frieden? Orientierungshilfen aus dem Neuen Testament.* 1983.

Walker, R. *Die Heilsgeschichte im ersten Evangelium.* FRLANT 91. 1967.

Walvoord, J. F. *Matthew: Thy Kingdom Come,* 4th ed. Chicago, 1980.

Wellhausen, J. *Das Evangelium Matthaei.* 1904.

Windisch, H. *Der Sinn der Bergpredigt,* 2d ed. UNT 16. 1937.

Wrege, H. T. *Die Überlieferungsgeschichte der Bergpredigt.* WUNT 9. 1968.

Zahn, T. *Das Evangelium des Matthäus.* Vol. 1 of *Kommentar zum Neuen Testament,* edited by T. Zahn. Leipzig, 1903.

Zeller, D. *Die weisheitlichen Mahnsprüche bei den Synoptikern.* FzB 17. 1977.

Notes

1.1 Literary-analytical Presuppositions

1. Cf. below, however, at Matt 5:1-2, 13, 15-16, 32; 7:2, 29; and elsewhere.
2. On the reconstruction of the Q source in detail, see Schulz, *Q*.
3. Bultmann, *Geschichte*, 222. The named distinguishing criterion is presupposed by the coherence criterion, which states that whatever objectively agrees with traditional material that was proved authentic with the help of the first criterion can be considered original (thus, for example, the words of Jesus that express an "exultation of eschatological feeling"; cf. pp. 110, 135).
4. With justification R. Walker designates the Gospel of Matthew as a "kerygmatic historical work" (*Heilsgeschichte*, 145). On the other hand, the alternative between "a manual of instruction for the church," which is to be accepted, and a "historical reconstruction of Jesus' life and sayings," which is to be rejected (Baere, *Matthew*, 5), is in no way fair to the Matthean intention and conception.

1.2 Types of Exegesis of the Sermon on the Mount

1. Cf. Martin Luther, "Wochenpredigten über Mt 5-7" (1530/32), WA 32 (1906): 299-544; also WA *Deutsche Bibel* 6 (1929): 26-38.
2. WA 32:300, 520; WA 52 (1915): 459-60: "This is the most common theology of popes and sophists."
3. Cf. WA 32:498.9ff; 499.1ff.
4. Ibid. 301.4: ". . . that they know no difference between the secular and the divine realm, much less what it is fitting to teach and to do differently in each realm"; cf. ibid., 389.
5. Ibid. 359.17ff: "Namely that through the teaching of the law we can become neither justified nor blessed, but only come thereby to knowledge of ourselves, how we are not able properly to fulfill one tittle out of our own strength . . . but must always crawl to Christ, who has fulfilled everything in the purest and most perfect way and given us his fulfillment, so that through him we exist for God, and the law cannot blame or damn us."
6. Augustine, Writings against the Pelagians 3.
7. Post-Reformation orthodoxy went further in the direction of doubt as to the realizability of the "Torah of Christ." One document indicative of this development is "Biblia illustrata," the exegetical masterpiece of Abraham Calov (1612-86), one of the main representatives of Lutheran high orthodoxy; it was directed against Hugo Grotius: "Since no one can fulfill the law in accordance with that [required] stringency, for this reason his pronouncements on the law only show our inability after the Fall and lead us to Christ, who has fulfilled the law in our place" (Annotata ad Matthaei Cap. 5 [1719], 191—I am indebted to my colleague J. Baur for this reference).
8. Martin Luther, *Vorreden zur Heiligen Schrift*, (Munich, 1934), 73; cf. also WA 32:305.7: "For he proceeds, therefore, not as Moses or teachers of the law

with commanding, threatening, and frightening, but in the friendliest fashion with pure charm and enticement and pleasant promises."

9. Thus, Schniewind, *Matthäus*, 73-75; Schlatter, *Matthäus*, 197; Jeremias: "Something came before" the demands of the Sermon on the Mount, namely, Jesus' sermon on the kingdom of God, his exhortation of filiation to the disciples, the self-attestation of Jesus in word and deed (*Abba*, 184-85).

10. Thus, for example, Kittel, "Bergpredigt"; C. Stange, "Zur Ethik der Bergpredigt," *ZST* 2 (1925): 37-74.

11. W. Elert, *Morphologie des Luthertums* 1 (1958), 25-31; F. Lau, "Luthers Lehre von den beiden Reichen," *Luthertum* 8 (1953): 46-49.

12. Literary expressions of the so-called "fanatics" are relatively rare; cf. P. C. Bauman, *Gewaltlosigkeit im Täufertum: Eine Untersuchung zur theologischen Ethik des oberdeutschen Täufertums der Reformationszeit*, Studies in the History of Christian Thought 3 (Leiden, 1968), 166, n. 1; cf. Berner, *Bergpredigt*, 13.

13. H. Zwingli, "Elenchus in Catabaptistarum strophas," in: Macaulay Jackson, *Selected Works of Huldreich Zwingli* (Philadelphia, 1901), 161; cf. Bauman, *Gewaltlosigkeit*, 150. Different, however, was the development of a violent group of Baptists who possessed a prominent representative in the leader of the Peasants' War, Thomas Müntzer, and also made possible the founding of the "heavenly Jerusalem" in Münster. This movement, understandably, forwent laying a foundation on the Sermon on the Mount and based its authority on the Old Testament.

14. Leo Tolstoy, *A Confession; The Gospel in Brief; What I Believe* (London: Oxford University Press, 1940).

15. Ragaz, *Bergpredigt*, 9.

16. Ibid., 191: "The will and order of God . . . are apparent in the Sermon on the Mount. It is nothing else. Whoever wants to do God's will, whoever wants to trust in God, must do it in the way of the Sermon on the Mount. And this will be the rock, for the individual person and for the community of people. The world is sand and stream; God is the rock, and Christ God's truth."

17. F. Naumann, *Ausgewählte Schriften* (1949), 132.

18. The problem of realizability represents a typical postbiblical and post-Reformation statement of a problem. Neither Matthew nor, say, Martin Luther asserted the realizability as such. Luther begins, instead, the other way around with the fact that the demands of the Sermon on the Mount have remained unrealized; cf. WA 32:469.16ff.

19. W. Herrmann, *Die sittlichen Weisungen Jesu* (1904), 3d ed. (1921), 25; cf. idem, *Ethik* (1909).

20. Herrmann's followers include Karl Barth and Rudolf Bultmann; both teachers were also influenced in regard to content by Herrmann's position; cf. F. W. Sticht, "Die Bedeutung Wilhelm Herrmanns für die Theologie Rudolf Bultmanns" (diss., Berlin, 1965); E. Busch, *Karl Barths Lebenslauf* (1975), 56-63; O. Merlyn, *Religion oder Gebet: Karl Barths Bedeutung für ein "religionsloses Christentum"* (1979), 14-17.

21. H. J. Holtzmann, *Neutestamentliche Theologie* 1, ed. A. Jülicher and W. Bauer, 2d ed. (1911), 241, 246, cf. 231-32.

22. Ibid., 248. Adolf von Harnack understood in similar fashion the beatitudes of the Sermon on the Mount, in which Jesus "radically linked his ethic and his religion and freed them from everything external and particular" (*Das Wesen des Christentums* [1950], 45). On the other hand, M. Weber exercises, in favor of an "ethic of responsibility," a surer critique of the "ethic of attitude" as an "absolute ethic of the gospel," since it relieves the Christian of the duty of "accepting responsibility for the (foreseeable) consequences of his action" ("Politik als Beruf. Geistige Arbeit als Beruf - Vier Vorträge vor dem

Freistudentischen Bund" [1919], second lecture, in M. Weber, *Soziologie. Universalgeschichte. Politik*, ed. J. Winckelmann [1973], 173, 175).

23. On the history of religion school cf. W. G. Kümmel, *Das Neue Testament: Geschichte der Erforschung seiner Probleme*, 2d ed., Orbis Academicus 3/3 (1970).

24. The works of Ritschl (1822-89), systematic theologian in Göttingen beginning in 1864, include *Die Entstehung der altkatholischen Kirche, Rechtfertigung und Versöhnung* 1-3, and *Geschichte des Pietismus* 1-3. See also J. Richmond, *Albrecht Ritschl: Eine Neubewertung*, GTA 22 (1982).

25. J. Weiss, *Die Predigt Jesu vom Reiche Gottes* (1892).

26. A. Ritschl, *Unterricht in der christlichen Religion* (1875), §9.

27. On this point Richmond places special emphasis in his study (*Albrecht Ritschl*, 145-46). He is fully aware of the connection between Ritschl's conception of the kingdom of God and the ideas of Kant and R. Rothe, but defends Ritschl against the misinterpretations of his followers and critics (ibid., 200-206).

28. Cf. Weiss, *Predigt*, 138-39, 143-44.

29. A. Schweitzer, *Das Messianitäts- und Leidensbewusstsein Jesu: Eine Skizze des Lebens Jesu* (1901); idem, *The Quest for the Historical Jesus*.

30. *Messianitäts- und Leidensgeheimnis*, 19. On the concept "interim ethic" cf. Holtzmann, *Neutestamentliche Theologie* 1, 241-48.

31. *Kommentar zum Neuen Testament aus Talmud und Midrasch* 1, 2d ed. (1956).

32. Kittel, "Bergpredigt," 584-85.

33. Davis, *Setting*. Cf., critical of this thesis, Strecker, *Weg der Gerechtigkeit*, 257-67.

34. Windisch, *Sinn der Bergpredigt*.

35. The book is divided accordingly: the first three chapters contain the historical exegesis of the Sermon on the Mount; chapter four, the theological.

36. Karl Barth, *The Epistle to the Romans* (London: Oxford University Press, 1933).

37. R. Bultmann, *Theologie des Neuen Testaments*, 8th ed. (1980), 599. In contrast to Barth, Bultmann also undertook methodological discussion of the theological meaning of the New Testament and worked out a hermeneutical program; cf. especially *Jesus Christus und die Mythologie*, GuV 4, 141-89.

38. R. Bultmann, *Jesus* (1923), 2d ed. (1965), 46ff.

39. G. Bornkamm, *Jesus von Nazareth* (1956), 87ff.

40. Bornkamm et al., "Bergpredigt," *RGG* 1:1050.

41. *Die Bergpredigt*, TEH 46 (1936).

42. Ibid., 12-13.

43. "In judgment and deed, those who follow after Jesus distinguish themselves from the world in their renunciation of possessions, of fortune, of right, of righteousness, of honor, of power; they become offensive to the world" (Bonhoeffer, *Nachfolge*, 88).

44. The monastic life was, to be sure, "a living protest against the secularization of Christianity," but it also became "the special achievement of the individual, to which the mass of church people could not be obligated" (ibid., 17).

45. "Finkenwalder Homiletik. Kausalität und Finalität der Predigt," in *Gesammelte Schriften* 4 (1961), 252.

46. The nonviolence propagated by Gandhi had its beginnings not only in the Sermon on the Mount, but also (and presumably earlier) in Indian Jainism; cf. O. Wolff, *Mahatma und Christus* (1955), 5.

47. *A Testament of Hope: The Essential Writings of Martin Luther King, Jr.*, ed. James Melvin Washington (New York: Harper & Row, 1986).

48. In the fifth thesis of the "Theological Declaration on the Present Situation of the German Evangelical Church," the Barmen Confessional Synod declared at the end of May 1934: "The Scriptures tell us that in this still unsaved world in which the church also exists, the state has the duty, under divine order and according to the measure of human insight and human ability, to provide for justice and peace with the threat and use of force. The church, in gratitude and reverence toward God, recognizes the benefit of this order. It remembers God's kingdom, God's commandment and righteousness, and thus the responsibility of the governing and the governed. It trusts and obeys the power of the Word, through which God upholds all things" (*Kirchliches Jahrbuch 1933-45* [1958], 65).

49. H. Gollwitzer, "Bergpredigt und Zwei-Reiche-Lehre," in Moltmann, *Nachfolge und Bergpredigt*, 93; cf. idem, "Bergpredigt und Zweireichelehre," in Brinkel, *Christen im Streit*, 93 ("brotherhood of humanity").

50. "Bergpredigt und Zwei-Reiche-Lehre," 98.

51. Ibid., 99.

52. K. Scharf, "Die Bergpredigt und eine sogenannte christliche Politik," in Brinkel *Christen im Streit*, 85-86.

53. Ibid., 86. Cf. also E. Käsemann, who understands the message of the coming divine dominion as an invitation to discipleship for the disciples and indeed as eschatological duty with political character, since it is a question of glorifying on earth the dominion of God ("Bergpredigt—eine Privatsache?" in Brinkel, *Christen im Streit*, 74-83, esp. 76).

54. Cf. H Schmidt, "Politik und Geist," *EK* 14 (1981): 214-15; and K. Carstens, "Zum Gebrauch der Bergpredigt," epd-Dokumentation 25 (1981), 1-2. On the peace discussion in the Evangelical Church, cf. on the one hand, the statement of the EKD (Evangelical Church of Germany) "Frieden wahren, fördern und erneuern" (1981), in which at the time of writing an atomic mobilization was "still" considered possible (p. 58); and on the other hand, the declaration of the Moderamen of the Reformed Union, in which the position rejecting atomic armament was raised to the level of a confession ("Das Bekenntnis zu Jesus Christus und die Friedensverantwortung der Kirche," 1982). The discussion on concretizing the prophetic promise of "swords into plowshares" (Isa 2:4; Mic 4:3; Joel 3:10) has a significance that reaches over the border with the German Democratic Republic; cf. W. Büscher, ed., *Friedensbewegung in der DDR - Texte 1978-82 (1982);* K. Ehring and M. Dallwitz, *Schwerter zu Pflugscharen: Friedensbewegung in der DDR* (Hamburg: Rowohlt, 1982).

2.1 5:1-2 The Setting

1. On the designation "Sermon on the Plain" cf. Luke 6:27 (ἐπὶ τόπου πεδινοῦ 'on a level place'.

2. Different also is Luke 9:28 (Mount of Transfiguration).

3. H. Schürmann, however, holds that the location of Jesus' speech on a mountain comes from the sayings source Q (*Das Lukasevangelium* 1, HTKNT 3/1 [1969], 318-19). According to J. Lange (*Erscheinen*, 394 Matthew is dependent on the mountain motif in Mark 3:13.

4. Cf. Schmauch, *Orte der Offenbarung*, 61ff.

5. Lange correctly sees a relationship between the Sermon on the Mount and the end of Matthew's Gospel: the speech delivers the "content filling" for 28:16-20 (*Erscheinen*, 404). On the mountain motif cf. also Matt. 4:8 (mount of temptation); also G. Lohfink, "Wem gilt die Bergpredigt?" *TQ* 163 (1983): 264-84.

6. J. Wellhausen raised against this hypothesis the objection that in the Old Testament conception Sinai is the seat of Yahweh, not Moses (*Evangelium Matthaei*, 13). Also, the childhood story of Matthew's Gospel confirms, despite an underlying relationship to the Moses narrative, that Jesus is understood not as a Moses redivivus, but as Son of God and son of David.

7. C. Schneider, *TDNT* 3:443.

8. Different is Lange's view that the mention of the people is to be ascribed to Matthean redaction (*Erscheinen*, 397, n. 14).

9. Cf. Matt 4:23-25.

10. Matt 8:23; 10:1; 11:1; 12:1-2; and elsewhere. This is in distinction to the use of μαθητεύειν ('make disciples'), which does not have the meaning of 'include in the circle of the twelve disciples,' but the more general meaning of 'make followers of Jesus' (cf. 28:19, the Great Commission; also 13:52, 27:57). Cf. at this point my investigation, *Der Weg der Gerechtigkeit* (191ff., 207, 223, 253-54), in which is established not only the historicizing tendency in Matthew's picture of the disciples—as U. Luz ("Die Jünger im Matthäusevangelium," *ZNW* 62 [1971]: 141-71) and N. Walter (*Zum Kirchenverständnis des Matthäus*, Theologische Versuche 12 [1981], 25-45) apparently hold—but also the ecclesiological function of Jesus' disciples in Matthew.

11. Cf. 26:40, 45 (the disciples asleep in the garden of Gethsemane); 26:69-75 (Peter's denial); 26:14ff.; 27:3ff. (Judas's betrayal and suicide).

2.2　5:3-20　The Opening of the Sermon on the Mount

12. Cf. also Jeremias, *Abba*, 182; by contrast, according to Burchard ("Versuch," 420, 432), 5:16 is to be taken as the theme of the Sermon on the Mount. To this end 5:17 and 7:12 are held to be the limits of the corpus of the Sermon on the Mount. Correctly seen here is the point that verse 16, as the application of the foregoing image sayings, makes an important assertion for the understanding of discipleship to Jesus. This, however, binds the verse to the following subsection, in which the relationship of law and righteousness is more closely defined. Verse 16 prepares for the theme of the Sermon on the Mount without being identical with it.

2.2.1　5:3-12　The Beatitudes

13. Cf. in particular F. Hauck and G. Bertram, *TDNT* 4:362-70; G. Strecker, *EWNT* 2:927; Str-B 1:189.

14. Cf. Matt 24:46-47: "Blessed is that servant whom his master when he comes will find so doing. Truly, I say to you, he will set him over all his possessions." Also, Kähler, "Makarismen," 232.

15. Cf. Michaelis ("π-Alliteration," 153ff.), who on this basis—although still not convincingly—also attributes Matt 5:5 to the primitive tradition.

16. The place of verse 5 in the order is not certain; Cod. D and other manuscript witnesses place the verse before the beatitude for the mourning (v. 4).

17. Frankemölle, however, holds that verses 5, 7-10 are redactional and also assumes redactional intrusion into verses 3 and 6 ("Makarismen," 67ff.).

18. On the question of the second or third person plural, Luke shows the second person (6:20-23), Matthew the third (5:3-10) and the second (5:11-12). In terms of form history, the problem of the original version is difficult to solve convincingly, for in Greek as well as Old Testament-Jewish literature beatitudes are found in both the third and second person. It is certain that the second person is documented for Q by verse 11-12, par. Luke 6:23-24, but the

idea that Matthew inconsistently introduced the third person cannot be made likely. Presumably, the discrepancy is based on the difference between the two versions of Q (Q[Matt] and Q[Luke]). Essentially, with the second person Luke emphasizes the beatitudes' character of direct address, while with the third person Matthew stresses the generally binding nature of Jesus' speech as proclamation.

19. Verse 4: παρακληθήσονται ('they shall be comforted'), verse 5: κληρονομήσουσιν ('they shall inherit'), verse 6: χορτασθήσονται ('they shall be satisfied'), etc.

20. Cf. also F.-W. Horn, *Glaube und Handeln in der Theologie des Lukas*, GTA 26 (1983), 121ff. Here it is demonstrated that the "Ebionite" sections in the Gospel of Luke belong entirely to the pre-Lukan tradition. This is of course also true of the first beatitude, and it is quite conceivable that through this acclamation Jesus expressed his solidarity with the poor and disfranchised.

21. Cf. Irenaeus, Her. 1 26:2. G. Strecker, addendum "Zum Problem des Judenchristentums," in W. Bauer, *Rechtgläubigkeit und Ketzerei im ältesten Christentum*, BHT 10 (2d ed., 1964), esp. 278-81.

22. BAG 1339, 3b and 1340; cf. also E. Bammel, *TDNT* 6:904; Ps 34:19: רוח רכאי (*dake ruach*) 'crushed in spirit,' 'of despondent mind'; 1 QS 11, 1:רוח רמי (*rame ruach*) 'proud' (in contrast to ענוה (*anawa*) 'her humility'). Zahn (*Matthäus*, 181ff.) and Schlatter (*Matthäus*, 133) also stress that it is a question of the human spirit; see also Dupont, *Béatitudes* 1:214-16; 2:19-51.

23. Cf. also Luke 18:9-14 (Pharisee and tax collector).

24. Cf. e.g., Augustine, De sermone domini in monte 1, 1:3 (Migne *PL* 34, 1231-32); Hieronymus, Commentary on Matt 5:3 (Migne *PL* 26, 34); John Chrysostom, Hom. in Matt 5:3 (Migne *PG* 57:224). On this point: Soiron, *Bergpredigt*, 146; J. Dupont, *Béatitudes* 3:399-411.

25. E.g., 18:4 (blessing the child): "Whoever humbles himself like this child, he is the greatest in the kingdom of heaven." The model quality of being a child consists not in the fact that the child is innocent, but in the fact that it is lowly and subordinated to adults. Humility is "subordination" (cf. also Jas 4:10).

26. Contrast E. Schweizer, *Evangelium*, 49.

27. 1QM 14:7: ענוי רוח (*anwe ruach*) 'who are of humble spirit' (parallel to: תמימי דרך [*temime däräch*] 'people who are completely changed').

28. E.g., Psalm 15; also Ps 24:3-6 (after the question, "Who shall ascend the hill of the Lord?" follows the answer: "He who has clean hands and a pure heart . . ."). Cf. H.-J. Kraus, "Psalmen," *BK* 15/1 (5th ed., 1978): 113, 196.

28a. Windisch, *Sinn der Bergpredigt*, 63, n. 1.

29. Versus Schniewind, *Evangelium*, 40-51; E. Thurneysen, *Die Bergpredigt*, 5th ed., TEH 105 (1963), passim.

30. Cf. also Matt 5:3 with Isa 61:1 and Matt 5:5b with Isa 61:7; also Zimmerli, "Seligpreisungen," 19. Yet the background in Isaiah is more important for the pre-Matthean tradition (versus Guelich, "Beatitudes," 431, according to which the Matthean redactional work has drawn in the Isaiah text).

31. With Schniewind (*Evangelium*, 43) one must point out that the messiah in the apocalyptic expectation of Judaism is a "comforter." At this point, the relationship with Isa 61:1 is especially close. It is all the more important to distinguish between the pre-Matthean tradition and the Matthean redaction.

32. Thus Bultmann, *TDNT* 6:43.

33. T. Rub. I 10 ("I grieved over my sins, for they were greater than had ever happened in Israel"). On this matter: K.-H. Rengstorf, *TDNT* 3:722-26.

34. Thus Frankemölle, "Makarismen," 71.

35. Cf. Eichholz, *Auslegung*, 35; Schweizer, *Evangelium*, 52; Koch, *Formgeschichte*, 53.

36. Thus F. Hauck and S. Schulz, *TDNT* 6:649.

37. On the translation of πραΰτης, cf. BAG, 1386-87; Weizsäcker, "Milde" (Lapide/Weizsäcker, *Seligpreisungen*, 8). In early Christian church discipline, the word is found in reference to congregational officers, who, faced with the angry outbreaks of others, are supposed to be πραεῖς ('considerate, composed'): Did. 15:1.

38. Thus is it presented in a real way in the Jewish apocalyptic: Isa 57:13; 60:21; Jub. 32:19.

39. Matthew spiritualized his sources in other ways also. There is no payment of the pious with earthly goods (19:29 vs. Mark 10:30; Jesus' mighty deeds occur "with a word" (8:8, 16); the first Evangelist avoids speaking of the manipulations of a miracle worker (vs. Mark 7:31ff.; 8:22ff.).

40. According to Schlatter, the phrase "hunger and thirst for righteousness" seems to make "visible the solid bond that united Matthew and his church with Paul." Righteousness is not the property of the pious, but the "gift of God," which a person "cannot produce, but only receive" (*Matthäus*, 137). Nonetheless, it is significant that Billerbeck can point to no rabbinic evidence for this interpretation; for "the old synagogue knows nothing of the inability of people to achieve, with their own strength, a fully valid righteousness before God" (Str-B 1:201).

41. Matthew likewise spiritualized the concept of poverty (v. 3); see above p. 32 and n. 22.

42. See below p. 139.

43. For a different view, cf. Lohmeyer, *Matthäus*, 87-88; P. Stuhlmacher, *Die Gerechtigkeit Gottes bei Paulus*, 2d ed., FRLANT 87 (1966), 188ff.; also E. Schweizer, according to whom the "righteousness of God" is the goal of human longing (*Evangelium*, 53). It is consistent with Pauline thinking that "righteousness" is a gift of God that is given to the pious at the end of life. Thus can the concept of "righteousness" in Matthew's Gospel be made parallel with Paul, according to G. Schrenk; on the other hand, however, the same author can acknowledge that Matthew understands "righteousness" as "acting for and before God" (*TDNT* 2:199).

44. For this interpretation of πεινᾶν and διψᾶν, there are numerous examples in Greek literature; Philo of Alexandria, for example, can speak of "hungering and thirsting for *kalokagathie*"; by that he means an active self-initiative for the highest goal of a Greek, for the attitude that realizes the good and beautiful (de fuga et inventione, 139-41). Cf. also Athenaeus (third cent. A.D.): ἴσχειν κελεύω χεῖρα διψῶσαν φόνον 'I order that my hand that thirsts for murder be strong' (10:43 Kaibel).

45. Cf. Lapide/Weizsäcker, *Seligpreisungen*, 8, 71.

46. In the background stands the Old Testament-Jewish, and also apocalyptic payment motif; e.g., Prov. 21:21 (LXX): "The way of righteousness and of alms will find life and splendor"; T. Levi 13:5: "Exercise righteousness on earth . . . so that you will reap [reward] in heaven"; also Isa 56:1; Matt 5:12.

46a. H. Cremer, *Biblisch-theologisches Wörterbuch des neutestamentlichen Griechisch*, ed. J. Kögel, 11th ed. (1923), 422.

47. Šabb. 151b (Str-B 1:203).

48. Cf. 1 Clem. 13:2: ἐλεᾶτε ἵνα ἐλεηθῆτε ('Be merciful so that you will find mercy!'); also Jas 2:13, where the future-eschatological aspect appears ("For judgment is without mercy to one who has shown no mercy; yet mercy triumphs over judgment").

49. E. Käsemann, *Sätze heiligen Rechts*, Exegetische Versuche und Besinnungen 2, 6th ed. (1970), 69-82.

50. Titus 1:15 ("to the pure all things are pure") clarifies the ethical component: those who may count themselves among the pure are those who also act accordingly in their deeds. To be sure, the Old Testament-Jewish wisdom asks: "Who can say, 'I have made my heart clean . . .'?" (Prov 20:9). Matthew is also familiar with absolution through the sacramental action of the congregation (cf. 26:28), but this is not central to his Gospel and is not mentioned in the Sermon on the Mount. If one understands the first Gospel "completely from the standpoint of post-baptismal doctrine" (W. Schmithals, "Evangelien, Synoptische," TRE 10:616), then such an interpretation is in tension not only with the "pre-" of the story of Christ, but also with the legitimation of the sacrament in Matthew's Gospel, which is conditioned by the specifically Matthean Christology (cf. also 3:15). "Pure" is the one who is addressed by Jesus' word, is called to good deeds, and accomplishes such deeds.

51. For a different view, cf. Hummel (Auseinandersetzung, 47, 75, and elsewhere; in contrast to this, Strecker, Weg der Gerechtigkeit, 244-45); modifying Hummel's position is that of U. Luz (ZTK 75 [1978]: 398-435, esp. 421; similarly, Schrage, Ethik, 143). Speaking against the thesis that the Evangelist Matthew belongs to a Jewish Christianity committed to the Old Testament-Jewish ceremonial law is especially the fact that there is no talk of a circumcision commandment in regard to the newly baptized Christians. Even the warning against "flight . . . on a sabbath" (24:20) is hardly sufficient proof, since according to rabbinical teaching the saving of human life can break the sabbath commandment (cf. Mek. Exod 31:13; T. Šabb. 15:11-17; P. Šabb. 14:14; Yoma 8:6).

52. Exod 24:9-11; 33:20-23, of Moses, who may see only God's back; Gen 32:30 (Jacob saw God face-to-face and remained alive).

53. For example, Isa 6:5 ("Woe is me! For I am lost; for I am a man of unclean lips . . . for my eyes have seen the King, the Lord of hosts!").

54. Plato, Phaedrus 250d, Republic 7:527d-e, Symposium 210, 211d-e; Aristotle, Ethica Eudemia, 7 15p 1249b 16ff., Ethica Nicomachea 10 7p 1177b 33. On this point cf. W. Michaelis, TDNT 5:321-22.

55. Sanhedr. 6b: Aaron "loved peace and pursued peace and made peace between one man and his neighbor."

56. Cf. Judg 6:23; 19:20; Dan 10:19.

57. Cf. Ps 84:11 LXX: where the glory of the Lord lives in the land, there will "righteousness and peace kiss each other" (and grace and loyalty meet each other); Jahweh's covenant of salvation is a כרית שלום (berith shalom, Isa 54:10), and the messiah bears the name of "Prince of Peace" (Isa 9:6; Mic 5:4). On this point see H. H. Schmid, Šalôm: "Frieden" im Alten Orient und im Alten Testament, SBS 51 (1971).

58. Mark 9:50; εἰρηνεύετε also in 1 Thess 5:13.

59. Jas 3:18 ("And the harvest of righteousness is sown in peace by those who make peace" = τοῖς ποιοῦσιν εἰρήνην). Thus, it is a characteristic of the "wisdom from above," which is said to be εἰρηνική ('peaceable': v. 17).

60. Ps 2:7; of Jesus at his baptism: Luke 3:22 v. 1. At this point cf. G. Fohrer, TDNT 8:344, 349-50.

61. Windisch ("Friedensbringer") points out that Roman emperors were named "sons of God" as well as "bringers of peace."

62. WA Deutsche Bibel 6:26-27.

63. Cf. above on 5:6.

64. On distinguishing two strophes of four beatitudes each, see p. 30 above.

65. According to E. Schweizer, here too one must think of the (entire) righteousness, which circumscribes discipleship in general (Evangelium, 56).

66. Versus H. D. Betz, who views verse 12 as a separate beatitude ("Makarismen," 9).

67. Even if this remains questionable in the individual case (and in distinction to the activity of the Christian scribes), M. E. Boring, perhaps correctly presumes in our text "the influence of the Christian prophets of the Matthean community" (*Sayings*, 206). The persecution admonition is widespread in early Christianity. Thus, the writer of First Peter especially addresses the suffering community in order to give them comfort in their persecution (1:5; 4:1ff.; cf. also Jas 1:12; 1 Thess 1:6; 2 Thess 1:4-6). W. Nauck would like to reconstruct from these texts a pre-Christian Jewish persecution tradition ("Freude im Leiden," *ZNW* 46 [1955]: 68-80). Nevertheless, this is probably only a situation that is asserted by analogy in Judaism (cf. the persecution presupposed in the books of the Maccabees; First Macc 2; Second Macc 6-7, 15).

68. Cf. also Matt 23:29-31 par. Luke 11:47-48: the scribes and Pharisees as sons of those who murdered the prophets.

69. 24:9*b*: "You will be hated by all nations (τῶν ἐθνῶν) for my name's sake"—the addition of τῶν ἐθνῶν comes from the first Evangelist (vs. Mark 13:13).

70. Cod. D it syr^{sin} Tert.

71. As opposed to the Lukan σκιρτήσατε (Luke 6:23), which translates literally the meaning of 'hop' or 'leap'; the word also appears in Luke 1:41, 44 (but not elsewhere in the New Testament).

72. Rev 19:7:χαίρωμεν καὶ ἀγαλλιῶμεν ("let us rejoice and exult").

73. Thus also Rom 5:3: "We rejoice in our sufferings"; cf. Jas 1:2; 1 Pet 1:6; 4:13.

74. According to this doctrine, the church administers these treasures, which are gathered from the "surplus works" of the saints and, above all, of Christ. As the body of Christ, the church let the *opera supererogativa* of its Head and its members pass to those who lack them. This occurs in connection with the Roman Catholic practice of indulgence, which is based on the "surplus earnings"; cf. *RE* 14:417-19.

75. Cf. also Steck, *Israel*, passim.

76. Presumably, verse 12*b* (par. Luke 6:23*b*) does not belong to the oldest tradition, for here, beside the promise of heavenly reward, a second reason has appeared. Wellhausen attempted to trace the difference between Matthew and Luke to an Aramaic original that had been read differently by each writer (*Das Evangelium Lucae* [1904], 24; *Einleitung in die ersten drei Evangelien* [1905], 36; differently in *Das Evangelium Matthaei* [2d ed., 1906], 36). Nonetheless, this attempt ran into contradiction and was later dropped by its originator (cf. Dupont, *Béatitudes* 1:246, n. 6; D. R. A. Hare, *The Theme of Jewish Persecution of Christians in the Gospel according to St. Matthew*, SNTSMS 6 [1967], 116, 174-75). It is also possible that in addition to the redactional ἐδίωξαν ('persecuted') and οὕτως ('so'), the words τοὺς πρὸ ὑμῶν also go back to Matthew, since they smooth the transition to what follows.

77. The expression ἔμπροσθεν τῶν ἀνθρώπων ('before men') is also of redactional origin in 6:1; the demand for good works fits into Matthew's overall conception; the verb δοξάζειν ('glorify')—also in 6:2; 9:8; 15:31—has only limited parallels; the designation of God as the "Father who is in heaven" comes from the tradition of the Matthean community.

78. B. Bek. 8b (Rabbi Josua ben Chananja answers such a question with a counterquestion: "Does salt spoil?"). We must regard as artificial exegetical attempts to demonstrate in the New Testament environment and presuppose for our text contaminated salt that has lost its power to season (on Cullmann, "Gleichnis," 193-94).

79. The verb μωραίνεσθαι has the meaning 'to become tasteless, useless, unusable'; in the background is the word μωρός ("foolish," "insipid").

80. It is an open question whether the salt saying on the lips of Jesus was intended to address the "spirit of readiness for sacrifice and self-denial as the *conditio sine qua non* for the disciples," as Cullmann believes ("Gleichnis," 199), and was an "admonition to readiness for sacrifice in discipleship," as Steinhauser asserts (*Doppelbildworte*, 349).

81. The image of being light has a broad religious-historical background; cf. T. Levi 14:1; also Str-B 1:237; H. Conzelmann, *TDNT* 9:310-43.

82. G. von Rad interprets the saying of the city on a hill ecclesiologically as a designation for the "eschatological community of disciples" ("Stadt," 447); similarly Schnackenburg, "Salz," 191; Campbell, "New Jerusalem," 363 ("the new community of Zion"). Different is Berger on 5:14: "pictorial reference to actual reality"; discipleship is a "necessity of nature" ("Stadt," 84).

83. A variant of Matt 5:14b is also found in the oxyrhynchus papyrus 1:37-42. Cf. on this discussion Steinhauser, *Doppelbildworte*, 338-39.

84. With verses 14b-15, Jeremias suggests a "double parable" (*Gleichnisse*, 89).

85. The Latin loanword *modius* ("bushel") designates a Roman measure of grain equal to 8.75 l. (about a peck).

86. "Lampe," 237ff. Versus Schneider, "Bildwort," 185; Steinhauser, *Doppelbildworte*, 361-63; cf., however, Hahn, "Worte," 112.

87. The contrast between *to light* and the presupposed *to put out* is brought in by Matthew; in Luke 11:33 and Mark 4:21 par. Luke 8:16, there is no mention of καίειν ('to light'); there it is a matter only of hiding the light (so also Mark 4:22; cf. Judg 7:16).

88. As often in the telling of a parable before the addition of the interpretation: 12:45; 13:49; 18:14; 20:16. Steinhauser sees correctly that the meaning of verse 16 sums up the Matthean interpretation (*Doppelbildworte*, 345).

89. The expression also occurs in 26:10 par. Mark 14:6 ("she has done a beautiful thing [lit.: a good work] to me"); cf. 23:5.

90. By contrast, Souček ("Salz der Erde") sets the indicative election of the community over against its commission, through which it must fulfill its being.

91. Cf. also Bonhoeffer, for whom this verse represents an appeal to the disciples not to hide themselves (*Nachfolge*, 96).

92. Cf. n. 12 above and regarding verse 20 below.

93. In this regard see below on verses 17 and 20.

94. Cf. below on 7:15ff.

95. Different from Luz, "Erfüllung," 415.

96. Under the influence of Mark 13:30-31; cf. also E. Schweizer, *Evangelium*, 64; Marguerat, *Jugement*, 114.

97. The ἀμήν-formula is often redactional; cf. 5:26; 8:10; 10:15; 11:11; 18:13; and elsewhere (versus Q); 19:23; 24:2 (versus Mark).

98. Verse 18d was perhaps formed by Matthew using a motif from 24:34 (par.).

99. Thus Ljungman, *Gesetz*, 42, 47.

100. Different from Luz, "Erfüllung," 420, n. 99; Hübner, *Gesetz*, 18.

101. Cf. here Lüdemann, *Paulus der Heidenapostel*, vol. 2 of *Antipaulinismus im frühen Christentum*, FRLANT 130 (1983), and A. Lindemann, *Paulus im ältesten Christentum*, BHT 58 (1979).

102. Of course, only in the expression βασιλεία τῶν οὐρανῶν is Matthean influence to be established with relative certainty; cf. 3:2; 5:3; 8:11; 11:12; and elsewhere.

103. Versus Heubült, "Beitrag," 144.

104. Käsemann, *Sätze*, 79. Concerning the disputing of statements of holy law by K. Berger, Luz correctly objects that legal character and wise admonition need not exclude each other; the first designates the situation in life (Sitz im Leben), the second the form-historical genre ("Erfüllung," 409).

105. Cf. S. Dt. 12:23 § 76; p. Qid. 1:58, 61*b*. Considered light commandments were, e.g., Deut 12:23 (prohibition of eating blood); Lev 23:42 (booth commandment); Deut 22:7 (commandment to release the mother bird). Heavy commandments include, e.g., Exod 20:12 (honoring parents); Gen 17:10 (circumcision).

106 *Evangelium*, 63.

107. The elative designates an absolute superlative without comparison ("very small"); the positive μέγας in verse 19b can be likewise understood ("very large").

108. Correctly: Broer, *Freiheit vom Gesetz*, 52-53.

109. Cf. Str-B 1:249-50; 4:2, p. 1138 (seven departments of the righteous in the Garden of Eden).

110. Thus Luz, "Erfüllung," 420.

111. With Hübner (*Gesetz*, 27), we can determine that the assertion of verse 18 (affirming the law) is "weakened" by the connection of verse 19 with verse 18; this is all the more true when one takes into account the superior position of πληρῶσαι ('fulfill') in verse 17 as relevant to the interpretation (ibid., 32-35, 234; cf. idem, *EWNT* 2:1166).

112. Luz holds that verse 20 leads from a Jewish conception of righteousness oriented toward the fulfillment of individual commandments (vv. 17-19) to a different understanding, which is expressed in the antitheses and defined by the commandment of love ("Erfüllung," 423).

113. The Sadducees were a privileged group in the political spectrum of Judaism until A.D. 70; for them only the old written law was obligatory; cf. here J. Wellhausen, *Die Pharisäer und Sadduzäer* (1874); E. Schürer, *Geschichte des jüdischen Volkes im Zeitalter Jesu Christi*, 4th ed. (1907); 2:475-89.

114. J. P. Meier lifts up the connection of Matt 5:17-20 with the antitheses. In his penetrating examination of our pericope, he convincingly establishes, concerning the Matthean concept of righteousness (cf. also above on 5:6, 10), that "dikaiosynē always and everywhere in Mt means one and the same thing: that ethical or moral conduct which is in keeping with God's will" (*Law and History*, 77). See also Dupont, *Béatitudes*, 3:211-384. Different still is M. Fiedler, who in his unpublished dissertation ("Der Begriff DIKAIOSYNE im Matthäusevangelium auf seine Grundlagen untersucht" [Halle, 1957]) rightly emphasizes the eschatological character of the Matthean righteousness, but he derives from it the conclusion that "it has its prerequisite and possibility in the action of the Messiah," and "only the community of the Messiah is capable of its realization" (Theologische Versuche 8 [1977], 68). Yet Matthew reflects neither on a possibility of righteousness through the Messiah nor on the enabling of the community to do right (cf. rather, e.g., Matt 13:24-30; 18:15-20; 25:31-46). B. Przybylski calls Matthew's conception of righteousness "essentially a Jewish concept" (*Righteousness in Matthew and His World of Thought*, SNTSMS 41 [1981], 123). His attempt to deprive the Evangelist of δικαιοσύνη as the typical characteristic of the disciples' behavior (114-15) lacks any basis whatsoever in the text.

2.3 5:21-48 The Antitheses

1. Lohse, "Ich aber sage euch."

2. Luke 6:27a (ἀλλὰ ὑμῖν λέγω 'but I say to you') cannot be made to support the assumption that Luke was familiar with the antithetical framework; rather, the position of the pronoun before the verb is typically Lukan (cf. 11:9; 16:9;

12:22). The ἀλλά corresponds to the preposed πλήν in verse 24 (cf. 11:41-42). In Luke 6:27a, only the words ὑμῖν λέγω are to be designated Q material (cf. Matt 5:44a).

3. In form, the parallel Mark 10:2ff. differs considerably from the antitheses in Matthew 5, and for this reason cannot be used in the tradition-historical derivation (vs. Berger, *Gesetzauslegung*, 587).

4. Bultmann was not willing to decide whether this antithetical triad was formed by the community or went back to Jesus (*Geschichte*, 157-58). E. Käsemann finds in the antitheses the heart of Jesus' proclamation: Jesus claimed to bring in the messianic Torah, and with this messianic self-consciousness, he stands in disagreement with the Torah of Moses ("Das Problem des historischen Jesus," *Exegetische Versuche und Besinnungen* 2:206).

5. Versus Käsemann (ibid.); also the concept "messianic Torah" is not to be presupposed for the time of Jesus (versus Davies, *Setting*, 108).

6. Thus, e.g., Str-B 1:235-36. Cf., however, O. Merk: "It refers to the Sinai generation and to all later generations who both receive the Sinai tradition and pass it on" (*Verantwortung*, 134).

7. These "Sanhedrins of the Twenty-three" were found in all places with more than 120 inhabitants, and they passed judgment on murderers in their district. The great Sanhedrin in Jerusalem, with seventy-one members, went into action only when one of the high priests was accused of a capital crime; cf. Sanh. 1:4-6, 17b; Mak. 7a and Str-B 1:257-58.

8. With reference to Exod 21:12; Lev 24:17; cf. J. Jeremias, *TDNT* 6:975; Chr. Dietzfelbinger, "Antithesen," 14-15.

9. According to a widespread apocalyptic view, murderers are subject to the just punishment of God: Rev 21:8; 22:15; Apoc. Pet. 25. The rabbinate can speak of the "court of heaven" (= of God), which reaches in where earthly courts cannot catch criminals; cf. Str-B 1:273ff.

10. The intention of the text is missed by attempts to weaken the original sense; for example: Jesus spoke out only against murder, but not against killing (corresponding to the difference between φονεύειν and ἀποκτείνειν). Here, it is a question of an inadmissible harmonization that leaves out of consideration the unconditionality and radicality of Jesus' eschatological demand.

11. Cf. Str-B 1:276ff.

12. Cf. the words γέεννα πυρός and ῥακά, which point to a Hebrew-Aramaic original content.

13. A secondary, ethicizing reworking is also recognizable in the variant reading εἰκῇ: everyone who is angry with his brother "without cause" shall be liable to judgment (v. 22a).

14. This rule also assumes "intentions of wisdom"; cf. Zeller, *Mahnsprüche*, 63.

15. Jeremias, "Lass allda deine Gabe."

16. Bultmann, *Geschichte*, 185. Cf., however, Zeller: "The fact that a parable in the form of an admonition is form-historically unique speaks, nonetheless, for the ... view that ... a common Jewish saying acquired subsequent eschatological meaning in its later stage through the addition of verse 26" (*Mahnsprüche*, 66).

17. Jeremias, *Gleichnisse*, 40.

18. According to Deut 22:22, adultery is punished by death; cf. Lev 20:10 and Mekh. Ex. 20:14; S. Lev 20:10; S. Dt. 22:22; Sanh. 7:9.

19. In accordance with the use of the passive μοιχευθῆναι (v. 32): a man who dismisses his wife causes her to commit adultery (namely, through her entering a second marriage, thereby destroying her first marriage).

20. Cf. Lv. R 23: Tr. Kalla 1; Berakh. 43b, 61a; Mak. 24 (Str-B 1:299-300);

versus E. Lohmeyer: Jesus was the first to give "an unconditionally binding rule" (KEK Sonderband, 2d ed. [1958], 128).

21. The parallel Mark 9:43-48 offers a more detailed version; thus, the annoyance of the foot is expressly carried out as a second example, the punishment of hell is clarified, the closing quotation (Isa 66:24) is added, and much more. One can hardly assume that the peculiarities of Matt 5:29-30 "are conditioned by that context and probably go back to the redactor" (Zeller, *Mahnsprüche*, 74).

22. γέεννα (see v. 22); also συμφέρει (~Matt 18:8-9: καλόν σοί ἐστιν); cf. LXX on Jer 33:14 (= 26:14 MT): συμθέρει = טוב (thob).

23. Thus also 5:39; the right hand is the more valuable; similarly, either the phrase "the right eye" is an assimilation, or it is presupposed that the right eye is the sharper (cf. Str-B 1:302; Grundmann, *Evangelium*, 161).

24. Cf. Git. 9,10.90aBar; p. Git. 9,50d,29; S. Dt. 24:1 § 269.

25. In opposition to Billerbeck, who identifies this concept with the "sexual sin" (Str-B 1:313), Hübner notes that such a limitation is not imperative; rather, it could also mean "offenses against the current good morals" (*Gesetz*, 52). Cf. also R. Neudecker: "Thus 'erwa as grounds for obligatory divorce covers everything that is 'nakedness' of the wife, beginning with certain bare parts of the body (easily interpreted as signs of a woman of loose morals) and reaching to the serious situation of adultery" (*Frührabbinisches Ehescheidungsrecht: Der Tosefta-Traktat Giṭṭin*, BibOr 39 [Rome, 1982], 5).

26. Even the concept ἀποστάσιον is not to be traced exclusively to Deut 24:1 but is also attested in Mark 10:4.

27. Thus E. Schweizer, *Evangelium*, 74; cf. on Deut 24:16-17 H. W. Wolff, *Anthropologie des AT*, 2d ed. (1974), 256; Baltensweiler, *Ehe*, 34.

28. An overview of the parallels produces the following synoptic picture:

Matthew 19:9	Mark 10:11-12	Luke 16:18
[9]*And I say to you; whoever dismisses his wife, except for unchastity and marries another commits adultery.*	[11]*And he said to them, "Whoever dismisses his wife and marries another commits adultery against her;* [12]*and if she dismisses her husband and marries another, she commits adultery.*	[18]*"Everyone who dismisses his wife and marries another commits adultery, and he who marries a woman dismissed from her husband commits adultery.*

The influence of Q on Matt 5:32 is to be seen in the expression πᾶς ὁ ἀπολύων ('everyone who dismisses'—KJV: "putteth away"; RSV: "divorces") in Luke 16:18. The argumentation from the man's point of view in the second half of the verse also goes back to Q; different is Mark 10:12, which presents the woman as the subject and perhaps reflects Roman legal practice.

29. The attempt to identify πορνεία ('fornication') with the Hebrew זנות (zenut 'consanguineous marriage') has little prospect, since this understanding is not otherwise attested in Matthew; vs. Baltensweiler, *Ehe*, 33; Fitzmyer, "Matthean Divorce Texts"; Meier, *Law and History*, 147-50. On the other hand, W. Rordorf correctly points to the discussion of the Pharisees according to Matt 19:3 and to the patristic interpretation ("Marriage," 196).

30. The avoidance of the term μοιχεία ('adultery') may be explained by the fact that in the context the verb μοιχεύειν has a legal meaning and designates, namely, the indictable offense; here, by contrast, it is a matter of the process, whose nature is to be established juridically.

31. On this matter: Schaller, "Sprüche" (bibl.). The restriction in 1 Cor 7:11a refers perhaps to a marriage that has already ended in separation (on H. Lietzmann, *An die Korinther* 1, HNT 9, 5th ed. [1969], 31).

32. Mark 10:12 expresses this connection from the viewpoint of the wife (see n. 28 above). The Lukan parallel belongs perhaps to the pre-Lukan sayings unit 16:16-18 (thus Polag, *Fragmenta*, 74; Schürmann, *Untersuchungen*, 137; versus Hoffmann, *Studien*, 54-55). According to F.-W. Horn (*Glaube und Handeln in der Theologie des Lukas*, GTA 26 [2d ed., 1986], 70th ff.), μοιχεία (v. 18, 'adultery') is parallel to φιλαργυρία (v. 14, 'avarice') and like the latter circumscribes, in the Lukan understanding, a basic prohibition of the law (cf. Luke 8:14; Acts 24:25).

33. Thus, the older Roman Catholic exegesis; cf. U. Holzmeister, "Die Streitfrage über die Ehescheidungsgesetze bei Mt 5:32; 19:9," *Bib* 26 (1945): 133-46; F. Vogt, *Das Ehegesetz Jesu* (1936). Speaking against this is, above all, the parallel Matt 19:9, which only with great difficulty can be interpreted inclusively. The newer Roman Catholic interpretation largely recognizes the exclusive character of the clause, yet still relates it either only to the separation of husband and wife or to a marriage that is illegitimate according to Jewish law (cf. n. 29 above and Schürmann, "Marginalien," 421-22). According to R. Neudecker, our text stands over the overall concept of "reconciliation" ("The Sermon on the Mount as a Witness to 'Inculturation': The First Two Antithetical Cases [Mt 5:21-32]," in *Inculturation: Working Papers on Living Faith and Cultures*, ed. P. Beauchamp et al. [Rome, 1982], 73-89).

34. Yet according to C. Dietzfelbinger, πορνεία marks the already accomplished breakup of the marriage. Therefore, with his stipulation, the Matthean Jesus reproduces the original sense of Deuteronomy 24: divorce is only possible when the marriage has broken up. If a man is faced with a marriage that no longer exists and dismisses his wife, he does not act against Jesus' absolute prohibition of divorce; and "even in 5:32b the prohibition of marriage to an illegally dismissed woman does not contradict Deuteronomy, since it speaks of the legally dismissed woman" ("Antitheses," 9). Nevertheless, in Jesus' understanding every divorce is illegal because it contradicts the divine creative will of God; hence, there can also be no talk of a dismissal that would be in harmony with original divine law.

35. Thus, it can be related, for example, to the Old Testament oath of purity, according to which the accused can, through a solemn assertion that contains the truth and no "false witness," reject an accusation made against him (cf. Exod 22:11). Also, the breaking of a vow is to be counted as perjury (Num 30:3; cf. Wis 14:28).

36. Another possible interpretation in BAG, 178-79; J. Schneider, *TDNT* 5:462, n. 32: ἀποδοῦναί τινι ὅρκον 'to discharge an oath,' that is, to swear to God a (true) oath. Here, however, the word *true* would have to be supplied.

37. Cf., however, the counterproposal of G. Dautzenberg, according to which the fourth antithesis goes back, not to Jesus, but to a secondary Jewish-Christian tradition ("Ist das Schwurverbot?"). Support for this comes from three points: (1) the antithetical form is artificial, since verse 33 brings no literal quotation; (2) thesis and antithesis are incongruous; (3) it is not a question of an intensification of the Torah nor of a suspension of the Torah, since verse 33 does not refer to an oath prescribed by the Torah ("Eid," 380-81). Nevertheless, the argument of artificiality or incongruity postulates an elegant antithetical form that cannot be reconstructed even out of the authentic first and second antitheses. Furthermore, verse 21b reproduces not just a prohibition of the Torah, but first of all a Jewish oral tradition (see above, p. 65). This leads ultimately, however, back to the Old Testament law and

makes tradition critique and Torah critique the same. In this, it is characteristic of the absolute prohibition of oaths that not just perjury is rejected, but any oath without exception, and that, thereby, the whole Old Testament-Jewish practice of oaths is called into question. It agrees essentially with the other ethical radicalisms of Jesus. That it was not observed in early Christianity (see n. 44 below) is something it has in common with other absolute demands of Jesus (cf. 5:44; 7:1).

38. Cf. Jas 5:12: "But above all, my brethren, do not swear, either by heaven or by earth or with any other oath, but let your yes be yes and your no be no, that you may not fall under condemnation." (Other parallels: Justin, Apol. 1, 16:5; Ps. Clem., Hom III 55,1; 56,3; XIX 2,4.)

39. Cf. the collection of texts by J. Schneider, *TDNT* 5:176-85, 457-67.

40. Cf. de decal. 84; leg. all. III 207; spec. leg. II 2, 4-5.

41. S. Westerholm correctly draws from our text the conclusion that "it is a misunderstanding of Jesus' intent to treat his words as a new statute" ("Jesus and Scribal Authority," ConBNT 10 [Lund, 1978], 113).

42. Cf. also 2 Cor 1:17: ". . . ready to say Yes and No at once" (P[46] and others).

43. Dautzenberg also recognizes that Matthew presents an "oath-substitute formula" that is supposed to avoid the decisive traits of an oath and strengthen the truthful assertion ("Eid," 381). The fact that the named supporting documents (except slav. Hen. 49:1-2 Rez. A, also b. Šeb. 36a; Mekh. Ex. 20:1; among others; cf. Str-B 1:336-37; M. Dibelius, *Jakobus*, 230-31) are to be assigned a relatively late date as literature cannot reduce their essential significance; cf. Banks, *Jesus and the Law*, 195.

44. Cf. also Dietzfelbinger, "Antithesen," 10. Early Christianity did not hold to Jesus' prohibition of oaths: Paul frequently appeals to God to witness an oath (1 Thess 2:5, 10; 2 Cor 1:23; 11:31; Rom 1:9; 9:1; Phil 1:8). According to Matt 26:64, Jesus himself made a sworn assertion before the high priest, and according to Matt 26:72, 74, Peter strengthened his denial through an oath. Matt 23:16ff. passes on a pre-Matthean Christian tradition that opposes the undisciplined use of oaths in Judaism.

45. Versus E. Schweizer, *Evangelium*, 79.

46. Cf. T. San. 25b; Meg. 28a; Berakh. 17a; Šabb. 88b (with quotation from Judg 5:31b). Other evidence, including Hellenistic-Jewish, in Zeller, *Mahnsprüche*, 57-58.

47. Cf. B. Qam. 8:6; Sanh. 58b.

48. The loanword μίλιον corresponds to the Latin *mille passum* (c. 1,500 m.); cf. Did. 1:4.

49. Thus, it goes back to the Q source; the verb δανείζεσθαι ('to borrow') is also in Luke 6:35.

50. On the synoptic agreements see above pp. 63 and 81-82.

51. The original location of 5:45 is disputed. According to S. Schulz (*Q*, 131), verses 46-47 interrupt the train of thought and are to be regarded as "tradition-historically later explanation" (thus also G. Strecker, "Antithesen," 67). It is also conceivable, however, that verses 46-47 originally presented a continuation of the Golden Rule (7:12 par. Luke 6:31), which was concluded by the general view of God's goodness (v. 45 par. Luke 6:35b). Luke 6:36 par. Matt 5:48 is not only the close of this section but also the transition to the next one (Luke 6:37ff.).

52. Cf. also 1 QS I 9-10; IX 21ff.; and tendencies in this direction in the Old Testament (Pss 31:7; 139:21-22).

53. Versus Jeremias, *Neutestamentliche Theologie* 1:206. The term was already present in Q, apparently as a circumlocution for hostile action (cf. Luke 6:27b).

54. Thus, 6:24 par. Luke 16:13; cf. Prov 13:24 and elsewhere; O. Michel, *TDNT* 4:690.

55. 10:22; 24:9-10; 5:11 par. Luke 6:22.

56. Thus Burchard, "Versuch," 423.

57. Like Luke 6:28, the Q source read ἐπηρεαζόντων ('who abuse'); cf. Schulz *Q*, 128.

58. Thus W. Foerster, *TDNT* 2:813-14.

59. Cf. Mekh. Ex. 23:4; T. BM. 2:26-27 (Str-B 1:368-69).

60. Cf. A. Bonhoeffer, *Die Ethik Epictets* (1968), 105 (reference to Seneca, Ant. 7:13, and Marcus Aurelius, ad se ipsum VI 27; VII 21; and elsewhere).

61. Cf. Prov 3:7; Joseph and Aseneth 28:5, 10, 14.

62. Cf. also Jub. 36:4, 9: "When you plan evil against your brother, you will fall into his hands."

63. Ber. 10a; Sanh. 37a; Midr. Ps. 41 (Str-B 1:370-71).

64. P. Pokorný correctly notes that Jesus' commandment to love one's enemy excludes every "vengeful attitude," and he surmises "that the hateful thoughts and expressions based on and strengthened by apocalyptic expectations form the concrete background for the demand to love one's enemy" (*Kern der Bergpredigt*, 25).

65. L. Schottroff expresses a different view in *Feindesliebe*, 218-21. Beginning with a call for social differentiation of the early Christian Jesus tradition, the author understands Matt 5:39-40 as a political apologia. From the Sermon on the Mount, she draws hermeneutical conclusions that are, in any case, open to discussion but also are revealed neither by Jesus' love-of-enemy commandment nor by Matthew's interpretation.

66. Cf. Plato, Leg. IV 713e, Phaedr. 253a/b, Theat. 176b; W. Michaelis, *TDNT* 4:664-66.

67. Cf. Matt 5:48 (ἔσεσθε) with the parallel Luke 6:36 (γίνεσθε).

68. In another sense for Jesus Christ; cf. 1:18-2:23; 3:17; 4:3, 6; and elsewhere. On this point see Grundmann, *Evangelium*, excursus 7, 236-42.

69. The expression τοῦ ἐν οὐρανοῖς ('who is in heaven') is Matthean (cf. 5:16; 6:1, 9; 7:11; 18:14).

70. The phrasing "on the evil and on the good . . . on the just and on the unjust" is in the form of a chiasmus (a + b . . . b + a) and is perhaps of pre-Matthean origin; thus Schulz, *Q*, 129.

71. This is shown by the terms ὕψιστος ('Most High'), χάρις ('thanks'), χρηστός ('kind'), and ἀχάριστος ('ungrateful'). The comments of Jeremias (*Sprache*, 144-45) attempting to demonstrate pre-Lukan terminology are not convincing.

72. Instead of the ancient terms τελῶναι ('tax collectors'—Matt 9:10-11; 11:19; 18:17; 21:31-32) and ἐθνικοί ('Gentiles'—Matt 5:46-47; 6:7; 18:17), Luke 6:32 offers the example of the ἁμαρτωλοί ('sinners').

73. Intended is the superterrestrial, heavenly reward (as in 5:12; cf. Luke 6:23, 35). Luke 6:34 has χάρις ('credit,' 'thanks') at this point without the idea of a gratuity (*Gnadenlohn*). At best, the question is whether there is a common underlying Aramaic tradition, so that μισθός ('reward') and χάρις ('thanks') can be understood as variant translations. Cf. Wrege, *Überlieferungsgeschichte*, 88ff.; Grundmann, *Evangelium*, 179, n. 146; versus van Unnik, "Motivierung," 295ff.; Hübner, *Gesetz*, 87.

74. Luke 6:32, 34. Perhaps Luke is thinking of the positive image of the penitent tax collector who is contrasted with the self-righteous Pharisee; cf. Luke 18:10 ff.

75. Cf. also Luke 7:29; 15:1; 19:1-10.

76. The word is περισσόν ('more'), as already in verse 37; like the preceding

μόνον ('only'), it is Matthean; the first Evangelist probably read in his source, as in verse 46: τίνα μισθὸν ἔχετε ('what reward have you').

77. Cf. 6:31; 7:12, 24; 22:21; and elsewhere.

78. Cf. 6:14, 16; and elsewhere.

79. According to widespread opinion (e.g., R. Bultmann, *Jesus*, 2d ed. [1965], 103) the words οἰκτίρμονες οἰκτίρμων ('merciful'—Luke 6:36) are secondary. In support of this, we could say that they anticipate the following context, the admonition against judging, and thus we have a Lukan transition. Yet the connection between Luke 6:36 and 37ff. is pre-Lukan. It belongs to the Q stage common to Matthew and Luke, since Matt 6:1-34 is recognizable as a secondary insertion. Moreover, οἰκτίρμων in Luke's Gospel is a hapax legomenon, so that pre-Lukan and pre-Matthean origin is to be presupposed.

80. Bultmann, *Jesus*, 102-3.

81. Ibid.

82. Cf. 1 QS I 8; II 2; III 9; VIII 18, 21; IX 6, 9, 19; also Braun, *Radikalismus* 2:43, n. 1.

83. Thus, correctly, Sand (*Gesetz*, 54-58, 208-9). On this basis, it is questionable to draw a straight line between the Sermon on the Mount and Syrian monasticism (say, with "wandering preachers" as the connecting link). Versus G. Kretschmar, "Ein Beitrag zur Frage nach dem Ursprung frühchristlicher Askese," *ZTK* 61 (1964): 27-67, esp. 57ff.; E. Schweizer, *Evangelium*, 129-30.

84. Cf. also Jas 3:2: the perfect person is "able to bridle the whole body." The cited texts in James prohibit understanding "perfection" in Matt 5:48 as a "gift"; such would not agree with the theological intention of Matthew, as can also be demonstrated in the redactional arrangement of the Lord's Prayer (to Schnackenburg, *Christliche Existenz* 1:137). E. F. Osborn correctly stresses that the Sermon on the Mount, even if one understands its instruction more as gift than as demand, expresses the "challenge to perfection" (*Ethical Patterns in Early Christian Thought* [Cambridge, 1978], 40). Thus is it confirmed by Rabbi Trypho, when he objected to "the teachings in the so-called gospel" that "no man can observe them" (Justin, dial. 10:2).

85. Against Stuhlmacher, *Gerechtigkeit Gottes*, 188-91; E. Schweizer, *Evangelium*, 85.

2.4 6:1-18 On Almsgiving, Praying, and Fasting

1. Other designations: "rules of piety" (Bultmann, *Synoptischen Tradition*, 156), "community catechism" (ibid., 141, n. 1), "cult didache" (Betz, "Kult-Didache," 446). B. Gerhardsson sees an "instruction on the spiritual service of sacrifice" in this section; he regards verses 1-6 and 16-21 as pre-Matthean and composed by an "early Christian rabbi" ("Geistiger Opferdienst," 73, 76).

2. Matthean vocabulary: προσέχετε ('beware'), ἔμπροσθεν ('before'); the infinitive construction θεαθῆναι ('be seen') with the dative is shown by 23:5 to come from the redactor Matthew; μισθὸν οὐκ ἔχετε ('you will have no reward') repeats almost literally the τίνα μισθὸν ἔχετε of 5:46.

3. Cf. under 5:6, 10, 20. Instead of δικαιοσύνην ('righteousness,' RSV: "piety") in 6:1, a large number of manuscripts attest the word ἐλεημοσύνην ('alms'), presumably under the influence of verse 2; weakly attested is the variant δόσιν ('gift'), which likewise cannot be considered original.

4. E. Schweizer, *Evangelium*, 88.

5. First expressed thus in Kerygma Petri 2 (first half of the second century); for further attestations see A. von Harnack, *Die Mission und Ausbreitung des*

Christentums in den ersten drei Jahrhunderten, 4th ed. (1924), 1:259-89; similarly Diogn. 1 ("new race").

6. See Schlatter, *Evangelist Matthäus,* 199-200.

7. Thus Tob 12:8: prayer, fasting, alms, righteousness; cf. Sir 7:10-11: prayer and alms.

8. Cf. above under 5:12, 46.

9. R. Bultmann, *TDNT* 2:482-85; cf. on the Jewish background: Str-B 4:536-58 (excursus 22).

10. Schlatter, *Evangelist Matthäus,* 201.

11. Cf. BAG, 1469; vs. Klostermann, *Matthäusevangelium,* 53.

12. Thus, e.g., Schniewind, *Evangelium,* 77.

13. E. Haenchen (*ZTK* 48 [1951]: 38-63), 58; more differentiated in D. E. Garland, "The Intention of Matthew 23," *NovTSup* 52 (1979): 96ff.

14. Cf. Dit. Syll. [2]845,7 (200v); M. Ant. 9:42; often Papyri and Ostraka; cf. BAG 167-68.

15. Cf. Clem. Al., Strom IV 138; Zahn, *Evangelium,* 264-65; G. Bornkamm, "Der Lohngedanke im NT," Aufsätze (1959), 80; D. Bonhoeffer, *Nachfolge,* 100 ("self-forgetting love"); Eichholz, *Bergpredigt,* 108-9; Schlatter, *Evangelist Matthäus,* 202 ("perfect selflessness"); E. Schweizer, *Evangelium,* 89. On this matter, see also M. Luther, *Evangelienauslegung 2. Teil. Das Matthäusevangelium (Kap. 3-25)* (1939), 125ff.

16. Even the parable of the Last Judgment (25:31-46) cannot confirm such a thesis, for the Judge of the world does not speak to the righteous about their unconscious doing of good, but rather explains to them that the good that they have responsibly done would turn out to be for him as the Christ and Judge of the world, without the doers of good being aware of this connection (as opposed to E. Schweizer, *Evangelium,* 312).

17. Cf. Wellhausen, *Evangelium Matthaei,* 25; Klostermann, *Matthäusevangelium,* 53. Ginza R I 104 (S. 17, 27ff.): "When you give alms, my chosen ones, do not bear witness to it. If you bear witness to it once, do not repeat it. If you give with your right hand, then do not tell your left hand. If you give with your left hand, do not tell your right hand."

18. Thus E. Schweizer, *Evangelium,* 87.

19. The concealment of right action (6:1ff.) stands in apparent contradiction to 5:16, according to which the disciples are to let their light shine before men, so that the people will see their good works and praise the Father in heaven. If the focus is on the difference between concealed and public, the result is an unresolvable antinomy between the doing before men of 5:16 and the doing in secret of 6:1ff. In truth, however, of decisive importance for our text is not the antithesis of concealed vs. public, but the difference between an attitude of hypocrisy that is directed toward the people and the deed of the right attitude, which occurs with a view toward God. The latter is also presupposed for 5:16, since the action before men is supposed to lead to the praise of God. The doing of good thus remains bound to God and does not serve the glorification of the doer. Fundamental in both cases is the view toward God, who vouches for the purity of human action. On this matter see E. Schweizer, "Der Jude im Verborgenen," esp. 92ff.

20. Cf. Prov 11:21; 12:7; 14:22; 15:6; 19:17.

21. Cf. 19:17 (redactional). Versus Schniewind, *Evangelium,* 54; E. Schweizer, *Evangelium,* 89-90 ("gift of love").

22. Braun, *Radikalismus,* 2:56 A; cf. also Merklein, *Gottesherrschaft,* 135 (bibl.).

23. On E. Schweizer, Evangelium, 88.

24. Cf. 1 Sam 1:26; 1 Kgs 8:22; Jer 18:20. Judaism is also familiar with the

kneeling position in prayer (Ps 95:6; 1 Kgs 8:54; Ezra 9:5) and with self-prostration in prayer (Gen 24:26; Exod 34:8).

25. The article is not found in Bezae Cantabrigiensis (D), Lake group (λ), Ferrar group (φ), old Syrian translations (sy^{cs}), Bohair translation (bo); cf. A. Huck and A. Greeven, *Synopse der drei ersten Evangelien*, 13th ed. (1981), 36.

26. Cf. Str-B 1:402.

27. New Testament hapax legomena: βατταλογεῖν ('to babble'), πολυλογία ('many words'). ἐθνικοί ('Gentiles') is only in pre-Matthean material (5:47; 18:17); εἰσακούειν ('to listen to') only here in Matthew's Gospel.

28. Cf. on ὁμοιωθῆτε ('be like'): 7:24, 26 (pre-Matthean?). On verse 8b: Matt 6:32 par. Luke 12:30.

29. Cf. G. Delling, *TDNT* 1:597; BAG, 273; BDR. § 40.

30. Ep. 31:5.

31. The use of the name *Our Father*, as well as the common German designation, *das Vaterunser*, comes from the Latin name, *Paternoster*, which is based on the first two words of the prayer.

32. Cf. Cyprian, *de dominica oratione*, CSEL 3/1, 267-94; Gregory of Nyssa, *de oratione dominica*, Migne, *PG* 44:1120-93; see also the introduction in Did. 8:2 ("Pray not as the hypocrites but as the Lord commanded in his gospel . . .").

33. The oldest post-New Testament witness is the quotation in Did. 8:2, which largely agrees with the Matthew text and directly or indirectly presupposes it.

34. Cf. also p. 123 below.

35. Thus the Byzantine text; the more important manuscripts ℵ B D and others do not have this addition.

36. It is based on Old Testament-Jewish doxological tradition, as it appears, e.g., in 1 Chron 29:11, and is also used in the New Testament (Rev 4:11; 12:10).

37. Thus Grundmann, *Evangelium*, 199; G. Schneider, *Das Evangelium nach Lukas*, ÖTK 3/2 (1977), 256; Jeremias, *Neutestamentliche Theologie* 1:189-90; idem, *Sprache*, 195. By contrast, J. Carmignac (*Recherches*, 23-26) and W. Ott (*Gebet und Heil*, 121-22) hold the Matthean version to be original; too apologetic is P. Fiebig (*Vaterunser*, 45-46), who claims both versions go back to Jesus himself.

38. According to K. G. Kuhn, the original language is Aramaic, and the individual verses were held together with end rhymes (*Achtzehngebet*, 30ff.).

39. Thus Vögtle, "Wir-Bitten," 345-47; also Schwarz, "Matthäus VI.9-13/ Lukas XI.2-4," 239. Cf. also the commandment to love one's enemy (5:44-48), to which—likewise in the pre-Matthean tradition—a rational substantiation (5:46-47) may have been added.

40. S. Schulz holds the Lord's Prayer to be a prayer form of the "oldest Jewish-Christian Q community of Palestine" (*Q*, 87, 93), even if it utilizes the oldest tradition (86). Goulder ("Composition," 35ff.) hypothesizes that Mark took up Jesus' general teaching on prayer and Matthew then shaped it into the form of the Lord's Prayer, which was shortened by Luke. Tilborg ("Form-criticism," 104-5) takes this thesis further by making "liturgical reflection upon the Gethsemane story" responsible for the origination of the Lord's Prayer within the Jewish-Christian community.

41. The Aramaic text is in G. Dalman, *Die Worte Jesu* (1898), 1:305; cf. Str-B 1:408, 418; Jeremias, *Neutestamentliche Theologie*, 1:192.

42. Text and commentary are in Dalman, *Worte Jesu*, 1:299-304; Str-B 4/1, 208ff. On Birkath ha-minim, see I. Elbogen, *Der jüdische Gottesdienst in seiner geschichtlichen Entwicklung*, 2d ed. (1924), 36ff., 51-52; *EncJud* 4/B, 1035-36; Davies, *Setting*, 275-76.

43. For the rest see Kuhn *Achtzehngebet*, 24ff.
44. Further examples in Carmignac, *Recherches*, 287-88; D. Flusser, "Qumrân and Jewish 'Apotropaic' Prayers," *IEJ* 16 (1966): 194-205.
45. Also 5:16, 45; 6:1; 7:11; 18:14; see p. 91 above.
46. Cf. S. Lauer, "Der Zeushymnus des Kleanthes," in U. Brocke, ed., *Das Vaterunser*, 156-62 and nn. 270-72. On the father image in the thinking and writing of Greece, see H. G. Gadamer and W. Lemke in H. Tellenbach, ed., *Das Vaterbild in Mythos und Geschichte: Ägypten, Griechenland, Altes Testament* (1976), 102ff., 116ff.
47. Faithful confidence expresses itself in the midst of despair with the prayerful cry, "For thou art our Father" (Isa 63:15-16; 64:7; Jer 3:4). According to L. Perlitt, the talk of God as Father is a question of not a primary but a secondary theme of Old Testament theology and does not belong in the "middle of the witness to God" ("Der Vater im Alten Testament," in H. Tellenbach, ed., *Vaterbild*, 50-101, esp. 97ff.).
48. Cf. G. Schrenk, *TDNT* 5:945-1014. As a prayer salutation it is also in the Eighteen Benedictions (Palestinian recension): 4th and 6th benedictions (Babylonian recension: 5th and 6th).
49. Cf. Jeremias, *Abba*, 15-67; Vögtle, "Vaterunser," 183-84. This negative evidence is, of course, relativized by D. Flusser's comment that rabbinical material on charismatic prayers is meager anyway (*Jesus in Selbstzeugnissen und Bilddokumenten*, rororo Bildmonographien [1968], 139, n. 162).
50. Thus in the Q tradition Matt 11:27 par. Luke 10:22 (absolute *Father*); cf. also 24:36 par. *My Father* is not found in Mark, but very often in Matthew's Gospel (7:21; 10:32-33; 15:13; 16:17; 18:10, 19, 35), as distinct from *your (plur.) Father* (6:32 par. Luke 12:30; Matt 5:48; 6:8, 15; 10:20, 29) and *your (sing.) Father* (6:4, 6, 18). *Our Father* is singular; it speaks of the common filial relationship of Jesus and his followers vis-à-vis God.
51. See p. 108 above.
52. Cf. J. Jeremias: "self-realizing eschatology" (*Abba*, 171).
53. Cf. As. Mos. 10:1; Midr. Hl. 2:13; Tg. Isa 31:4; exception: Tg. Micha 5:8.
54. It is uncertain whether we are to read here ἐλθέτω (thus Nestle-Aland[26] and H. Greeven, *Synopse*—also in Luke 11:2) or ἐλθάτω (Nestle-Aland[25]; Huck-Lietzmann, *Synopse*, ad loc.; cf. Matt 10:13). On the varying forms of the aorist, see BDR § 80-81.
55. Cf. also the first petition in Marcion ("May your Holy Spirit come upon us and cleanse us"), which appears in a few manuscripts as the second petition of the Lord's Prayer.
56. M. Luther, *Kleiner Katechismus*, BSELK, 513: "God's kingdom will probably come of itself without our prayer, but we ask in this prayer that it also come to us."
57. The conclusion that it is a question of a formation by Matthew (thus B. W. Bacon, *Studies in Matthew* [London, 1930], 276; Kilpatrick, *Origins*, 21; G. Barth, *Überlieferung*, 65, n. 3; Schulz, *Q*, 86, n. 202) is not convincing since both θέλημα ('will'; also Luke 22:42 par. Matt 26:42; Matt 12:50 par.) and οὐρανὸς καὶ γῆ ('heaven and earth'; Matt 5:18 par. Luke 16:17; Matt 11:25 par. Luke 10:21; Matt 24:31 par. Mark 13:31) are attested as pre-Matthean.
58. Rather, it is significant that in 'Abot 2:4, the recommendation is given to do God's will so that (!) he will do the will of humanity; even if this is not a prayer text, the divine-human relationship is still understood as a contractual one (cf. Str-B 1:420).
59. ὡς . . . καί 'as . . . so' (BAG, 1173); cf. Gal 1:9; Phil 1:20; Acts 7:51.
60. Cf. Eichholz, *Bergpredigt*, 122-23; also Luke 22:42.
61. Versus P. Billerbeck: "Where God hallows his name in the world, there

humankind acknowledges the dominion of God, and where God's dominion achieves recognition, there God can carry out his will, which is a gracious will for the salvation of the world" (Str-B 1:410). The close relationship between the three petitions is asserted by Calvin: "The three petitions stand in close relationship to each other, for the hallowing of God's name and the coming of his kingdom are always tied together; and to his dominion belongs this above all: that his will be done" (*Gospel Harmony*, Opera, vol. 45, CR 73, 196).

62. Cf. Luke 12:35ff.; 17:20ff.; 21:7ff. On this topic see H. Conzelmann, *Die Mitte der Zeit*, 5th ed. (1964), 193ff., esp. 217ff.; Schneider, *Evangelium nach Lukas*, 358-59.

63. F. Preisigke, *Sammelbuch griechischer Urkunden aus Ägypten* (1915), 1:5222 (n. 5224); ἐπιουσ . . . perhaps equals τὰ ἐπιούσια (what is determined for the day, i.e., the daily ration); cf. Lohmeyer, *Vaterunser*, 97ff.

64. Cf. BAG, 587-88; BDR. § 132:2; C. Müller, *EWNT* 2:68-77.

65. Thus Lohmeyer, *Vaterunser*, 107-8; Carmignac, *Recherches*, 192ff.

66. In the sense of ἡ ἐπιοῦσα (add: ἡμέρα) 'for the following day'; Schol. Pind. Nem. III 38; Acts 7:26; see also BAG, 562-63.

67. Thus Jeremias, *Neutestamentliche Theologie*, 1:193-94: "Bread of the time of salvation"—corresponding to the understanding of the mealtime fellowship of Jesus' disciples as an "anticipation of the final meal."

68. Cf. P. Vielhauer, "Judenchristliche Evangelien," in E. Hennecke and W. Schneemelcher, *Neutestamentliche Apokryphen in deutscher Übersetzung*, 3d ed. (1959), 1:95.

69. Cf. W. Foerster, *TDNT* 2:591.

70. Matt 6:34; here the usual αὔριον ('tomorrow').

71. Cf. M. Luther, *Kleiner Katechismus*, BSELK, 514: "Everything that belongs to bodily nourishment and need . . ."

73. Cf. Schulz, *Q*, 90; Schürmann, *Gebet*, 101ff.

74. Thus also J.-W. Taeger, *Der Mensch und sein Heil. Studien zum Bild des Menschen und zur Sicht seiner Bekehrung bei Lukas*, SNT 14 (1982), 32.

75. Matt 6:12b τοῖς ὀφειλέταις ἡμῶν ('our debtors'); Luke 11:4b: παντὶ ὀφείλοντι ἡμῖν ('everyone who is indebted to us').

76. Cf. Rom 4:4; similarly ὀφειλέτης has the meaning of 'debtor'; also Matt 18:24.

77. The Aramaic equivalent חובא (*choba*) can likewise have the double meaning of an 'owed sum of money' (literal) and a 'sin' (figurative); cf. F. Hauck, *TDNT* 5:565.

78. Ὡς has both a comparing and a substantiating function; cf. BAG, 1773-74.

79. Thus, Jeremias presumes an Aramaic present perfect; it would have the meaning, "as we have thereby forgiven" (*Abba*, 161).

80. Cf. Jeremias, *Neutestamentliche Theologie*, 1:196; Schulz, *Q*, 92. Different is Vögtle, "Wir-Bitten," 355-58 (discussion of the literature).

81. According to the rabbinical view, God does not tempt the godless but the righteous (cf. Str-B, 1:135 on Matt 4:1a).

82. Cf. M. Luther, WA 5:204.26 (Operationes in Psalmos 1519-21): "*ad deum contra deum confugere*" ("to flee from God to God").

83. b. Ber. 60b.

84. Thus, e.g., Schulz, *Q*, 82, n. 202. For linguistic analysis see the following; the verb ῥύεσθαι ('to deliver') is found only here in the Gospel (apart from the quotation in 27:43).

85. Cf. 1:1-17 (3 times 14 generations); 5:3-9 (7 pre-Matthean beatitudes); 23:1ff. (7 woes).

86. At this point, the Matthean composition is different from the assertion of

the seventh of the Eighteen Benedictions (Palestinian recension): "Look at our misery and lead our cause and deliver us for your name's sake" (Str-B 4/1, 212). Here "misery" designates the distress of the scattered; thus, this petition is connected with the national hope of the Jewish people.

87. Mark 11:26 is weakly attested by the manuscripts, and in critical editions is mentioned only in the notes. Mark 11:25, on the other hand, is without objection in terms of manuscripts yet is linguistically Matthean (parallels: Matt 5:23-24 and 6:14; ὁ πατὴρ ὑμῶν ὁ ἐν τοῖς οὐρανοῖς 'Your Father in heaven' is found only here in Mark's Gospel). Thus, dependence on Matthew's Gospel is probable: verses 25 and 26 are early and late post-Markan glosses.

88. Vögtle, "Vaterunser," 194.

89. Cf. the Luther's interpretation in the *Kleiner Katechismus* of 1529: "Amen: what is that? That I should be certain that such petitions are pleasing to the Father in heaven" (BSELK, 515).

90. On the understanding of prayer in Luke's Gospel, cf. Schneider, *Evangelium nach Lukas*, 262-64 (bibl.).

91. On σκυθρωποί ('dismal') cf. H. Bieder, *TDNT* 7:450-51.

92. Thus can the Greek play on the words ἀφανίζουσιν and φανῶσιν be imitated; since our text describes the attitude of the hypocrites in caricaturing fashion, a relatively strong choice of words is to be preferred for the translation.

93. D. Zeller (*Mahnsprüche*, 73-74) correctly emphasizes that verses 16-18 are essentially different from the rejection of fasting by Jesus in accordance with the discussion of Mark 2:18-19 and are not authentic; see p. 102 above.

94. Yoma 8:1; cf. also Str-B 4/1, 77-114 (6th excursus: "Vom altjüdischen Fasten").

2.5 6:19-7:12 Individual Directives

1. Cf. W. Zimmerli, "Zur Struktur der atl. Weisheit," *ZAW* 51 (1933): 185.

2. Cf. Schulz, *Q*, 142-43; Jeremias, *Sprache*, 218.

3. Perhaps a chewing insect, say, a woodworm; less likely = ἰός ('rust'); cf. Jas 5:3; BAG, 294.

4. Less likely is the digging up of hidden treasures; The derivation from διῶρυξ ('ditch') contributes to the understanding of the verb διορύσσειν ('dig through').

5. Cf. 4 Ezra 7:77; Apoc. Bar. 14:12; 24:1; t. Pea 4:18; Str-B 1:429-30.

6. The reading σου ("your") in Matthew (vs. the plural in Luke 12:34) is probably a Matthean transition to verse 22.

7. καρδία ('heart'), as seat of the human will, is also in 5:8.

8. The idealized description of renunciation of possessions in the early community (Acts 2:24-25; 4:32ff.) is not typical for the ethic of the Evangelist Luke; see F.-W. Horn, *Glaube und Handeln in der Theologie des Lukas*, GTA 26 (2d ed., 1986), 36ff.

9. Cf. Schulz, *Q*, 470; E. Schweizer, *TDNT* 7:1054-55; G. Harder, *TDNT* 6:555-56.

10. J. Becker, *Die Testamente der zwölf Patriarchen, Jüdische Schriften aus hellenistisch-römischer Zeit* 3/1 (1974), 82 (T. Iss. 4:6).

11. The incomplete main clause τὸ σκότος πόσον ('how great [is] the darkness') draws a conclusion *a minori ad maius* and contains a rhetorical question; the presumed answer is "Extremely great!"

12. Cf. the blessing of the eye witnesses in Luke 10:23-24 (par. Matt 13:16-17) and the eschatological cry of alarm, "He who has ears to hear, let him hear" (Luke 8:8 par.).

13. Presumably secondary vis-à-vis Luke 11:34-36; thus Schulz, *Q,* 469.

14. Midr. Ps 17 § 8 (66a) and elsewhere; Str-B 1:432.

15. This logion reads almost the same in Matthew and Luke; the exception is Luke's introduction of οἰκέτης ('servant'), motivated by the attachment to the parable of the Unjust Steward (16:1ff.), for 16:13 is the redactional conclusion of that pericope.

16. Str-B 1:433.

17. This opposition is also presupposed in Logion 47 of the Gospel of Thomas: "It is impossible for a man to ride two horses and draw two bows, and it is impossible for a servant to serve two masters. Or he will honor the one and offend the other."

18. In personified locution also in 2d Clem. 6:1; on this issue cf., in addition to the literature given above, F. Hauck, *TDNT* 4:388-90; H. Balz, *EWNT* 2:941-42. On the problem of rich and poor in the New Testament, see esp. Jas 1:9ff.; 2:1ff.; 5:1ff.; Luke 6:20-26; 12:13-32; 16:19-31.

19. Cf. above under 5:3.

20. Cf. in detail Schulz, *Q,* 149-52.

21. For a discussion of research cf. Zeller, *Mahnsprüche,* 83, n. 213.

22. At this point, Luke has the admonition to the "little flock" not to fear (12:32), which presumably already belonged to the Q^{Luke} text; cf. Polag, *Fragmenta Q,* 62; vs. Schneider, *Evangelium nach Lukas,* 284.

23. Against Klostermann, *Matthäusevangelium,* 62; Schniewind, *Evangelium,* 91.

24. Thus K. Bornhäuser, *Bergpredigt,* 149ff.; Schlatter, *Evangelist Matthäus,* 227.

25. The 1st person singular λέγω ὑμῖν ('I tell you') also appears in Luke 12:22 (Q) and Matt 6:29 (Luke 12:27); like the antitheses (5:22, 28, 32, 39, 44), it presupposes the eschatological authority of Jesus as Lord of the church.

26. The opposition of ψυχή and σῶμα is attested before Socrates and seems to be connected with Greek thought; cf. E. Schweizer, *TDNT* 7:1026, 1054-55.

27. In both cases the dative is a *dativus commodi;* cf. BDR. § 188, n. 1.

28. The statement form in Luke 12:23 is presumably secondary; likewise Luke 12:29 vs. Matt 6:31.

29. Here, the text of Matthew's Gospel is probably more original than the Lukan κόρακας ('ravens'); on the other hand, like Luke 12:24, Matthew probably read θεός (instead of ὁ πατὴρ ὑμῶν ὁ οὐράνιος 'your heavenly Father'), as suggested by Matt 6:30; cf. Schulz, *Q,* 150.

30. Cf. Seneca, de remed. fort. 10: "The birds lack nothing; the cattle live for the present"—which, of course, presupposes a Stoic understanding of nature and humanity; for further examples see R. Bultmann, *TDNT* 4:597, n. 19.

31. Cf. *Qidd.* 4:14: "Have you ever seen a wild animal or a bird practicing a trade?" Of course, this and other texts understand anxiety as the punishment for sin (see Str-B 1:436-37).

32. Normally, ἡλικία is translated as 'span of life'; the related concept πῆχυς ('cubit') seems to suggest an understanding of 'stature.' Yet the latter meaning is found in the New Testament only in Luke 19:3. On this issue: J. Wettstein, *Novum Testamentum Graece* I (1752; rpt., 1962), 334; J. Schneider, *TDNT* 2:942. Since the contextual train of thought is broken, verse 27 (par. Luke 12:25, together with Matt 6:28a) is presumably a secondary addition that was already present in the Q tradition common to Matthew and Luke.

33. With this comparison, naturally, the text does not intend to take a position on work or to glorify doing nothing as opposed to working. The Bible knows both: the plague of work (Gen 3:17-18) as well as its dignity (Ps 104:23); cf. Eichholz, *Bergpredigt,* 144; G. Agrell, *Work, Toil and Sustenance,* (Lund, 1976).

34. The expression recalls Ps 102:15 LXX, where χόρτος ('grass') and ἄνθος τοῦ ἀγροῦ ('flower of the field') are used as images for transitory human life.

35. In Matthew's sense = 'nonbelievers'; cf. 17:20; Strecker, *Weg der Gerechtigkeit*, 233-34.

36. Luke follows a universalist tendency when, in the parallel, he speaks of "all nations of the world" as opposed to the community as the "little flock" (12:30, 32).

37. Thus Grundmann, *Evangelium*, 217.

38. Thus also Ps. Clem. R II 20:2 and III 20:3 L.

39. Epict. I 9:19; Seneca, ep. III 3:1; cf. Klostermann, *Matthäusevangelium*, 64.

40. Accordingly, one prays for the bread necessary for today, not for tomorrow (see above under 6:11).

41. Cf. here and in the following Schulz, *Q,* 146-49.

42. Thus Merklein, *Gottesherrschaft*, 242. In general, ἵνα in New Testament language is used finally, not consequently; cf. BDR § 388-89; E. Stauffer, *TDNT* 3:323-33: the consequent or causal meaning of ἵνα is "seldom or meaningless" in the New Testament. Also on this issue: A. A. F. Ehrhart, *Politische Metaphysik* (1959), 2:36: Epict., Fragm. 60.

43. Similarly in rabbinical tradition; cf. Rüger, "Mit welchem Mass," 174ff.

44. Against Wellhausen, *Evangelium Matthaei*, 30. Also, no connection is to be made at this point with the Jewish legal practice of the rabbis and the Qumrân community; thus correctly, Braun, *Radikalismus*, 2:92, n. 2. Cf. also the fundamental recognition of judging on the basis of human merit as well as on the part of God in the rabbinical literature: Šabb. 127a Bar; Meg. 28a; Str-B 1:441-42.

45. Sota 1:7: "With the measure with which a person measures, he will be measured" (by God).

46. Cf. Sota 3:1 and elsewhere (Str-B 1:444ff.).

47. Cf. b. Arak. 16a Bar: "I would be surprised if there were anyone in this generation who would accept correction. If someone said to him, 'Get that speck out of your eye,' he would answer, 'Get that log out of your eye.'"

48. Even attempts to reconstruct an Aramaic protologion (cf. Jeremias, *Abba*, 83-87) do not lead to convincing explanations; according to G. Schwarz, Jesus originally directed his saying, "Do not put your rings on dogs, and do not hang your pearls on swine," toward female disciples ("Matthäus VII 6a," 24).

49. With reference to Matt 7:6, the Didache presents a secret ecclesiastical discipline related to the sacrament: "No one shall eat or drink from your Eucharist except those baptized in the name of the Lord, for even for this reason the Lord said, 'Do not give dogs what is holy'" (Did. 9:5; cf. 10:6).

50. Thus Hieronymus, Comm. in Mt 1, on 7:6 (CChr. SL LXXVII 42); among the representatives of this interpretation, whom Hieronymus does not mention by name, is the apologist and Bishop in Asia Minor, Theolphilus of Antioch (2d cent.); cf. idem, Comm. in Evangelia I 45 (CorpAp VIII 285); also 2 Pet 2:22, where with a quotation from Prov 26:11, those who have fallen from faith are compared with dogs and swine.

51. Cf. G. Strecker, *Das Judenchristentum in den Pseudoklementinen*, TU 70 (2d ed., 1981), 44-45, 50.

52. Through the Lukan connecting formula κἀγὼ ὑμῖν λέγω ('and I tell you'), the Q parallel Luke 11:9-13 is appended to the parable of the Importunate Friend (11:5-8), and beyond that to the Lord's Prayer (11:1-4—see p. 127 above). The original location in Q can no longer be determined.

53. Zahn, *Evangelium*, 309-11.

54. E. Schweizer, *Evangelium*, 110; Steinhauser, *Doppelbildworte*, 74.

55. Schniewind, *Evangelium*, 98; Grundmann, *Evangelium*, 223-24; Bornkamm, "Aufbau," 419-32.

56. Cf. on the future use of the present BDR. § 323.

57. Included in the wisdom background is the indirect demand of Prov 8:17 ("I love those who love me, and those who seek me diligently find me"); cf., furthermore, the instruction of the Stoic philosopher Epictetus: ζήτει καὶ εὑρήσεις 'seek and you will find' (I 28:20-21; IV 1:51). Prophetic influence can be substantiated from the formula "what man of you" (v. 9); see Isa 43:13; 50:10; Hag 2:3; Greeven, "Wer unter euch . . . ?" esp. 99ff.; Schulz, *Q*, 63, 163. Versus D. Zeller: "the means of a challenging, wisdom-like debate" (*Mahnsprüche*, 84).

58. Instead of ἀγαθά ('good'—v. 11*b*) Luke 11:13*b* reads πνεῦμα ἅγιον ('Holy Spirit')—doubtless a secondary reading, for ἀγαθά is attested for Q by Matt 11*a*.

59. By comparing Matthew and Luke the Q version can be reconstructed as follows: (καὶ) καθὼς θέλετε ἵνα ποιῶσιν ὑμῖν οἱ ἄνθρωποι, οὕτως καὶ ὑμεῖς ποιεῖτε αὐτοῖς '(and) as you wish that men would do to you, do so to them.'

60. Lun-Yü (Dialogues of Confucius), 551-479 B.C.: Tzu-kung asked and spoke, "Is there a word according to which one can act during one's whole life?" The master spoke, "Is it not reciprocity? What you do not wish anyone to do to you, do that to no other" (Lun-Yü XV 24, according to *Konfuzianische Bildung und Bildwelt*, selected and translated by V. Contac, Bibliothek der Alten Welt [Zurich, 1964], 25). See also L. J. Philippides, *Religionswissenschaftliche Forschungsberichte über die "Goldene Regel"* (1933), 48-49.

61. Herodotus (d. c. 425 B.C.) III 142; cf. also Hom Od V 188-89 (see n. 69 below).

62. Dihle, *Goldene Regel*, 103; see also G. B. King, "The Negative 'Golden Rule,'" *JR* 8 (1928): 268-79.

63. Tob 4:15 ("You shall do to no one what you hate"); Ep. Arist. 207; Philo, Hypothetica (Eus., praep. Ev. VII 7:6); Sir 31:15 ("Value your neighbor next to yourself, and be considerate in everything").

64. T. Naph. 1:6; Tg. Yer. I Lev 19:18.

65. Thus J. Jeremias, "Goldene Regel," *RGG* 2:1688; G. Schneider, "Die Neuheit der christlichen Nächstenliebe," *TTZ* 82 (1973): 257-75, esp. 275.

66. Correctly: Burchard, "Liebesgebot," 52 and n. 56; Nissen, *Gott und der Nächste*, 399.

67. Cf. the negative version in Did. 1:2 beside the commandment of love of enemy (1:3; also Acts 15:20, 29 v. 1.); both versions are used indiscriminately in Apost. Const. VII 2:1; also in Pseudoclementine; positive: Hom XVII 35:5; VII 4:3; XI 4:4; negative: Hom II 6:4; VII 4:4; XIX 19:8; Rec VIII 56:7; for others see Dihle, "Goldene Regel," 107-8.

68. Philippides, *Forschungsberichte*, 48.

69. Ep. Arist. 207: "'What is the teaching of wisdom?' The other one answered: 'As you yourself do not want to suffer anything bad but to participate in everything good, if you act thus in regard to subordinates and evildoers, if you gently rebuke respectable people; for God acts with gentleness in regard to all people.'" The information that the Epistle of Aristeas offers only a "rule of common sense" (E. Schweizer, *Evangelium*, 112) cannot substantiate the thesis of the uniqueness of the positive version in the Christian tradition. Cf. also 2 Enoch 61:1; Hom Od V 188-89 ("but I certainly think and plan nothing different from what I would have in mind for myself if the same thing affected me").

70. Tg. Yer. I Lev 19:18; negative and positive versions are connected also in

Aboth R. Nathan 15-16: "May the honor of the other person be as dear as your own! . . . That teaches that what is pleasing to one's own honor should also be pleasing to the honor of another; and since one does not want vile gossip to come out against one's own honor, one should also want to bring forth no vile gossip against the honor of another" (Str-B 1:460).

71. Bultmann, *Synoptische Tradition*, 107.

72. Correctly: H. Schürmann, *Das Lukasevangelium* 1, HTKNT 3/1 (1969), 351; H. Conzelmann, *Grundriss der Theologie des Neuen Testament* (Munich: Kaiser Verlag, 1967), 139; Merklein, *Gottesherrschaft*, 244-45.

73. Cf. I. Kant, *Kritik der praktischen Vernunft* (1788), *Gesammelte Schriften*, ed. Preussischen Akademie der Wissenschaften (1908), 30.

74. Thus Merklein, *Gottesherrschaft*, 244. The fact that one cannot produce a precise proof for the thesis that the Golden Rule is a component of the proclamation of the historical Jesus makes clear by example how limited the possibilities are of discovering appropriate criteria for inferring the authentic Jesus material and of using them to achieve assured results; cf. also p. 13-14 above ("Literary-Analytical Presuppositions").

75. Matt 5:39*b*-42 par. Luke 6:29-30; Matt 5:46-47 par. Luke 6:32-34 (see also pp. 83-92 above).

76. Against the interesting surmise of Dihle, *Goldene Regel*, 113-14.

77. πάντα ὅσα ('all that') in 28:20 is redactional; otherwise it is in Matthew's special material: 13:46; 18:25; ἐάν ('if') has an iterative meaning as in 10:11; cf. BDR § 380, 1*b*.

2.6 7:13-27 Closing Admonitions and Parables

1. This connection is indicated in the Didache when the teaching of the two ways (Did. 1:1) is interpreted through the double commandment of love and the Golden Rule as the "way of life" (1:2); cf. J. P. Audet, *La Didaché. Instruction des Apôtres* (Paris, 1958), 259-60. That is the way the author of the Didache interprets the Gospel of Matthew; his interpretation cannot be validated for the original connection between Matt 7:12 and 7:13.

2. Cf. Jeremias, *Sprache*, 231-32. The Greek words ἀγωνίζειν ('strive'), θύρα ('door'), ζητεῖν ('seek'), and ἰσχύειν ('be able') can be traced back to Luke. Versus Hoffmann Πάντες," 195; Merklein, *Gottesherrschaft*, 137. According to G. D. Kilpatrick (*Origins*, 22-23) Matt 7:13-14 is a combination of Q (Luke) and the presumed M source of Matthean special material.

3. Cf. W. Michaelis, *TDNT* 5:48-56; on Greek-Hellenistic models, see Klostermann, *Matthäusevangelium*, 69; critical thereof is Michaelis, ibid.

4. Cf. 4 Ezra 7:7-8; Apoc. Bar. 85:13; 1 Enoch 91:18-19; 2 Enoch 30:15; T. Asser 1:3-4: "Two ways has God given to humankind, two decrees and two ways of acting and two places. . . . He gives two ways, the good and the evil. . . ." Cf. also the blessing-curse concept of the Qumrân community; see P. von der Osten-Sacken, *Gott und Belial* (1969), 108ff., 214ff.

5. Cf. Did. 1-6. Also see W. Rordorf, "Un chapitre d'éthique judéo-chrétienne: les deux voies, + † *RSR* 60 (1972): 109-28; M. J. Suggs, "The Christian Two Ways Tradition," in *Studies in New Testament*, FS A. Wikgren, NovTSup 33 (1972), 60-74 (esp. 69-73).

6. See Aboth 2:9; Berakh, 28*b*; Mekh. Exod 14:28; S. Dt. 11:26 § 53; O. Böcher, *Der johanneische Dualismus im nachbiblischen Judentum* (1965), 79-82.

7. Hence H. Braun judges our text to be a "genuine word of Jesus . . . even if in this word the special conversion terminology is missing" (*Radikalismus* 2:32, n. 10).

8. This future-eschatological announcement has a Johannine parallel in the

present-eschatological announcement in the Gospel of John that the Paraclete as the Spirit of truth convicts the world of sin and proclaims judgment (John 16:8-11). According to A. J. Mattill the term τεθλιμμένη ('narrow') in verse 14a reflects the eschatological θλίψεις ('tribulations'), including persecutions, which threaten the community on its way into the kingdom of God ("The Way of Tribulation," 531 ff.).

9. Cf. 4 Ezra 8:3: "Many are created but few are chosen."

10. Against E. Schweizer, *Evangelium*, 118. The term *find* corresponds to the image of *seeking*, as is presupposed here and expressly named by Luke (13:24; cf. Matt 7:7-8; Epict. I 28:20 [see above, p. 149 and n. 57]); thus, the word may not be interpreted in terms of dogma.

11. See Schulz, *Q*, 316-18.

12. Ibid., 318.

13. Cf. Deut 13:2-6; Mic 3:5; Jer 23:9ff.; E. Osswald, *Falsche Prophetie im Alten Testament*, Sammlung gemeinverständlicher Vorträge und Schriften 237 (1962); in the New Testament esp. in later writings: 1 John 4:1; 2 Pet 2:1; and elsewhere.

14. Schlatter, *Evangelist Matthäus*, 512. According to D. Hill it is a question of "Pharisees" who threaten the community from without and not of an intracommunity phenomenon ("False Prophets," 342ff.).

15. R. A. Guelich's exegesis shows that imagination knows no bounds when one does not observe that with verse 21 the theme of false prophecy is dropped again (see below). According to Guelich the false prophets are to be identified with nomistic Jewish Christians, who with a "touch of irony" are reproached for their ἀνομία (cf. v. 23). These are the Jewish Christians who in the years 67-70 had fled from Jerusalem to Pella (*Sermon*, 26, 402-3). Yet in all probability the Pella tradition is a legend; cf. G. Lüdemann, "The Successors of Pre-70 Jersualem Christianity. A Critical Evaluation of the Pella-Tradition," in E. P. Sanders, ed., *Jewish and Christian Self-Definition: The Shaping of Christianity in the Second and Third Centuries* (London, 1980), 161-73, 245-55.

16. Thus, e.g., G. Barth, "Gesetzverständnis," 68. Versus, however, Sand, *Gesetz*, 100.

17. Cf. the parallel formulation in 10:34; see p. 53 above.

18. The threat is asserted in προσέχετε ('beware'), but from this imperative (cf. also 6:1; 10:17; 16:6ff.) or from the following ἔρχονται ('come'), which likewise points to the future, one cannot deduce that we are dealing here with an actual encounter of Matthew with a particular antinomian group (on Marguerat, *Jugement*, 187-88).

19. Cf. Acts 20:28-29; 1 Pet 5:2-3; John 10:1ff. On the Old Testament background: Pss 77:52; 79:2; 99:3 LXX.

20. Cf. also O. Böcher, for whom the metaphorical "wolves" characterize the prophetic false teachers as people who are possessed by demonic powers ("Wölfe in Schafpelzen," 424).

21. Luke 6:44b is different: thorns/figs, bramble bush/grapes, without a difference in the basic content of the assertion. On the tradition history of this "double image saying" and on the (secondary) parallel in the Gospel of Thomas (log. 45), cf. Steinhauser, *Doppelbildworte*, 79-96 (bibl.).

22. Cf. F. Lundgreen, "Pflanzen im Neuen Testament," *NKZ* 28 (1916): 816.

23. Cf. Gen 3:18; Hos 10:8; in the New Testament also Heb 6:8; further, Herm., sim VI, 2:6-7; and elsewhere.

24. Thus the rhetorical question in verse 16b presupposes the answer "No!"

25. An assertion of principle is as little to be assumed here as, say, in 7:11 (see p. 150 above) or in 12:34; versus A. Schlatter, who wants to work up a difference between the human understanding of Jesus and that of the

Pharisees: Jesus places "being before willing and doing, while the Pharisaic teaching of freedom, on the other hand, saw in the willing the real process on which the condition of humanity is dependent" (*Evangelist Matthäus*, 256).

26. Cf. Clem. Al., Strom. 44:1-3; E. Osborn, *Ethical Patterns in Early Christian Thought* (Cambridge, 1978), 48-49; idem, *The Beginning of Christian Philosophy* (London, 1981), 267ff.; W. Bauer, *Rechtgläubigkeit und Ketzerei im ältesten Christentum*, BHT 10 (2d ed., 1964), 137ff. On the topic: "The artist is known by the works" (2 Enoch 42:14).

27. Did. 11:8-12:

> [8]But not everyone who speaks in the spirit is a prophet, unless he has the morals [τρόπους] of the Lord. For by their morals will the false prophet and the [true] prophet be recognized. [9]And no prophet who orders a table in the Spirit eats from it, unless he is a false prophet. [10]But every prophet who teaches the truth is a false prophet if he does not do what he teaches. [11]Every tested, true prophet, who acts in accordance with the earthly mystery of the church but does not teach how to do everything that he himself does, shall not be judged by you, for he has his judgment with God; for so did also the ancient prophets. [12]But whoever says in Spirit, give me money or something else, to him you shall not listen. But if he says you should give to others in need, then shall no one judge him.

28. Correctly: Marguerat, *Jugement*, 192.

29. This includes οὐ πᾶς ('not every one'; cf. 7:24, 26), εἰσελεύσεται εἰς τὴν βασιλείαν τῶν οὐρανῶν ('shall enter the kingdom of heaven'; cf. 5:20, redactional; 18:3 par.), τὸ θέλημα τοῦ πατρός μου τοῦ ἐν τοῖς οὐρανοῖς ('the will of my Father who is in heaven'; 11 times in Matthew); Schulz, *Q*, 427-28.

30. This could be inferred from 2 Clem. 4:5: the summons to observe the commandments of Jesus (cf. Matt 7:21) is linked with the announcement that otherwise the "evildoers" will be thrown out (cf. Matt 7:23; Bultmann, *Synoptische Tradition*, 122). Of course, this can confirm the pre-Matthean unity of our text only if we can be certain that 2 Clem. does not presuppose Matthew's Gospel. Yet a use of the First Gospel directly or indirectly (thus H. Köster, *Synoptische Überlieferung bei den Apostolischen Vätern*, TU 65 [1957], 109ff.) also by 2 Clem. 4:2 (reference to Matt 7:21 as well as the Matthean concept of righteousness) seems to suggest itself.

31. Cf. also above under Matt 7:13-14 par. Luke 13:23-24. Versus Schulz, *Q*, 425.

32. This applies not only to verses 22a and 23a but also to the essential part of the remaining vocabulary: προφητεύειν ('proclaim') is redactional in any case in 11:13, although there it is related to Old Testament prophecy; 15:7 par. and 26:68 par., on the other hand, are traditional. On δαιμόνια ἐκβάλλειν ('cast out demons') cf. 9:33-34 (S); 10:8 par.; 12:24, 27-28 par. δυνάμεις ποιεῖν ('do mighty works') occurs only at this location.

33. Trilling, *Israel*, 189.

34. This can also be seen in our text in the parallel between λέγων (v. 21: 'saying') and ὁμολογήσω (v. 23: 'I will declare'—see below).

35. E.g., Matt 8:2, 6, 8, 21, 25; 9:28; 14:28, 30; and elsewhere.

36. E.g., 12:38; 22:16, 24, 36; thus the *rabbi* ('master') form of address is also found only in the mouth of the betrayer (26:25, 49). Enlightening is the change in form of address in the words of discipleship: The "scribe" addresses Jesus as "teacher" (8:19), but one of the "disciples" says "Lord" (8:21).

37. Str-B 1:910-11 (on Matt 23:3) shows that placing human deeds over

words has a Jewish background. For the Hellenistic environment cf. Diogenes Laertius, vitae philosophorum VI 28.

38. The connection between belonging to Jesus and doing God's will is also asserted in the Nazarene Gospel (fragm. 6): "If you are at my side and do not do the will of my Father in heaven, I will push you away from me" (P. Vielhauer, "Judenchristliche Evangelien," in E. Hennecke and W. Schnee-melcher, *Neutestamentliche Apokryphen* 1 [3d ed., 1959], 95); cf. also 2 Clem. 4:5.

39. At this point Jesus speaks for the first time in Matthew's Gospel of God as "my Father"; thus also 11:27 par.; 20:23; 25:34; 26:29, 39, 53 redactional. On the Father-designation see above under 6:9.

40. ἐκείνη ἡ ἡμέρα ('that day'; Heb. הַהוּא יוֹם = *yom hahu*) in the Old Testament is the day of Yahweh's judgment (Isa 2:11, 17; cf. Zech 14:6); also Matt 24:36; 26:69 par.; Rom 2:16; Acts 17:31.

41. Cf., say, Paul and the glossolalia phenomena in Corinth (1 Cor 14), also the appearance of early Christian prophets (Acts 11:27; 13:7; 21:10; and elsewhere).

42. Cf. Str-B 1:469.

43. The concept ἀνομία is synonymous with ἁμαρτία, as H Räisänen correctly states (*Paul and the Law*, 214, n. 57).

44. See above under 7:13-14.

45. Cf. Matt 8:1–9:34: ten miracles of Jesus; see H. J. Held, *Überlieferung*, 189ff.; G. Strecker, *Weg der Gerechtigkeit*, 175-77.

46. Cf. H. Schürmann, *Das Lukasevangelium* 1, HTKNT 3/1 (1969), 38ff.

47. The Matthean conception, as opposed to the Lukan, may presuppose Palestinian conditions. On house building in ancient Judaism cf. G. Dalman, *Arbeit und Sitte in Palästina* (1942), 7:62ff.

48. Cf. Schulz, *Q*, 312-14.

49. Jeremias, *Gleichnisse*, 140, n. 1.

50. Thus E. Klostermann, HNT 1, 71 (reference to Matt 13:20-21).

51. Cf. Jeremias, *Gleichnisse*, 43, n. 1; Grundmann, *Evangelium*, 243.

52. Cf. A. Jülicher, *Gleichnisreden*, 2 vols. (2d ed., 1910), passim.

53. In the indirect sense also in Matt 11:25-30; cf. H. Schulte, *Der Begriff der Offenbarung im Neuen Testament*, BEvT 13 (1949), 13ff.; Dibelius, *Formge-schichte*, 279-84; H. Becker, *Die Reden des Johannesevangeliums und der Stil der gnostischen Offenbarungsrede*, FRLANT 68 (1956), 53ff.

54. See above under 7:13-14.

55. Aboth Rabbi Nathan, 24 (Str-B 1:469).

56. Pirque Aboth 3:17.

57. According to D. Flusser Jesus was also speaking in 7:24 of the "words of the law" (*Gleichnisse*, 99-100), a conjecture that has no basis in the text.

58. Cf. the redactional οὖν ('then') in verse 24, as well as the Matthean demonstrative τούτους in verses 24 and 26.

59. Matthew intends no parallel between our text and the use of the word *rock* in regard to Peter (16:18). Yet every hearer of Jesus is basically like Peter if he puts his trust in the word of the Preacher on the mount and bases his existence upon it. He can even become the "rock" of the church; on this extended interpretation cf. the ecclesiological assumption of the saying on the power of the keys (16:19) in 18:18.

60. As opposed to Luke 6:47-48, the future ὁμοιωθήσεται ('he will be like') is consciously used by Matthew in order to point to the future nature of the final event; cf. also 25:1 and, on the other hand, the aorist ὡμοιώθη ('it was like') in 13:24; 18:23; 22:2.

61. Cf. the verb τελεῖν ('finish'), which also appears in Matthean closing and

transitional formulas in 11:1; 13:53; 19:1; and 26:1—versus πληροῦν ('fulfill') in Luke 7:1 and 22:16.

62. Cf. above under 7:24, 26; also Num 16:31.

63. See above under 5:1.

64. The genitive of the personal pronoun ('their') is redactional in contrast to Mark 1:22; cf. also Matt 4:23; 9:35; 10:17; 12:9; 13:23; further, 11:1; 23:34; and Mark 1:39; 7:9, 13.

3 Outlook

1. Exod 21:12; Lev 24:21; Num 35:16ff.; cf. Str-B 1:254-75.

2. Versus P. Lapide, "Bergpredigt—Theorie und Praxis," *ZEE* 17 (1973): 369-72, esp. 370 (reference to Derech Eretz 10: "Whoever publicly shames the face of his neighbor is like one who sheds blood"; cf. Str-B 1:282).

3. Cf. Job 31:1; Sir 23:4-5; 26:9-11; Ps. Sol. 4:4-5; T. Iss. 7:2. Prov 6:24-25; Sir 9:5; Lev. R. 2.

4. Cf. Sh. Talmon—D. Flusser, "Early Christianity and Jewish Territorial Doctrine," in *Christian News from Israel*, Ministry of Religious Affairs, 25/3/19 (Jerusalem, 1975): 137ff.

5. A. Loisy, *L'Évangile, et l'église* (Paris, 1902), 111.

6. Cf. I. Tödt, "Die Feinde lieben. Politik mit dem Gebot Jesu?" *EKL* 14 (1981), 504-5. On this issue, see K. Griewank, *Das Problem des christlichen Staatsmannes bei Bismarck* (1953).

7. Within the framework of his distinction between the private and public person, and with reference to the Sermon on the Mount, Luther stressed for both areas the responsibility of the Christian for third parties, which is rooted in the commandment of love and carried out in various forms. Cf. the sermon on Matt 5:38-43 (1530/32), WA 32:386-95, v.a. 390.33; "Von weltlicher Obrigkeit" (1523), WA 11:246-80, esp. 255.13, 256.2ff.; and the writing "Ob Kriegsleute auch in seligem Stand sein können" (1526), WA 19:616-62, esp. 625.

8. Cf. here D. Bonhoeffer: "Humanly speaking, there are countless possibilities for understanding and interpreting the Sermon on the Mount. Jesus knows only a single possibility: simply to go out and obey. Not interpret or apply, but do, obey. Only in this way is Jesus' word heard. But again, not to speak of doing as an ideal possibility, but really to start doing" (*Nachfolge*, 131); further, cf. the "Zehn Artikel über Freiheit und Dienst der Kirche" edited by the Konferenz der Evangelischen Kirchenleitungen in the German Democratic Republic (*Kirchliches Jahrbuch* 1963, ed. J. Beckmann, 181-86, esp. 181).

Subject Index

Admonition, 29, 39, 41, 49-50, 52, 60, 68, 78, 80, 82-84, 89, 110, 113-14, 118, 120, 125, 131-33, 136-37, 140-41, 144-46, 149, 153-54, 156-58, 160, 164-65, 167, 176, 179, 184

Antitheses, 14-15, 27, 56, 60-95, 120, 143, 174-76, 180, 184

Apocalyptic, 19, 31, 39, 41, 43, 46, 50, 72, 108, 112, 115, 122, 131, 143, 149, 157, 160-61, 163, 166, 170, 179, 181. *See also* Kingdom of God; Eschatology

Authority (power), 26, 31, 34, 55-56, 62, 65, 71, 76, 78, 94, 110, 113, 115, 120, 137, 154, 170, 172-73, 179

Brother, 23, 66-67, 89, 92, 120, 125, 145-47, 153, 174, 176. *See also* Neighbor

Christology (Jesus Christ; Lord; Son of God), 11, 14, 21, 25, 33-36, 43, 45-53, 55-56, 58-59, 61-62, 65, 70, 76, 82, 94, 111-12, 114, 120, 123-29, 145, 147, 157-59, 162, 166-67, 171-72, 178-79, 183-84

Comfort (comforter), 29-30, 33-37, 178

Commandment, 15, 17, 41, 57-58, 62-65, 68, 70-71, 73-74, 76-77, 82, 87, 93, 98, 112, 130, 141, 143, 152, 155, 157, 165 (n. 30), 174-77, 180, 183-84. *See also* Law; Love commandment

Community (church), 13-14, 19, 23, 29, 34, 36, 42-47, 49-51, 53-54, 56-58, 60, 67-70, 74-76, 80, 82-84, 88-89, 91, 93-95, 97-98, 102, 104, 110-14, 115, 117-29, 135, 137-38, 141, 145, 147-48, 153, 157-62, 164-68, 170, 172-74, 177-81, 183-84

Compliance, 82-85, 87, 153, 155, 176, 178, 182

Creation (Creator), 76, 79, 90-91, 95, 109, 119, 137-41

Decision, call to, 21, 26, 72, 135, 153, 156, 158, 167, 170-71. *See also* Repentance

Disciple, 22, 24-26, 48-51, 53, 60-61, 69, 83, 92, 98, 118-19, 122, 127, 135, 137, 140, 145, 149, 166-67, 185. *See also* Community

Discipleship, 22, 33, 39, 42, 47, 49-53, 59-61, 92, 94, 110, 119, 122, 127, 131, 134-35, 139-41, 143, 149, 154-55, 166, 172, 177, 179, 182-83

Eschatology, 19-21, 25-26, 31, 33-38, 42, 45-46, 50, 53, 56, 59, 61, 65-66, 68-69, 71, 75-76, 78, 84, 89, 94, 101, 104, 109, 112-18, 120-35, 129, 131, 140, 143, 149, 153-54, 157-58, 160-61, 168, 171-73, 175-79, 181, 184. *See also* Apocalyptic

Ethic of attitude, 18, 21, 66, 151, 183

Faith, 22, 43, 108, 110-12, 122, 133, 137-38, 141, 147, 178

Fulfillment. *See* Realizability

Gentile Christians, 12, 44, 56-58, 107, 147. *See also* Jewish Christians

Gentiles, pagans, 60, 79, 92, 97-98, 104-5, 109-10, 127, 138, 147, 151

Gnosticism, 147

Good works, 31, 38-39, 46-47, 50-53, 60, 86, 92, 98, 100-101, 112-13, 121, 125, 128, 132, 152, 164-68, 170-71. *See also* Reward

Gospel, 16, 22, 33-34, 179. *See also* Law

221